"A passionate, wonderful and illuminating love story, *GIANT STEPS* is everyone's book: personal, intimate, honest, a rare and caring and unflinching portrait."

DR. WAYNE W. DYER

"A fascinating book with a view of helping people that is filled with love and great promise."

ALAN ARKIN

"About the kind of love everyone secretly wants but is afraid to ask for...a liberating book; the perfect gift for someone who's hurting inside."

Los Angeles Times

"I wish Barry Kaufman's *GIANT STEPS* had been around when I was growing up. But it still arrives in time to be of help, not only to children from broken families but for all of us who care about the very real problems young people face coming of age in our sometimes beautiful, but nearly always difficult world. This is a gentle and loving work with wide appeal."

ROD MCKUEN

GIANT STEPS

Barry Neil Kaufman

A Fawcett Crest Book
Published by Ballantine Books

Copyright © 1979 by Barry Neil Kaufman

All rights reserved under International and Pan-American Copyright Conventions. Published in the United States by Ballantine Books, a division of Random House, Inc., New York, and simultaneously in Canada by Random House of Canada Limited, Toronto.

ISBN 0-449-21569-0

This edition published by arrangement with Coward, McCann & Geoghegan, Inc.

Printed in Canada

First Fawcett Crest Edition: May 1981

FAWCETT CREST • NEW YORK

A Fawcett Crest Book
Published by Ballantine Books
Copyright © 1979 by Barry Neil Kaufman

ISBN 0-449-21569-5

This edition published by arrangement with Coward, McCann & Geoghgan, Inc.

Printed in Canada

First Fawcett Crest Edition: May 1980
First Ballantine Books Edition: February 1983
Eighth Printing: October 1990

IN CELEBRATION OF THEA:
MYSTERIOUS, IMPISH, ARTISTIC, ALWAYS LOVING
...A SPECIAL LIGHT IN MY LIFE.

THESE YOUNG PEOPLE
DIDN'T JUST WALK,
THEY TOOK GIANT STEPS.

CONTENTS

PREFACE

Dawn. Jonathan. David. Robertito. Angie. Jeanette. Dominique. Sammy. Their young faces and bright eyes are always with me now; alive, caring and open—so very different from the assortment of masks which camouflaged their thoughts and feelings initially. I think each of them had believed that a journey into their own worlds would result in a ferocious battle with the all-too-apparent difficulties and hidden miseries. Instead, they learned to confront the demons without swords or the benefit of armor. The fist became an accepting hand. As they embraced themselves with a more living and non-judgmental attitude, their changes and movements were not small, barely perceptible gestures . . . they were observable, joyful, giant steps.

*   *   *

In my previous book, *To Love Is To Be Happy With*, the attitude and principles of The Option Process, a lifestyle we live and teach, were present as they might be taught to others; the attitude and method explored in depth and then applied to many different life experiences, from guilt to trusting ourselves, from love relationships to sex, from health to psychic experience, and so on. The publication of that book and the one prior to it, *Son-Rise*, which detailed the rebirth of our son from a supposedly irreversible situation, afforded me the wonderful opportunity to talk and share with people all around the country through mass media, individual lectures and talks. And as I have tried to give to others something of what I know, they, in turn, have enriched me. Somehow, I wanted this book to reflect that enrichment in content and form.

Often, a story is the perfect metaphor to convey all the possibilities, beauty and meaning one person might want to communicate to another. So perhaps, rather than outline concepts and ideas, I would like to allow each child, in the details of his or her story, to be for you what he or she has been for me: teachers, friends and challenges to my own humanity. When allowed to go with themselves and find their own truths, in many ways, they know all there is to know. Their movements are very special and uplifting experiences.

I would like to punctuate the word "uplifting," for these young people become testaments to the power within each of us as they confront events and circumstances no different from ones we or our own children might face: Dawn, a teenager avoiding fears about her own sexuality by becoming overweight; Robertito, a different child dismissed as hopeless by those who encounter him; Jonathan, a youngster imprisoning himself in an attic to stop his continued dependence on drugs; David, the seven-year-old punished and condemned as disruptive and unruly by everyone except the seventy-three-year-old man who befriends him; Angie, the delicate, strong-willed young girl trying to absorb the shock of rape and the resulting pregnancy by taking a very unpopular position; Jeanette, a child unwilling to assert herself despite being dismissed by teachers as shy and stupid; Dominique, the inner-city youngster trying to survive the anger and rejection resulting from her parents' impending divorce; and Sammy, trapped in the silence and plastic smiles of a family stumbling through the trauma of dealing with a dying parent.

Since each story, inevitably, is so separate and special, ranging from the immediacy and irrevocable breakthrough of a one-day encounter to the more studied evolution spanning a period of months, I have assembled them as mini-books within a book, though the thread of Option is evident in each. Although most of these individual journeys have been disguised to ensure the privacy of each child and *condensed for purposes of presentation*, the aim is to present a before-during-and-after vision of each young person's experiences and growth resulting from his or her exposure to an accepting attitude and participation in the dialogues.

In *To Love Is To Be Happy With*, the examples illustrated the disconnecting of the networks of unhappiness, but seldom explored the outreach effects of the Option experience. In this book, each child's evolution, although specific and detailed, becomes more than a freeze-frame for the environment-at-large; it is an opportunity to depict the widespread implications for the person observing and confronting his options . . . for in changing and freeing himself, he also begins to change and free others by simply touching them with a loving and accepting hand.

Children are born from us; they are not owned by us. They are not possessions. The fact that they are little does not mean they are less. They are free spirits for us to love and enjoy. For all of us, children can be a beautiful experience . . . doorways into our own humanity.

PROLOGUE

Several years ago, a dear friend of mine died while on an operating table. His heart and respiration stopped during a relatively minor procedure. Because of the heroics of a team of surgeons and nurses, he was revived within a short time. In the recovery room, he shared with his family and friends a very strange and wonderful occurrence which he had experienced at the time of his death. His story duplicated, with amazing consistency, other accounts recently documented by researchers and clinicians.

In great detail, he described the sensation of, somehow, being released by his physical nature, as if the essence of what he traditionally called *himself* floated freely outside of his body. He heard the quick, frenzied instructions exchanged by the medical personnel who participated in the bold attempt to revive him. He felt no panic, but only a quiet, protected movement . . . like a balloon drifting easily through gentle air currents.

The noise in the room became muffled; individual voices and the clanging of metallic instruments melted into one continuous hum. Then, he felt himself eased downward into a dark tunnel which surrounded him like warm water, soothing and comfortable. His sense of peace was overwhelming. The visual aspects of his travel appeared quite definite, though he did not think of himself as seeing through his eyes. At the end of the tunnel, he encountered an intense yellow-white light. Although he sensed an incredible power and intelligence in the light, he refused to name or label it, becoming slightly embarrassed with the implications of his words.

As he bathed in the energy of its glow, he heard a question, not one asked of him verbally, but one which bubbled from within. He felt more receptive at that moment than during any other time in his life. The question was quite simple and direct: Was he happy or unhappy about the life he lived and, whatever his response, why did he feel that way?

Several people in the room became very upset with his story. "My God," one woman exclaimed, "who would want to be asked such a question when you died? Surely there would be so many things left undone . . . and what about all the regrets? What a horrible question to be confronted with."

'No, no," he assured them in a soft, mellow voice. He had heard this question in a way he had never heard such a question before. The tone felt so loving and accepting. No implied accusation or judgment. He knew, whatever his answer, it would be for his own enrichment . . . to come to his own truth and understanding. Rather than running away, he found himself welcoming such an awareness. His eyes displayed a comfort defying the skepticism and fears of those in the room.

Whether he had experienced a dream, a fantasy, or, in fact, another kind of journey we all know very little about, I found myself awed and excited by his words—for his experience mirrored in tone and attitude a central aspect of The Option Process, a life-affirming perspective which has helped us dramatically modify and reorder our own lives. It begins with a very simple, loving and non-judgmental dialogue, precipitated by questions similar in content and mood to the one my friend heard.

In our own personal Option journeys, less flamboyant though no less beautiful, we have learned to dispense with most of our discomforts and fears by uncovering and discarding the beliefs which fuel them; beliefs which we have been taught, which we have adopted and which we can change.

From such an exploration, a very special attitude has evolved: "to love is to be happy with," an accepting and non-judgmental way to embrace who we are . . . not as the result of any dogma or theory, but simply by viewing, understanding and accepting our feelings and behaviors rather than judging and condemning them. In such a pursuit, we can often observe that all of us, although perhaps tripping and stumbling at times, are doing the very best we can, the very best we know how based on our beliefs. That awareness, joined with the delight of experiencing ourselves as our own experts, can present us with the unique opportunity to redefine and recreate ourselves—a very open-ended and joyful activity.

Living Option and teaching it became a way of life. We witnessed people doing dramatic and wonderful things for themselves in areas they had previously considered difficult or unsolvable. We experienced our own lives as a mellow and easy movement, quite different from the stormy and troubled days before we understood how we operated and how easily we could change.

And then... the birth of our third child, Raun Kahlil, whom others would come to view as a "horrifying," "hopeless" and "disastrous tragedy." It was through our encounter with this very special human being that we fully realized that the accepting and loving vision, which had become the cornerstone of our existence, was not only a powerful philosophy and an effective teaching technique, but also a beautiful and special gift of living.

Although this book, basically, will portray the inspiring stories of young people (and, in some cases, their parents) who have used Option to deal with questions frequently confronting young people in such areas as sexuality, self-worth, drugs, discipline, abortion, rape, divorce, a dying parent, I would like to share our experience with our son, as well. His story is very much an Option experience and suggests the endless possibilities which might be present in any situation if we suspended our judgments and moved without fear, trusting ourselves.

Delivered naturally, without drugs or instruments, our son entered the world easily; a beautifully and well-formed little boy whose delicately chiseled features and doll-like appearance captivated all who crossed his path. Yet, in contrast to the serenity of that visual impression, he cried day and night for the first month after his birth, during which time he almost lost his life as the result of a severe ear infection, dehydration and other complications that resulted in his confinement in a pediatric intensive care unit.

Though Raun seemed to develop normally after this initial difficulty, by his first birthday we noticed a growing insensitivity to audio stimulus as he became less responsive to his name and other sounds. During the following two months, this behavior was compounded by his tendency to stare and be passive. He preferred solitary play rather than participating in our family activities. When we lifted him into our arms, he dangled limply. Our questions and visits to several pediatricians yielded little reaction, except vague assurance he would outgrow his peculiar manners.

Within the next two months, our son slipped behind an invisible, impenetrable wall, oblivious to all human contact. He occupied himself with a series of self-stimulating rituals; either rocking back and forth, hour after hour, or spinning every object in sight for periods sometimes lasting an entire day. He smiled at blank walls with little reference to the external world around him. His fingers moved repetitiously against his lips. He did not develop language . . . no words, no pointing gestures. No expression of wants—never once indicating a desire for food or to be changed or to be lifted from his crib. Totally withdrawn. Totally self-stimulating.

At seventeen months of age, he was formally diagnosed as a classic case of autism, traditionally a subcategory of childhood schizophrenia, considered the most irreversible of the profoundly disturbed. Although others had reclassified autism as a brain-damage situation of indeterminate cause, they, too, viewed the dilemma as basically hopeless and irreversible. Even the literature supported their point.

And yet, despite those who would condemn him and extend their soft voices of sympathy, we saw in our son a very special and beautiful human being, with his own dignity and unique qualities.

Wanting more for him and ourselves, we began a journey around the country to observe and explore different alternatives. Most programs were little more than experiments. Whether dedicated to psychoanalysis, sensory conditioning or behavioral techniques, they reached only a few children in each one hundred. Their successes, ironically, meant the one or two youngsters who learned to function on a very primitive level. The overwhelming majority spent their lives in faceless institutions.

We encountered professionals who administered electric shock treatments with cattle prods on children under five because a doctor, teacher, or parent deemed their behavior unacceptable. Other boys and girls were enclosed in portable black closets, with no windows, as part of aversion therapy. Some were strapped to the backs of chairs to prevent them from rocking and flapping their arms.

The more we observed, the more polarized we became. Our entire lifestyle stood in dramatic contrast to even the most "humanistic" programs which, despite their avowed sensitivity, still approached these children with disapproval.

And so we trusted our own inclination and decided to create our own program based on the philosophy of Option and grounded in the attitude of "to love is to be happy with." We would approach our son without conditions to which he had to conform, without expectations which he had to fulfill, and most significantly, without judgments defining his actions as good or bad. Our awareness suggested that in terms of his present abilities, Raun, as all of us, was doing the best he could.

Rather than force him to conform or adapt to our world, rather than disapprove of him, we decided to join Raun in his world with love and acceptance, to understand and know his universe by participating. Working with him during his every waking hour (eighty hours each week), we began by imitating him on a global scale—not just a strategy or tactic, but sincerely being with him; rocking when he rocked, spinning when he spun, flapping when he flapped. Several doctors labeled our effort a tragic mistake since we supposedly supported our son's bad behavior. Yet for us, good and bad had no useful meaning in our thrust to make contact with this very different little boy. All we wanted to do, initially, was to find a way to say: "Hey Raun, it's okay wherever you are. Hey, Raun, we love you."

As we continued observing and accepting his world, we lavished him with affection and caring while introducing gentle visual and auditory stimulation. We knew, if he would ever communicate or function in our world, it would have to come from him. In effect, we wanted to create a world so easy, so loving, so responsive that he might find himself drawn to us and motivated to push beyond his obvious difficulties and dysfunctions. We included both our daughters, Bryn and Thea, as facilitators and loving mentors for their brother as well as training others as teacher-therapists, using the principles and attitude of Option as our tool.

Though we worked with our son for several years, within the first year, this dysfunctioning, totally withdrawn, self-stimulating, functionally retarded and "hopeless" little boy became a social, highly verbal affectionate and loving human being displaying an intellectual capability far beyond his years. Today, at five years of age, he attends a regular kindergarten class in a regular school. More socially and verbally sophisticated than his peers, Raun Kahlil enjoys and learns from the environment he touches easily, sharing his excitement and joy with everyone around him.

As we have come to embrace ourselves and those we love with the attitude of "to love is to be happy with," and explore the universe from a non-judgmental perspective, we become the children of Option. And since children provide the literal focus for this, The Second Book of The Option Process, their stories have compounded meaning and implication.

Why children now? I could say this book is born out

of my deep involvement and respect for young people and articulates awesome transformations of children who have been exposed to Option not only as an educational and therapeutic technique, but also as a lifestyle alternative. I could also point to the relevance of the journeys of these children, for in their explorations and evolvements, we can watch the mirrored reflections of ourselves. Both these answers would be accurate, but somehow incomplete.

The seeds of who we have become were initially planted in our childhood. The exploration of our beliefs and the rechoosing can almost be characterized as an undoing and unlearning. The child's world presents us with a unique opportunity to witness rapid and meaningful changes precipitated by a loving and accepting attitude.

A child, unlike his older counterpart (you and me), has not yet spent years ingesting and acting on the beliefs he has adopted and empowered. His constellation of judgments and expectations are still relatively newly acquired and flexible. He has not expended endless energy and time defending or protecting who or what he is. In many ways, he is much closer than most of us to the searching, open, spontaneous, welcoming and happy infant he once was.

As we become more conscious of the food we feed our children (from sugar-infested candy to breakfast cereals with red dye), and as we try to remedy the situation, a non-judgmental perspective can give us a new clarity and insight into the profound effects and underlying messages of the beliefs which we have also been freely feeding our children—beliefs which unfortunately are no more productive or "real" than the artificial flavoring and coloring which have infiltrated most of the commodities in our diet.

* * *

PROLOGUE

Awareness and wanting bring change. Beginning with our youth is beginning with ourselves. This, then, sets the vision for this sharing.

THE BOOK OF DAWN

The winding road edged past antique colonial structures, carefully preserved remnants of another century. An old woman, dressed in grey overalls and workboots, raked the ground beside the stone wall. Down a steep incline on the opposite side of the street, people gathered around a large duck pond. The sound of sea gulls and geese splintered through the air.

Since our jeep towered above neighboring cars, driving it always provided me with a special panorama. In the distance, brake lights glared, igniting the red beacons in back of every vehicle like an endless series of falling dominos. The traffic came to a complete halt. Trapped in this log-jam of metallic dinosaurs steaming and hissing in place, I jumped from our truck, then sat atop the front fender. The sun solarized halos around the edges of the trees as it descended over a rooftop.

A group of high school students, busily chattering

to each other, passed by. A tall, thin girl separated from her friends and walked directly toward me. Her electric-blue eyes danced in their sockets.

"Hi, it's me," she said. A slight challenge filtered through the matter-of-fact declaration. I smiled, remembering a telephone conversation of almost two years ago which began with those exact same words.

* * *

"Hi, it's me," the voice barked at the other end of the phone.

"Well, hello, 'me.' I don't recognize your voice, so would you like to tell me who you are?"

"Come off it. My mother told me to call at five."

The clock indicated five forty-five. I flipped through a small pile of papers, chuckling to myself, amused by my own lack of organization and my caller's demand for instant recognition. After leafing through a collection of torn pages and folded notes, I quit the search and asked: "Can I help you?"

"No." Her voice seemed less self-assured.

"Do you want to help me?" I asked, aware my question sounded comical though my intent was serious.

"No," she replied.

"Oh, then why are you calling?"

"Because I have to!"

"What do you mean by 'have to'?" I asked.

"It's very simple," she lectured. "If I didn't call you, my mother was going to turn me over to my uncle who threatened to ship me off to some shrink. So I had no choice."

"Oh," I said, realizing the identity of the caller. "I guess you could have decided to be 'shipped' off to a shrink."

"I didn't want that, obviously," she said. "That's precisely why I'm calling you."

"Then did you 'have to' call me or did you *want* to call me?"

No immediate answer to my question. I could hear her swallowing; then she cleared her throat. "I guess I wanted to," she whispered.

"Okay . . . what now?" I inquired.

"Shit! This is stupid. You know damn well why I called."

"Do you really think so? I know why your mother wanted you to call. She had her reasons, but what are yours?"

"I'm supposed to make an appointment," she said.

"Are you asking for one?"

"Yes, damn it!"

"Okay," I answered. "Knowing and asking for what we want can be a beautiful experience."

"Sure, sure!" she said. "Before we set a time. let's talk about something. My mom called you very accepting. I want to see how true that is! I don't intend to sit in any room staring into somebody's face for an hour. Can we meet at the duck pond in the old town?"

I had had many sessions with some of my students in that same park. My response came easily. "Sure, if you'd like."

"On my terms," she continued.

"It's your session."

"Good," she said.

"Wednesday, at four," I suggested. "Is that okay for you?"

"Uh-huh. What do you look like?"

"Six feet, three inches tall, stocky, bearded, longish brown hair, large nose." I found myself laughing at my own description.

"Are you that funny-looking?" she said.

"To some people, perhaps. And you, how will I know you?"

"Well, now," she teased. "I will wear a black jacket with a lily-white collar."

"Fine. I'll be sitting on a bench just beside the lower pond."

"Is that all?"

"Yes," I said. "Unless you want to ask or say something else."

"No."

"Okay, then, I'll see you Wednesday."

"Wait," she said. A long pause. "My name is Dawn."

"Hi, Dawn. Many people call me 'Bears,' a nickname my wife and children gave me."

"I'll call you Kaufman, or do I have to call you Mr. Kaufman?"

"Whatever you'd like," I said.

"Okay, Kaufman. I'll see you Wednesday."

Entry in Dawn's Diary, May 3

Called the fuck yesterday. He sounded much softer than I expected, but I won't like him. His wife and kids call him Bears—how touching. Maybe he was the head keeper at the Bronx Zoo. I hate this! I hate this! I don't want to talk to anyone, I don't *need* to talk to anyone. Nothing's wrong with me. Damn her. My father was willing to forget it, but she had to keep pushing. Between her and Mr. Potter, you'd think I use the needle. Tina and I must've looked pretty stupid sitting together on the john puffing away—we couldn't stop laughing all the way to the principal's office. All I could think of was ice cream and Goober's Chocolate Covered Peanuts. Noah asked me out Friday. I sure know what he wants. Chubby Dawn or is it fat Dawn. I don't really look at myself in the mirror any more. Only Allen's my real friend. I think. The lecher, Mr. Thomas, keeps looking at Jill's tits, he's afraid to stare at Lisa since she told him to buzz off. Someone ought to cut off his prick and hand it back to him in a shoe-box. I passed Karen in the hall after gym. I couldn't look at her. I made believe I didn't see her, but I know she knew I did. I'm so mixed up about Karen.

The sky hovered low over the park as I waited for Dawn for that first session. A thin silver mist enveloped the open meadows, obscuring sharp edges, muting bright colors. I gazed across the field leading up to the road. I scanned the area around the pond. No girl with a black jacket topped by a lily-white collar. I sat down on one of the wooden benches hesitantly. Within seconds, the almost imperceptible haze penetrated my pants. The winged population, flitting about, drew my attention away from my moist skin. Two boys threw a Frisbee back and forth. A group of small children charged across the meadow toward an old wooden bridge. Ten minutes drifted by. Still no sign of Dawn. Again, I searched the entire park area. I suppressed an inclination to leave. "On my terms," she had said, and I had agreed.

The loud hawking cries of sea gulls surrounded a teenage girl who systematically threw handfuls of popcorn high into the air. Her body moved gracefully, though her face appeared curiously fixed. Her denim jacket rippled around her waist. Her thighs pressed against the seams of her jeans. Obviously overweight she had tried to push her body into clothes made for a more slender form. Although she stood several hundred yards away, I detected her glancing in my direction several times. Curious, exploratory, secretive glances. *Dawn*, I thought to myself, instinctively identifying her.

In response to my steady gaze, she turned her back toward me, then proceeded to move down a path hidden from my vision. Another twenty minutes elapsed. Suddenly, the same young girl appeared directly opposite me on the other side of the pond. This time, she pulled a bread loaf from a large paper bag. With each three pieces thrown to the ducks, she stuffed one piece into her mouth. Even now, my image of her chewing the white bread remains vivid. Her mouth moved mechanically, as if disconnected from her body.

As I rose from the bench, she looked directly at me, extended her arm, then pointed to her wrist. She held up what appeared to be seven fingers. And then I knew. Seven more minutes remained in our session—or nonsession. I sat down again and watched her continue feeding the ducks. In exactly seven minutes, she turned and left the park.

> *Entry in Dawn's Diary, May 10*
> The smug bastard just sat there on the bench, looking so cool. But I knew he must've felt like a jackass, looking around for the black jacket and white collar. What an easy mark! I think I'm going to like this... it's like leading a dog around by the nose. I knew it about noble Noah. He was all hands. He's so gross with all those pimples. All he had on his mind was fucking, but I don't fuck, not any more. Boy, was he surprised when I slapped him. So was I. Janet and Darleen are running a course on women's lib in the free school—they keep pushing me to attend. I'm not interested in their flag waving. Besides, Chris said Janet and Darleen are homos. Suzanne went on and on about her big-deal fabulous Saturday night with Howie. And if it's not Howie, it's Craig or Marsh or

Jimmy. She must have the most experienced
tits in the whole school. What a cock-teaser!
I told her to shut up. She called me jealous.
Disgust was more like it. But she was right,
I was jealous. Besides Allen, who doesn't
count, pimple-face Noah is the only person
who asked me out in two months. It's kind
of sad spending Saturday night masturbating in front of the television set. Dragon lady
Doris is still on my back, even after my session (ho-ho) with Kaufman. I do what she
wants and it's still not good enough. First
she asked me about Noah, then when I said
I didn't want to talk about it, she asked me
what I was hiding. You should have seen her
face when I told her I was out fucking telephone polls.

Our second session began much like the first, with
the exception of my choosing a different bench to sit
on. Dawn returned with bags of popcorn for the birds
and another loaf of bread for the ducks. No hello. No
good-bye. Yet our awareness of each other had grown
more intense.

Entry in Dawn's Diary, May 17
I did the whole scene with Kaufman in the
park. I thought he'd come over and start
bitching about how we're supposed to talk
or something ... but he didn't. I wonder what
his game is—well, I can hold out as long as
he can. Funny, but he does look like a bear.
And he still puts on that cool, relaxed, just-
sitting-in-the-park bit. I haven't seen Karen
lately. Maybe she's sick, but I don't want to
call her. Sometimes I think I'm going crazy.
I had a weird daydream in class yesterday.

Noah was standing by the window. I imagined him telling everyone how he fucked me. He made up this whole big bullshit story. All the kids laughed. Then he said he put a Coke bottle up me because I couldn't get enough since I was so oversexed. So I ran up and pushed him out the window. I was glad when I heard him scream, glad when he went splat on the sidewalk. But then, when I looked at his face on the ground, it wasn't Noah at all, but Jonathan, my first boyfriend. I can't stand Jonathan, I can't stand Noah, and I can't stand the Dragon Lady.

During our third meeting, Dawn drifted within ten feet of the bench. Her blue eyes locked with mine. Defiant, yet soft. Angry, yet sensitive. Wanting to run away, yet wanting to come close. I smiled at her, genuinely touched by her special presence.

Immediately, she turned and walked away. At the end of our time period, from across the pond, she looked at me and did something amazing. Dawn waved, though her face remained fixed, expressionless. She reminded me of the journey with our son, Raun, where even the most simple actions had been undertaken with great difficulty.

Entry in Dawn's Diary, May 24
I don't know why I did it, but I waved to him today. Charity—I didn't want him to get too lonely. Oh, who the fuck cares! Kaufman said on my terms—well, he'll have to suffer through it. When I came close to him, he sat there smiling like some big idiot. He almost felt genuine, like he liked me. I wanted to kick him in the face and hug him at the same time. Who would have believed anyone would

have put up with me. The Dragon Lady keeps pressing about the sessions. I wish she'd just bug off. My father complained I'm not making any progress. That's a laugh! Now he even wants me to see a shrink. My mother said I needed a loving friend not a doctor. A loving friend? How the hell would she know? Maybe I'm a lot crazier than anyone knows.

The fourth time we met in the park, our session began in its traditional manner. I sat on the bench alone. She wandered leisurely across the field beside the road. But instead of feeding the birds at a distance of two hundred yards, Dawn strolled over to the bench and, without ceremony, sat down. I watched her face, noticing an almost imperceptible fluttering in her eyelids. Her lips were sealed tight, as if locked closed so they would not betray her.

Then, without facing me, she said: "This is stupid, isn't it?"

"What do you think?"

"Hey, Kaufman. I know your game. Answering my questions with your questions." A talking Renoir painting. Statuesque against the treed background, Dawn's large full form seemed light, almost buoyant. Her unusually rosy cheeks displayed a natural elegance tempered only by the strain of anger.

"It doesn't matter what I think ... it's your session," I said. "What do you think?"

"I think it's absurd," she said, smiling. She jumped from the bench and began to walk away. She stopped, hesitated, then returned. Looking at me as if she were about to cry, Dawn asked timidly: "Is it okay to do what I'm doing?"

I nodded and said, "Sure, but is it okay with you?"

Regaining her composure, she sat down again. Her

face hardened, her lips curled at the edges. "You're a funny egg, Kaufman," she said, flaunting a sarcastic grin. "I'd thought you would have had the smarts to leave by now." She scrutinized my face carefully, searching for anger, annoyance, disapproval ... anything to substantiate her fears. "Well, aren't you going to respond?"

"Why does it matter?"

"Because it does, it does." Her forehead furrowed. She tapped her fist on the bench mechanically. "Say anything ... anything, but not another stupid question."

I wanted to ask her why questions disturbed her so, but I didn't. Somehow, I found myself searching for one clear statement. "Okay, Dawn. We each do the best we can, which is precisely what you and I are both doing at this very moment. Each in our own way."

A soft smile broke through her fixed facade. Then, quickly, her face clouded as she applauded weakly. "That's very good ... very, very good. I give it at least a C plus. I'm big on rewarding effort," she heckled, nervously rising from the bench. "Now I'll tell you something equally profound. I'm leaving early today. Ta-ta." Without once turning back, she walked steadily away.

Entry in Dawn's Diary, May 30
It's hard to stay away from the stuff. I think half the students in school are high all the time. Between periods, you get stoned just walking into the bathroom. Tina and I shared another joint. Fuck my mother. Darleen was stoned out of her mind. When we got back to health class, she flashed her tit ... just pulled the big sloppy thing right out of her shirt, even with Mrs. Freed stand-

ing there. Everyone was on the floor. Freed was so embarrassed she made believe she didn't see it. I got cramps this morning, guess I'm getting my period. What a pain! Oh, yes, dear paper, some news about my sessions with the Bear. That big creep got me to talk to him, but I turned it around and he fell for it. I'm not going to get sucked in. Dumb! They think you're dumb! I can't stand his eyes, they're so soft.. . .

The fifth session began very differently. Dawn walked directly over to me, sat down and grinned slyly. Though still stiff in her body movements (she folded her arms across her chest like an indignant general), she, nevertheless, seemed more vulnerable, more willing to show herself. "You know what, Kaufman? I don't even *have* a black jacket with a white collar." We smiled at each other. Dawn began to giggle, a silly, beautiful little-girl giggle. As I began to laugh with her, she stopped herself, almost choking in the process. She skillfully threw another internal switch, displaying the dazzling control she always exercised over herself.

"I thought about what you said last week," she said. "You know, about how we all do the best we can. I decided to change your mark; it really rated a B plus."

Shifting her position, Dawn turned her back toward me before continuing. She stretched her arms, then folded them over her head. "I wanted to sit on this bench from the very beginning." Her voice deepened. "I really did. Somehow, I know you knew that." Releasing her arms, she leaned back, squeezed her eyes tightly and blew noisily through her lips. "Okay, Kaufman, what do we do next?"

"What do you want to do?"

"Well, we might as well get on with it."

"On with what?" I asked.

"Doing what you do. Finding out what's wrong with me," she said.

"I don't find out what's wrong with anyone. That's just a judgment. What I know to do is to ask questions... questions which come from what you say. In a real way, they're really your own questions. And you can do with them what you choose. There's no place to go, Dawn, except where you decide to go."

"Come off it, Kaufman. That's a crock of shit. You want to reshape me into my mother's silly vision of the good little fifteen-year-old virgin who never smokes, never stays out late, never disagrees. Well, too bad, I like being me!" She began to cry, but quickly stopped herself. "Damn, damn!"

"What are you angry about?" I asked.

"About you, about me, about letting myself sit here, about talking to you!"

"What is it about being here on this bench, about talking with me that gets you so upset?"

"I don't know." She pivoted on her thigh, again facing in the opposite direction. Her body rocked back and forth in a slow rhythm.

"Well, why don't you guess at an answer," I suggested.

"Somehow, you're different... I think. But, maybe it's a trick."

"What's a trick?"

"Your being here, letting me decide about these sessions, not criticizing the way I spent all the time feeding the birds. It's really scary!"

"What is?"

"To have it left so open. Maybe I'll do something terrible, maybe I'll say something unforgivable... that's what the Dragon Lady is afraid of!"

"Who's the Dragon Lady?"

"Shit! It's just a private thing, between me and myself. Forget I said it."

"Okay," I continued. "Before, you said if it's left so open, maybe you'll do something terrible. What do you mean?"

"It's my mother."

"What's your mother?"

"The Dragon Lady, of course. That's my nickname for her," Dawn said sheepishly. "I don't know what I really mean by terrible. All I've ever heard is that I don't know. 'You can't let Dawn decide, because she'll fuck up.' I always lose. I'm either too young or too stupid. Like I'm a complete asshole. So maybe when I finally get the chance to do whatever I want, maybe it'll be true."

"What will be true?"

"That I don't know anything, that I'll just do stupid, awful things."

"Do you believe that?"

Dawn cried again. This time she allowed it. Hard, dry sounds echoed from her throat as her shoulders trembled. After a minute, she straightened her back and busily wiped the tears from her eyes. "I guess I do believe it. It's like thinking something is twisted inside."

She rose to her feet, then put the palm of her right hand in front of my face; a gentle gesture, edged with unspoken desperation. For the moment, this little girl/young woman wanted my silence. After taking three deep breaths, she withdrew her hand and said: "Could we walk as we talk?"

As we moved down the path, Dawn broke from her sluggish gait into a full run. Her excess weight dragged at her arms and legs. At a distance of fifty yards, she looped gracefully around a cluster of pines, ungracefully lost her balance and fell face down into the grass.

Bouncing to her feet within seconds, she charged back, finally rejoining me. "One minute," she panted, holding her index finger in the air. A thin film of perspiration laquered her forehead. "Now, let's go on."

"We often have reasons for what we believe, Dawn. Why do you believe if you just did what you wanted, you would do awful things?"

"Because I've already done them!"

"Done what?"

"I don't want to talk about it."

"Why not?" I asked.

"Because I just don't want to." Glancing at her watch, she said, "Besides, the session is about over. Goodbye, Kaufman, I've got to get home." Without looking at me, she jogged down the path and disappeared over a small hill.

> *Entry from Dawn's Diary, June 2*
> I almost did it, almost told him. God, I can't tell anyone. Somehow that'll make it even more real, more terrible. My session with Bears went quickly this time. I guess that's because we talked. The crying didn't feel too good. He deals pretty straight (I think, I hope). He never flinches—I like that. There's something so easy about his voice. I think he likes me. I must be careful, very careful. I don't even tell Tina about the sessions. I miss Karen. She's back in school now, but we haven't talked. Another run-in with the Dragon Lady. She smelled pot on my clothes when I came home from school today (she still never explained how she became such an expert in smelling marijuana). Bang! Off she went. Didn't even ask, just assumed I smoked my head off all day. She wanted to know if I discuss my *problem* during my ses-

sions. I told her there wasn't any *problem* to discuss. That jerky, spaced-out bus driver. Randy, didn't say anything when Greg lit up. In minutes, everyone sucked on their weeds. The bus reeked of the stuff. And I didn't touch a thing. Well, next time, damn her, I will. What's there to lose, I'm always being accused anyway. I wish she'd trust me. I hate her fucking guts sometimes. Big laugh this week on Jill. She's nauseous every morning. Guess what that means! Noah asked me out again. He doesn't give up. Next time he tries to feel between my legs, I'll piss on his hands. Darleen did another one of her bits this week. This time in Chem. 302. She told Mr. Sawyer she had been working on an experiment for several weeks and wanted to show the class. At the head of the room, she bent over, put a match to her ass, and farted. Wow, what a flame! Far out! Everyone got hysterical. So now you know what they do at the women's lib meetings, besides . . . Angie said she once saw Darleen mouthing it with Pam. A group of dancers performed in our Humanities class. One of them was terrific. I couldn't keep my eyes off her. She had such a beautiful body, she moved so . . . Oh, God, I don't know what I'm saying anymore.

* * *

Prior to our next session, Dawn called. I barely recognized her voice, even after she identified herself. A soft, humming quality permeated her words. "Where do you usually Option with people?" A direct question. My first response, though accurate, was just a bit too glib."Everywhere. Wherever I ask questions with a loving and accepting attitude. In the kitchen. At school. On a subway. In the park." Her forced laughter protested the commentary. I then described a favorite place; a little one-room glass house sitting on top of a hill behind the house in which my family and I live. My daughter, Thea, our impish eight-year-old resident artist, lettered a sign for the building as a surprise gift for me. Delighted with her own handiwork, she taped it squarely in the middle of the front window. "Big Bear's Happy Option Home ... love Thea." Dawn wanted her next session on the hill. I agreed, although I had developed a fondness for the park as a place to explore and share.

When she arrived on Wednesday, her face seemed sallow again. Looking around like an interior decorator, Dawn affected a haughty British accent. "Not bad, my dear Kaufman, but certainly not great. So this is where you do it. Not as middle class as I thought it would be. I give it a B minus." Dropping the pose, she pointed excitedly at a photograph of a war-weary soldier, vintage early 13th century, holding an infant in his arms. "Wow, is that you?"

"No. But I took the photograph. It's a favorite of mine."

"Oh," she smirked, "some hidden talents." Tapping the typewriter on a side table, she asked: "Do you write your books up here, too, or just rent yourself out for secretarial work as a side-line. No need to answer, wouldn't want to embarrass you." She ground her teeth absent-mindedly. Her eyelids fluttered nervously.

"Where do I sit?"

"Wherever you want," I suggested.

Dawn dropped heavily onto the couch opposite me, threw her shoes on the floor, and placed her bare feet theatrically on the coffee table between us. Her toes quivered, dancing to a hidden electrical current.

"Okay, Kaufman, I'm ready."

I nodded.

She ground her teeth together again before speaking. 'I wanted the session here because I feel more serious about it." An awkward smile rippled across her face.

"What do you want to work on? Is there something you're unhappy about?"

"You get right to the point, don't you? Let's talk about fat."

"What about fat?"

"I can't stand this any more," she said, fingering the flesh around her waist. "I can't stand the way I look."

"What is it about your looks that upsets you?"

"I'm unattractive. Nobody gives me a second glance, except Noah, of course, and that's like being desired by a leper. What a shitty way to be."

"What do you mean?"

"It's like with Allen. We've been friends for years. He always tells me about his love-life problems with Tina or Lisa. I'm like his sister, and a go-between. He never once looked at me the way he looks at them."

"And how do you feel about that?"

"Fucking miserable."

"Why?" I asked.

"Then all I do is end up thinking."

"What do you mean?"

"I keep thinking about when I wasn't fat and when I wasn't alone."

"What about that time, Dawn?"

Her hands rubbed her thighs nervously. She kept wetting her lips. "Well, I might as well go through it. If I don't do it here, I'll do it when I leave. About two years ago, I met this boy, Jonathan. He was older than me, had great looks...something very special about him, at least I thought so. We went out several times. The petting got pretty heavy. I got scared, but he wanted to go further, to do everything. He said it would be alright. All I could remember is how much it hurt. He seemed cold afterwards, said I wasn't very good at it. I couldn't stop crying. I asked him to talk to me, but he just walked away. I know you're going to think this is stupid, but I went to him the next day and told him I'd be better, that I'd read this book on how to make love. He smiled—boy, what a sucker I was for a smile—and said he'd give me another chance. I must've been out of my mind. Begging him to do it. Well, I lied to my mother that weekend so I could stay out until twelve. We parked along Shore Road. And," she stopped. Her voice quivered. "And, he put on the inside dashboard light. I was too scared to ask him what he was doing. We both pulled down our pants and he pushed it into me. It hurt so much, I thought I'd go out of my mind. I tried to move up and down like the manual said, but he had me pinned against the steering wheel. I kept praying it would be over." As Dawn talked, tears flowed down her cheeks. "He kept pushing against me. Finally ... finally, he stopped. Suddenly, oh God, I realized there were faces pressed against the windows of the car ... familiar faces!" She moaned. The cry erupted from some dark, hidden place. The blood drained from her face as she hyperventilated.

"Dawn, watch me," I said, as I cupped my hands in front of my mouth. "Breathe into your hands, like this. Go ahead, it'll help you catch your breath." In a couple of seconds, she regained control of her breathing.

Crying, pounding her fist on the table, she continued. "You know what that bastard did? He had invited his friends to watch ... that's why he put the dash lights on. The rest is such a blur. I wanted to kill him. I wanted to kill myself." Dawn stood up and leaned against the glass door. "Two days later, right in front of the school building, he tried to apologize. Do you believe that? It's like saying, 'Gee whiz, sweetheart,

I'm sorry I cut your throat.' So I kicked the bastard in the balls."

"What about that experience disturbs you most right now?"

"I think,..." She stopped herself, swallowing noisily. "Every time I think about it, I hate myself. I got sucked in so easily. I'm so damn gullible."

"Why is that disturbing?"

"I asked for it. Literally, I did. I even went back for more. That's scary."

"What's scary about it?"

"Kind of proves the point, doesn't it?" Dawn concluded.

"What point?"

"My mother's always worrying about me like I'm an idiot, always reminding me. And she doesn't know half of it. Oh, God, there's got to be something terribly wrong with me."

"Do you believe that?"

"How else could that have happened?"

"What do you think?"

"Anyone who'd let that happen to them can't be all there. A screw is missing. Something's out of whack."

"What do you mean?"

"I can't quite explain it," she said, "but I scare myself."

"How?"

"I keep going over that incident with Jonathan. No matter how I try, I can't make it alright... like I'm sick or something." Clasping her hands tightly over her eyes, she continued. "His fucking smile. The dashboard lights. Those squashed faces against the window." Suddenly clenched fists slammed on the table.

"Why are you so angry?"

"I hate them, I hate them, I hate them, I hate them, I...hate me."

"Why, Dawn?"

Tears flooded her eyes. "Why didn't I know? Why didn't I see it coming?"

"What would your answer be?"

"Oh, no," she yelled, waving her hand, "it's a little too pat to say I was a dumb thirteen-year-old, naive and all that shit."

"Why is it too pat?"

"Because there's got to be something more, something wrong with me," she insisted.

"Can you find that 'something'?"

"No."

"Then why do you believe it's there?"

"I don't have any reasons. I just do."

"Why would you want to believe something which creates so much unhappiness if you don't have any reasons to believe it?"

"Sounds stupid, doesn't it? But I still feel unhappy about it." She sighed.

"What are you afraid would happen if you weren't unhappy about it?"

"Oh, Christ, maybe then I'd do it again, get taken again and again."

"Why do you believe that?"

"I don't know. I can't ever forget how I felt, how I hate him."

"What are you afraid would happen if you did?"

"It's the same answer. Then it might happen again."

"Are you saying by being unhappy or in pain, you somehow protect yourself from letting this happen again?"

"Yes," she said, "if I let it be okay, then maybe I won't be as careful as I should."

"What are your reasons for believing that?"

"I don't know. I really don't."

"Do you think you can be comfortable with yourself

about what happened and still watch out for yourself?"

"I'm not sure."

"You want to think about it?"

She closed her eyes and spoke in a whisper. "I guess I could be relaxed and still take care of myself. I know much more now, especially right now!" A faint smile creased her face. "It's getting clearer and clearer. It's just amazing!"

"What is?"

"To realize maybe I don't have to be unhappy or angry and drive myself crazy to take care of myself. To know, when I took a look, there really wasn't anything wrong with me. Really, that's weird. I kind of feel free. It's not scary any more." She stretched like an infant just awakened, filling the room with a loud, throaty sigh. Her arms grabbed at the space around her, then fell completely relaxed by her sides. No fluttering eyelids. No quivering toes. "We sure moved a long way from where we started. What does all this have to do with my being fat?"

"What do you think?"

Dawn laughed.

"Do you want to share it?" I asked.

"Uh huh! I just realized I've been heavy for almost two years. I started gaining all the weight not too long after that night with Jonathan. I guess it connects, but I don't know how. Can we go through it again?"

"Sure. What is it about being fat that makes you unhappy?"

"That I won't be attractive."

"And why would you be uncomfortable if you weren't attractive?"

"Then boys won't ask me out."

"And how would you feel about that?"

"Awful. Because then I'd be alone. Shit, we've come a full circle; we're in the same place!"

"Are we? Before you said that when you were alone, you thought about the incident with Jonathan and how painful it was. Right now, if you were alone, would you still be thinking about it?"

"No. And if I did, the pain's gone. It would be okay to be alone now."

"Then if fat meant unattractive which meant being alone—and now being alone isn't an unhappy place any more, would you be unhappy about being fat?"

"I guess I wouldn't. But that doesn't mean I want to be fat. I still want to be thin."

"Sure, but there's quite a difference between them. Being unhappy about being fat is trying to move away or run away from what you fear. Focusing, doing what you can to be thin, is moving toward what you want. Away versus toward.

"I understand what you said, but as I listened, I realized I can't really see myself thin."

"Why not?"

"Maybe my metabolism has changed."

"Do you believe that?"

"Not really."

"What are you afraid would happen if you were thinner?"

"Nothing. Well, that's not true...I mean I didn't say the first answer which popped into my head. I was going to say prettier. But that's stupid. Why would I be afraid of being prettier, especially since that's what I've said I wanted all along?"

"What might be frightening about being prettier?"

"It's crazy. I just saw myself thin—a lot of guys would start asking me out."

"What about that would frighten you?"

"Oh, wow! The more invitations, the greater the risk of getting sucked in again."

"Do you believe that?"

"No, not any more, not now." Tears filled her eyes. "I see. I see. So Jonathan and my fat are very much connected. What a crazy way to protect myself."

"Crazy? I don't think so. Painful—perhaps. Remember what I said to you that first time we talked? That we each do the best we can? Maybe now that becomes clearer. Your anger, your fat, represented the best way you knew how to take care of yourself."

"I don't want to do it that way any more," she said. "I don't need to do it that way any more. I feel so, so un...un-angry."

The intensity of her smile energized the room. Her clarity dazzled me. Sometimes we dismiss the insights of a child or teenager because of his or her age, but whether we're five, fifteen or fifty, we all know. To witness that 'knowing" come to life is an awesome experience.

"Dawn," I said as she put her shoes on, preparing to leave, "you once said you didn't think you could make it alright, that you were sick or 'something.' Perhaps, from what you've discovered for yourself today, you can know there is nothing sick or unapproachable or unchangeable in any of us—not in you, not in me. Those are just beliefs, judgments; they're only true as long as we believe they're true."

"Thanks for today," she whispered.

"There's no thank you due to me, not in the way you might mean it. Whatever happened for you today, you did. I could tap your shoulder to show you a sunset. If you were busy, you might just ignore it. But then, again, you might turn and be thrilled by a glorious sky. Well, what you did when you watched the sunset, you did for yourself. If you turned, you chose to turn. If your body tingled, if you felt joy, that's how you responded to what you saw. All I did, all anyone can ever do, is tap you on the shoulder."

Her eyes glowed. Her lips parted in slow motion, but emitted no sounds. She kept nodding her head. Very quietly, she left the hilltop house.

Entry in Dawn's Diary, June 10

Can't possibly describe my session with Bears yesterday. I feel so different, so high— higher than I ever felt on grass. Hope it lasts. Wanted to tell him at the very end of the session, but I couldn't bring myself to talk about it. My voice disappeared. I knew it wouldn't make a difference to him (I hope not), but I still wanted to say it. Maybe next time I'll be ready. Funny how he's always ready. Last night my mother did her usual hysterics bit. I did a really weird thing—a first! Instead of screaming back, I just felt like kissing her, which is exactly what I did. She looked at me flabbergasted (I think that's how you spell it), then stormed out of my room. This morning, Noah stopped me in the hallway before my second class. You know, if you really try, you can find some clear skin between all those pimples. He kept asking me if anything was wrong because I treated him so nice. I pushed myself to watch Karen get off the bus this morning. I still have trouble looking at her. I think she has the same problem because she never looks at me either. Chris said Jill isn't pregnant. Who cares!

Entry in Dawn's Diary, June 14

Finally made up my mind about the hilltop house and called Kaufman today. Switched my sessions back to the park. He never asked why, but I wouldn't have told him anyway. I think I say too much on the hill. Thought about Jonathan today, it's wierd to feel so different—finally!!! I let Noah kiss my nipples. He's so darn serious that I couldn't keep a straight face. When I kept laughing (it tickled), he said I blew his concentration. You'd think he was taking a test. Jill's nauseous again, everybody—she's a regular one-girl soap opera. They invited those dancers back to our Humanities class. I couldn't watch that girl, the one who was so special and terrific last time. Kept looking away. Told Mr. Jenko I felt sick, spent the rest of the period with Tina and Chris in the lunchroom.

Warm sunshine mixed with a cool northern wind. The trees arched, their limbs dancing in the breeze. Once again we came back to the park. Dawn gave no reasons for choosing to have her session here again, but I imagined she wanted to change gears, to slow the process down. It would be her way of making this work. So many of us rush to judgment; labeling what we see as resistance, regressions, steps backward. When we hike, then pause to rest or even backtrack to find our way again, the pause and the backtracking are integral aspects of the hike. Clearly, the pause is part of the movement.

My early arrival allowed me extra time to squat on the grass and face the hot sun with my eyes closed. Images of the parched, sun-baked face of Thomas Eagle Feather, an old Black Foot Indian I met in western New Mexico, surfaced beneath my lids. We hammered silver together in the shadow of a sacred Indian mountain. He talked of shaping his life to the flow of nature, orchestrating his movement in harmony with the elements. Eagle Feather would have applauded this moment.

Suddenly, a dark shape blocked the sun. I waited for it to pass, but it persisted in hovering over me. It felt natural for my eyes to open, but somehow they remained closed.

"Perfect. Don't move, Kaufman. Your eyes, keep them shut," Dawn said. "I like you squatted on the grass; it's more natural than the bench though I do think you're getting a pot belly. I want to tell you some things, but you can't look at me. And don't ask me why you can't look at me."

"I'm very comfortable with my eyes closed. So go ahead, I'm all yours." From the rustling of her clothes, I knew she had sat opposite me on the grass. The familiar sound of grinding teeth reverberated in my ears.

"Last time," she said, "I told you about Jonathan and me—remember?"

"Yes."

"I watched you. You didn't blink an eye. Well, I have some other things to say. First, five days before the incident with Jonathan, I gave Stephan Kelb a blow job—he said I was great. Second, I not only smoked pot, but I sniffed coke once. Third, I used to think about killing my mother with a kitchen knife. Fourth, I used to think about killing myself. Fifth, I think my father's an asshole. So is God." Dawn paused, allowing for the reaction which never came. "Sixth, I once hit my younger sister with a stick from behind and told my parents she fell. Seventh, I called Maria Sanchez a spic. Eighth, I tell a lot of lies. Ninth, I...I. There is no ninth. I've told you enough. Well?"

"Well what?"

"What do you think?"

"You seem to be talented at making lists," I observed.

"Come on, Kaufman, do your thing!"

"Oh, I thought that's what I've been doing."

"Bull...sitting here with your eyes closed while I vomit at the mouth. All you've been doing is listening."

"Not just listening, Dawn...accepting. Maybe that's what you've been doing too." My eyes opened. Dawn avoided my gaze, bowing her head slightly toward the ground. Then, in a jerking spastic movement, she snapped her head erect and smiled; a warm, open, infectious smile.

The remainder of the session focused on her relationship with her mother. She realized her anger stemmed from the fear her mother might be right. Working that through, she then questioned the nature of her mother's love...anger as a statement of caring. Dawn concluded unhappy people act in unhappy ways, which says nothing about her mother's loving her or wanting to love her more.

> *Entry in Dawn's Diary, June 17*
> Hadn't realized how much I'd changed, how differently I saw my mother, until last night. She wouldn't quit, ranting and raving about my irresponsibility. I didn't say a word. I just listened. She looked so sad, so miserable. When she finished, I asked her what about what I did made her so unhappy. I couldn't believe my voice. It sounded like his. And I wasn't playing a game, I was really there. Wow, she answered me—right off! I asked another question. We talked until four in the morning! She talked about her mother for the first time. She'd been an alcoholic who died in an institution before I was born. My mother cried. We cried together. It was the most beautiful night of my life.

We continued the dialogues in the park. From time to time, she tested my attitude with provocative statements, stretching her imagination to be as vulgar as possible. Sharp four-letter words appeared as little delicacies, sprinkled occasionally throughout her descriptions. But her belligerence had dissipated; the anger had almost disappeared.

In a discussion about Noah, the question of responsibility for someone else's unhappiness arose. Could she make Noah unhappy? Reviewing the genesis of her own feelings with Jonathan and her mother and how she felt completely different when she changed her beliefs, Dawn reaffirmed that only she could make herself unhappy, thus only Noah had the power to make himself unhappy.

She mentioned a girl named Karen for the third time in two weeks. Dawn strained to soften her voice, almost successfully camouflaging her anxiety. Only once did her references to Karen generate a direct question, one which centered on her discomfort about avoiding her friend or former friend. She flatly refused to answer, choosing instead to redirect the dialogue.

Entry in Dawn's Diary, Aug. 14
I keep trying to enjoy it with Noah. No luck. It scares me. Darleen pushes me to join her women's group. Why me? Everyone started to notice the weight I've lost. Tina wouldn't believe me when I said I wasn't dieting—I could hardly believe it myself. And wouldn't you know it—Allen, old platonic friend Allen actually asked me out. I told him he's losing his marbles. He said I act differently now. We had a fight in the lunchroom. I accused him of being a chauvinist, into my ass and tits now that I'm thinner. He laughed in my face, said I looked just as huge as ever, said I'd have to lose a lot more than six pounds to get his vote for having an acceptable body.

Fuck him! Funny, but I can now observe myself becoming unhappy—like I'm outside of my body. Yet so many of the old situations don't bother me any more. My mother and I had such a fabulous weekend. She's so different with me. I'm so different with her. And we're both so different with my father. Even he's changing. Angie and Chris asked me to their party on the 22nd. I had a great talk with Jill, but she's so fucked up about sex. Look who's talking! Karen keeps slipping into my conversations with Bears. I look forward to the sessions. They really clean out my head...I mean (sorry, teach), *I* really clean out my head. He's great, he let's me pick it up and leave it anywhere I want. Maybe it's time to go back to his little house on the hill.

The sliding glass door squeaked as she slid it open. Dawn smiled weakly, while remaining outside. I could hear her teeth grinding. She did that every time she was about to allow herself to make a new discovery. Without coming inside, she closed the door again, sat on the floor of the deck and stared at me through the window. Then she disappeared, only to return minutes later with flowers in her hand. Making a bold entrance into the room, she immediately grabbed my empty tea cup and used it as a vase. Dropping onto the couch opposite me, Dawn removed her shoes and whimsically placed her feet on the coffee table. An instant replay of our former meeting within these walls.

"Now to business," she said. "I want to talk about Karen."

"Okay, what about Karen?"

"It's hard to begin," she sighed. "Karen has always been my dearest, dearest friend. We used to go every place together . . . shopping, the library, the movies, the city. We could talk for hours and hours and hours. There's nothing we couldn't say to each other. I told her everything, even about Jonathan. We were real friends. Tina's nice and so is Suzanne, but with Karen, it was special. And now I can't look at her."

"Why can't you look at her?" I asked. Several minutes passed without a response. "Dawn, what are you feeling?"

"Very uncomfortable."

"Why?"

"Because of what I am," she hissed, her voice raspy.

"What do you mean?"

"This isn't just anything, you know." She eased herself off the couch and leaned against the window. Suddenly, she whipped around with clenched fists. I thought she was going to scream, but then, in a hushed tone, she said: "I'm a lesbian."

"What do you mean?" I questioned.

"Shit, Kaufman, you know damn well what I mean," she shouted. "A dike. That's what I am, a dike, a homosexual, a lesbian!"

"Those are words, Dawn. They mean different things to different people. What do you mean when you call yourself a lesbian?"

"Well, I'm not talking about when two girls hold hands." She paced the room nervously. "Three months ago my parents went to Chicago for the weekend. Rather than get shipped off to my aunt, they agreed to leave me home if Karen slept over. We stayed up talking till three in the morning. Then, we decided to swap backrubs. I did hers first. Then she did mine." A long pause. Her breathing became labored, her throat tensed. "It felt so good, so damn good. Suddenly, I realized she had slipped her hands under me. When she touched my breasts, I thought I'd die. I didn't move. She kept at it. One thing led to another. There we were, naked, hugging each other, touching each other—everywhere." Blood flushed her face.

"Dawn, what is it about that experience that is so upsetting to you?"

"I don't want to be a lesbian!"

"Then why do you believe you are?"

"Doesn't that prove it? I slept with a girl," she said, "not a guy."

"If you smoked a joint or sniffed cocaine, as you once mentioned you did, does that make you a junkie?"

"No, of course not," she declared.

"Okay, then if you are sexual with another girl, why would you call yourself a lesbian?"

Dawn sighed. "There's more. When I watched a ballet company perform in school, I couldn't keep my eyes off the lead dancer—and the lead dancer was female."

"What do you think that meant?"

"That shows me I must really be gay."

"How so?"

"It's not natural to be attracted to women, to people of your own sex."

"Why do you believe that?"

"Are you kidding? Because . . . because that's what I've been taught, that's what everyone believes."

"Sure," I said, "someone taught it to you. And, perhaps, many others believe the same thing. But each of us would have our own reasons for believing it. So the question remains the same. Why do you believe it's not natural to be attracted to women?"

"You mean it is?"

"What do you think, coming from you?" I asked.

"I guess when I think about it, I don't really believe it. Before this happened with Karen, I could watch Billie Jean King play for hours and enjoy looking at Gracie Slick wiggle her ass all over the stage. Then, it seemed okay."

"What's the difference now?"

"I know something about myself that I never knew," she said.

"Which is?"

"That it's in me, the lesbian thing. And what about Noah? I let him touch me and rub me and kiss me. I wanted to love it, but nothing happened."

"What do you mean?"

"I didn't get excited. I do much better masturbating."

"Why do you think you don't get excited?"

"Because I'm not into guys?"

"Is that a question or an answer?"

"Both, I guess. I don't know," she said, "if I'm into men any more."

"Why don't you use Noah for an example, since he's the one that doesn't excite you?"

"Oh, this is stupid, the whole discussion. Noah's a lousy example. He's kind of a nice slob, but I'm not into him, his head or his body. It's so uncomfortable."

"What is?"

"To try to turn yourself on to someone who doesn't interest you."

"Why would you want to do that?"

A smile momentarily surfaced on her face. "That's a good question, Kaufman. If I made it with Noah, it would change what happened with Karen."

"How?"

"Well, it would show me that men *do* excite me. But look what happened, I can't get turned on by a man."

"Why do you believe if Noah doesn't turn you on, then no man can turn you on?"

"I guess that really wouldn't follow. Maybe if Greg or David asked me out, it would be different."

"So are you saying it doesn't mean that?"

"Yes. It doesn't follow. I could still like other boys and not be excited by Noah. But that doesn't erase what happened. That doesn't un-make me a lesbian."

"How do you feel when you call yourself a lesbian?"

"Shitty. Unhappy."

"Why?"

"Because I don't want it this way," she said.

"Not wanting something to be a certain way is very different from being unhappy about the way it is. What are you afraid would happen if you weren't unhappy about what you and Karen did?"

"Then we might do it again."

"Oh, are you saying by being unhappy, you'll make sure you won't do it again?"

"Yes. Starts to sound silly after a while, doesn't it?"

"Let's follow it through. Why do you believe you have to get unhappy to prevent yourself from doing what you don't want to?"

"I don't believe that," she sighed. "But I guess I did when I said it. It's the same thing I did with the experience with Jonathan. Drove myself crazy, so I'd take care of myself. I certainly don't have to do that." Dawn nodded her head. "It's getting clearer, but I'm still confused."

"Okay. What are you confused about?"

"Why I did it?"

"Can you answer that?"

"No, not really," she said. "No more than I can answer why Janis and I used to play doctor and feel each other up when we were seven. No deep, dark reasons. I guess we were exploring."

"Why is this different?"

"Because I'm older."

"And why would that make it different?"

"It wouldn't, I guess. Maybe it's just the word. Lesbian. It's like calling it bad."

"Why would you do that?"

"It's the whole thing again. If it's bad, it means: don't do it! But deep down, I don't think what Karen and I did was bad." She nodded her head and smiled broadly. "I can't believe I said that. What we did wasn't bad."

Her eyes glazed over. "I thought if I admitted that, it would confirm I wanted to be with women. But it doesn't. Even after the experience with Jonathan, I'd like to still try to be with a boy. Not to prove anything, like with Noah, but just to relax and give myself a chance."

"How are you feeling?"

"Remember when I realized there was nothing wrong with me...that's how I feel. Freed. I want to see Karen and tell her I'm no longer afraid to be her friend. I missed her. Don't ask me why, but I really feel happy."

I put my hands up in a surrender gesture and smiled.

"Kaufman," she said, "I think I'm done. I mean finished. I don't know how to say it. I feel clear, happy. For the first time in my life, I trust me. What do you think?"

"Why do you ask?"

"I want to know if you agree with me."

"Will it matter whether I do or don't?"

She began to laugh. "No, not really. Do you have to talk to my mother first?"

"Do you want me to?"

"No, I don't think it's necessary. Right to the end, huh, Kaufman. Having me make all the decisions."

"You always decided anyway. Only now you're happier and more trusting of yourself in making those decisions."

She inhaled a deep breath and stretched her arms above her head.

"Well, since there's no diploma, how does it end, I mean, how do I leave?" she asked.

"It's customary to leave through the door," I volunteered.

Dawn's laughter ignited mine. We stood there like two little kids, shaking our heads at each other.

"Okay," she said, "but I won't say goodbye." She squeezed my hand tightly and left.

*   *   *

To face Dawn for the first time after two years was an exhilarating experience. Everything about her sparkled. Her thin statuesque body accented her considerable height. Her eyes danced merrily.

"I never forgot anything," Dawn declared. "I wanted you to know that; it all really stuck with me."

"I can see that in your eyes," I said.

"Thanks for tapping me on the shoulder," she whispered. We both laughed.

"Now I know why there was a traffic jam here today."

Her group of friends, waiting impatiently for her on the sidewalk, suddenly became very vocal. They called to her. Dawn motioned for them to join her. As they approached, a young man took her arm with obvious affection. "I'd like you all to meet—to meet Bears," she said as she winked. Then Dawn introduced Jesse, her boyfriend, Cal and Ted.

The girl beside Ted smiled warmly at me. Her eyes seemed moist. She glanced at Dawn, then shook my hand. "I'm Karen. It's very special for me to meet you."

"For me, too, Karen," I said.

"We really got to go," Jesse insisted. "Nice meeting you." We exchanged goodbyes. Though the group moved toward the sidewalk, Dawn lingered another moment.

"Karen and I use your book all the time. I even got Jesse reading it. He's really a beautiful person." Her lips parted to form a word, but she hesitated, frozen in the midst of her thought. Then she released herself. "I have something I want to send you."

Jesse shouted for her in the distance.

"Hey, thanks for sharing these couple of minutes with me," I said.

She squeezed my hand and left. I watched her walk briskly with her friends. In an uncharacteristic gesture, she looked back and waved to me. I also waved, but my focus was rudely interrupted by blaring horns. The road had been cleared and the cars had started moving. I slipped off the fender, prepared to continue my journey into the village.

A week later I received a small package from Dawn, a very special gift. It contained copies of all the entries made in her diary during the time we talked together.

THE BOOK OF ROBERTITO

It had become almost ritual for Roberto (Roby) Soto. After lunch with his family, he returned to his shoe store only to watch the second hand of the large wall clock advance spastically, recording the passage of time in apparent slow motion. At precisely four o'clock, he smiled nervously as he turned his store over to his cousin. The waiting Thunderbird, polished once a week at a local garage, used to be a source of great pride, a symbol of his social and economic arrival after climbing out of the gutter in a small village in central Mexico and attending the school with pesos scrimped and saved from menial jobs. After several more years of employment, sometimes maintaining several jobs simultaneously, he moved north with his young wife and used his savings to open a small business.

His mind drifted as he drove down the crowded streets of Encinada, a small fishing village on the west coast of Mexico. Quaint Spanish-style buildings mixed awkwardly with glass-faced discount stores, supermarkets and gift shops. Music blared from busy twenty-four-hour bars. Old school buses, belching black clouds, carried residents through the town filled with tourists from the United States. Negotiating through the traffic, Roby's soft eyes registered a fatigue which does not come from hard work. The joy of living had been compromised. Though he tried to maintain his traditional focus on family and business, he found himself increasingly consumed by what he had once anticipated would be a beautiful, natural and easy experience.

Negotiating the final stretch of heavy traffic, Roby envisioned the last daily mail delivery from the States. For nine consecutive working days, he had come to the post office in search of a package. He parked his car in front of a donkey painted like a zebra with black and white stripes. The cart behind the animal contained a family of smiling visitors posing for a color Polaroid portrait. A uniformed postal employee waved and called to Roberto Soto when he entered the building. The package had finally arrived.

He waited until he sat alone in his car before stripping off the wrapping paper. His eyes filled with tears. There had been so many unfulfilled promises, so many painful dead-ends. At a psychiatric research center in Houston where they had last taken their son for help, a young graduate student, remembering the Sotos, forwarded an article to Roby which appeared in *People* Magazine. It detailed the story of a young family who had successfully developed a unique program for their special child who had similarly been dismissed by the professional community as incurably ill. Hope or another false start? Having the article translated into Spanish, Roby and his wife, Francisca, read and reread the piece. A notation about a book written by the father led him to further research. Another month passed until a friend had acquired the book for him in the United States.

Roby opened the package with great care. A little boy's porcelainlike face filled the cover of the book. His dark penetrating eyes mirrored those of his own son. Large, bold type and various quotations filled the front and back of the jacket. Roby cursed his inability to read English as he threw his car into gear. His heart pounded; tiny beads of sweat gathered at his hairline. He drove slightly south of the city to reach the house of Maestro Jaime Ankrom, a teacher and translator.

Señora Ankrom invited him into the entrance hall and offered him a cool drink. Roby shook his head. Within minutes, Jaime Ankrom appeared, greeting Roby with great formality and respect. He had grown to care for the Sotos and their strange little boy. On many occasions, he had translated papers and articles for them. The magnitude of this project considerably escalated his involvement. Jaime nodded his head, reaffirming his commitment to translate the book within six weeks as agreed. "Six weeks," Roby thought to himself, "six weeks is another lifetime." Propriety squelched his inclination to request faster delivery. But Jaime understood Roby's sense of urgency and canceled some of his own students in order to translate the book within three weeks.

* * *

The neatly typed pages contained a story and message radically different from everything else they had read and been told. Instead of pushing and pulling the child to conform to appropriate behaviors designated by some doctor or text, the couple from New York entered their son's world; joined him in his so-called bizarre behaviors with a loving and accepting attitude which defied any previous notions about dealing with such a situation.

As Roby and Francisca read the translated manuscript, they took a roller-coaster ride through someone else's life. They felt inspired and enriched for the first time in three years. Their own plight had taken them first to Mexico City, then to hospitals and universities in several American cities, including Los Angeles, Chicago and Houston. Their son, Robertito, had participated in three programs which ultimately yielded no results.

Though the boy was labeled alternately as brain-damaged and retarded, the diagnosis most frequently suggested was infantile autism, traditionally a subcategory of childhood schizophrenia, an irreversible condition of the profoundly disturbed and psychotic. Many of these children, often totally withdrawn behind some invisible and incomprehensible wall, spend their lifetimes drugged on Thorazinne as they rock back and forth in their own feces, alone and forgotten on the cold floor of an institution. The prognosis for Robertito conformed to that dismal picture.

Yet the Sotos kept looking, kept trying. Though confused by the regimen and disapproval techiques of behavior modification, they entered Robertito in such a program after numerous professional recommendations. The year of involvement yielded no visible or lasting results. They tried "patterning," a method of sensory conditioning which attempts to have a child relive all the developmental stages in the hope he might regain some lost step. They watched with discomfort as doctors wrapped their son, then three years old, in a rug, pulling it back and forth across a room. They viewed Robertito being forced to crawl like an infant, his screams ignored by a staff dedicated to executing a textbook treatment for autistic and brain-damaged children. Again, no differences could be detected with the exception of a noticeable increase in anger and unhappiness. The Sotos also tried orthomolecular medicine (megavitamins) without success.

Roby and Francisca decided to try to contact the people in New York, determined to fully understand and, perhaps, institute what appeared to them as a very special and unusual alternative.

Jaime sent a telegram on their behalf. Weeks passed by with no answer. Another telegram also yielded no response. They followed up the wires with two letters. Finally, they resorted to the telephone, uncomfortable about so directly invading someone else's privacy. A house-sitter answered. She considerately acknowledged receipt of the telegrams and letters, explaining the family had never received them since they were out of the country. She assured them an eventual response would be sent when they returned at the end of the month, though she cautioned the Sotos about expecting a fast answer in view of the rapid accumulation of mail from around the world which also awaited a reading and a reply. At the beginning of the following month, they received a lengthy reply from New York offering assistance.

Huddled around the phone, these two eager parents sputtered in Spanish while Jaime translated everything into English for their long-distance recipient. "He says," Jaime told Roby and Francisca, "the attitude is the most important consideration. He wants you to know they will do what they can to share with you and teach you whatever you want to learn, but—and the emphasis is strong on this point—there can be no promise of miracles, no assurances there will be any changes whatsoever. The child is the unknown which we all must respect."

Francisca held her hand over the mouth, wanting to shout their response. She had always felt so isolated in her love and affection for the little boy most others regarded with disdain.

"Yes, yes, they understand you exactly," Jaime declared, straightening his back authoritatively as he continued to talk loudly into the receiver.

Elaborate preparations were made for the New York journey. Roby hired Jaime to accompany them as their translator. The Maestro shifted his teaching schedules, making himself readily available. Roby then arranged for his cousin to handle the store in his absence. Francisca bought little Robertito new clothes, anxious to do everything possible to make sure her son would be liked and accepted.

They drove to San Diego for a direct flight to the East Coast. Staring eyes, pointing fingers and hissing whispers marred their short delay in the airport terminal building.

Robertito's dazzlingly large black eyes rolled from side to side like marbles in their almond-shaped sockets, finally resting to stare absent-mindedly at his own hands flapping like a bird beside his head. High cheekbones accented the width of his face. All his features seemed sculptured to perfection; the strong chiseled nose, the delicately arching lips, the copper-colored skin; even the straight black hair neatly trimmed in bangs formed an expertly styled bowl shape around his face. Robertito could have been an exquisite picture postcard for his native Mexico, a beautiful four-year-old little boy with a startlingly handsome and haunting presence.

Yet all this beauty, all this physical perfection cast a very different shadow after only a few minutes of contact. Sitting in the chair beside his parents in the San Diego airport, Robertito Soto never once looked at anyone in the room. He never once moved his lips to speak; never once stopped flapping his hands beside his head. When his mother tried to adjust his four-button vest, he shrank away from her touch, seemingly lost behind vacant eyes. From time to time, he made loud, peculiar, infantile sounds like a ventriloquist, hardly moving his lips or altering his fixed facial expression.

*   *   *

SUNDAY EVENING —The Arrival

The fire licked the bricks behind the mesh screen. The easy, muted horn of Miles Davis filled the room with its special melody; an old jazz aroma from an early nineteen-sixties album. Our daughters played back-gammon. Intense and competitive Bryn, just eleven years old, dangled her head and arms over the side of the couch as she energetically threw the dice, converting an otherwise mellow game into the mini-Olympics. She threw her arms into the air and shouted in response to the high score of double sixes. Then she turned to me, smiled her triumphant victory smile and returned to the game. Thea, poised gracefully on crossed legs, giggled at her sister's outburst. Though she participated enthusiastically, she maintained only a limited investment in winning. Thea embraced her world in a more ethereal and mystical manner than her older sister. The moment-to-moment involvement excited her far more than the outcome.

A small city of wood blocks jutted majestically sky-ward from the shaggy rug. Raun, our four-year-old ar-chitect-in-residence, busily constructed houses and towers and office buildings just west of the coffee table and south of the fireplace. His eyes beamed at the rising structures. Occasionally, he solicited our help for his more delicate designs. Suddenly, Raun paused, looked directly into my eyes with a silly grin, then charged at me like a bull. I intercepted his thrust with my arm, tossing him gently into his mother's lap. Immediately consumed by Suzi's kisses, Raun giggled and screeched. On his feet within seconds, he asked me to "slap me five," which triggered a short series of comic antics.

The piercing ring of the telephone cut through the music. Suzi motioned to me, indicating Jaime Ankrom as the caller. We exchanged a smile, knowing we were about to embark on another journey with another special child.

"Hello, Jaime. Welcome to New York. How was the trip?"

"Good, the plane ride was very pleasant," he said.

"And the Sotos and little Robertito?"

"They, too, had an enjoyable flight. We have made hotel accommodations for tonight at the airport. The Sotos would like to know what time after work would you be available to meet with them."

"Oh, wow," I said, awed by the realization they had traveled thousands of miles for, perhaps, an evening meeting of only several hours. "Suzi and I will be available for you all day tomorrow and, if you want, the next day and the next. We've cleared an entire week." I listened to him translate my words.

"The Sotos are very grateful to you and your wife for your kindness. They say we can arrive any time. What is most convenient for you?"

"Nine in the morning would be fine. And, Jaime, please tell them we will try to share what we know and are happy, very happy to do it," I said. Again he translated the words, then closed our conversation with a rather succinct goodbye.

Something about the tone of their telegrams and their letters excited both Suzi and me. To translate *Son-Rise* into Spanish, then hire an interpreter and fly with their son to New York represented a special determination. Though I have carefully responded, in some personal form, to each letter amid the hundreds we received each month, the process of making ourselves available to teach and help by sharing our vision and attitude formed the most difficult task. Without the support of funds and grants, which we continued to solicit, our involvement in this area began to seriously drain our financial resources. Nevertheless, we chose to continue as long as possible, also working with schools and early childhood developmental centers wanting to adopt our perspective and techniques.

Before the Sotos' arrival, Suzi and I spent hours discussing optimum conditions for working with them and Robertito. Since they traveled more than three thousand miles to see us, we decided to try to be with them on a marathon basis, which differed from our previous involvement with special children and their parents. Usually, our input with them was limited to single visits or a series of full-day sessions spanning several months. Although we had witnessed immediate and spectacular changes in some children, in most situations we felt hampered by limited time or the lack of consistency in the child's total environment.

A grant might have enabled us to help parents surround their children with a network of loving and accepting mentors giving sensitive and responsive input around the clock, seven days a week . . . a critical component of the program which facilitated our son's rapid and amazing rebirth. An idea evolved, but not yet delivered. For the moment, with the Sotos, we would do what we could . . . not by mourning what wasn't, but by celebrating what was.

MONDAY—The First Day

Sasha arrived first, her black shirt tucked neatly into her black pants, a green knapsack strapped tightly to her back. She might have been a pallbearer in a military funeral or a renegade Bohemian from a Greenwich Village which no longer exists. Yet a soft, almost vulnerable smile tempered her harsh appearance. Sash had volunteered to help with meals and the care of our children while we worked with the Mexican family. Since Bryn, Thea and Raun attended school until three in the afternoon, she delighted in having the opportunity to observe.

Several minutes later, a taxi deposited the Soto party at our front door. Jaime Ankrom bowed slightly as he shook my hand, then Suzi's. His plaid sportsjacket framed a starched white shirt and tie. Wisps of hair barely covered his huge head, which sheltered deepset eyes and offset thick jowls. With great dignity, he introduced Roberto Soto, a tall, handsome man in his late thirties. Dressed more casually in a walking suit, he bowed his head humbly as he took my hand.

Francisca, tall and full-figured, waited with her son. Her short, red-brown hair dipped just beneath her high cheekbones, accenting her classic features. She carefully searched our faces before being introduced. Her penetrating eyes peered boldly into ours. A hesitant, half-smile fluttered across her face.

Robertito bounced rhythmically up and down on his toes. He made a clicking sound with his tongue as he pulled at his mother's hand, obviously trying to release himself from her grip. Francisca resisted, knelt down and addressed him with great affection. Her subtle eyebrows and animated face accented each thought. But her words fell on deaf ears; her warmth never penetrating the invisible wall encapsulating her son. A great sadness clouded her eyes as she rose to her feet. Holding back tears, she avoided looking at us directly.

Still unresponsive and mute, Robertito continued flapping his free hand in the air.

Our guests seated themselves stiffly on the couch in the living room; we faced them in silence. Only soft smiles passed between us for those first minutes. Their sensitive faces rippled with moments of anxiety. Francisca tried self-consciously to stop her son's flapping hands on several occasions.

Suddenly, Roby swallowed noisily, then cleared his throat. He pulled a pile of documents from a large leather briefcase which he carried, and began to recount in detail their experiences with Robertito. Jaime meticulously translated each word, each detail, even the implicit attitude between the words. Roby gestured emotionally as he spoke. Each time he glanced at his son, his voice cracked, his eyes watered.

In combination, the papers presented a confusing computer-like smorgasbord of conflicting reports and diagnoses. Three described Robertito as definitely autistic with a grim prognosis. Two labeled him authoritatively as severely retarded; one further suggested the boy was uneducable. Another hypothesized brain damage resulting from an undetected case of encephalitis. The most recent report talked vaguely about an atypical schizophrenic condition complicated by unknown bio-chemical irregularities. Pages and pages filled with complex four-and five-syllable words; abstractions grounded in theoretical judgments, several of which were concluded after only fifteen minutes of testing. Yet, not one of these clinical work-ups clearly suggested a mode of treatment. Not one analysis captured by description or inference the particulars of the child facing us.

As his father spoke, little Robertito sat awkwardly on the couch. He moved his body like an infant just learning to sit upright. An occasional murmur erupted from his throat. The incessant hand-flapping continued unabated. And yet, his face appeared serene.

"Señor Soto says these reports have not been very useful," Jaime translated. "No more useful than all the programs the boy has participated in."

"Ask him why he chose to show them to us in such detail." Another pause for the necessary translation.

"He says he wanted to illustrate that they care very much for their son and did not come here as ... how do you say, ah ... as innocent or naive people."

I nodded my head, peering first into Roby's eyes, then into Francisca's. We, too, had once jumped through the same hoops to no avail.

Quietly, like a cat, Sasha slipped into the room carrying a tray of coffee and tea. She also brought a large glass of juice for Robertito. Francisca led her son immediately into the kitchen, fearing he might suddenly decide to throw the glass or dump it on the couch. Often, when he finished drinking, he would relax his hand in an absent-minded fashion, allowing the cup or glass to simply drop to the floor. When they returned to the living room, Suzi sat on the rug beside Robertito. She stroked his leg very gently. When he pulled away, she smiled, slowly withdrawing her hand. Robertito increased the flapping motion.

As I turned to address Jaime, I realized when any of us spoke, we looked at the Maestro instead of each other. Bending forward, I purposely faced Roby and Francisca as I talked. "Jaime, tell the Sotos that I very much would like to look at their faces when we talk, that our eyes carry very important messages for each other. Tell them our words are just one way to speak."

As Jaime translated, they smiled, nodding their heads affirmatively.

"And I will address you directly," I continued. Then I turned to Jaime. "Instead of saying 'they say' or 'Señor Soto says,' would it not be more direct just to speak their words?"

"Señor Kaufman, the role of interpreter is new for me," Jaime said. "I usually translate written matter. Your suggestions are helpful I will learn these fine points ... ah, on-the-job." He smiled, enjoying his own ability to use idiomatic expressions.

"Okay," I laughed, deciding to make one last suggestion. "I want to address you by your first names. Please feel free to do the same. In our home, we're very informal. For the next few days, we will be one family with one common purpose."

Jaime considered my words, but insisted on addressing me and Suzi more formally as a sign of respect. The Sotos welcomed the warmth.

We decided to work directly with Robertito the mainder of the day, at least until dinner. Then, in the evening, we could deal with Roby and Francisca exploring their feelings and attitudes, all significantly related to any program they would institute for their son. We preferred to be alone with Robertito, without any distractions. We offered the Sotos our car to transport them to a local hotel. Jaime gallantly dou bled as chauffeur.

Suzi led Robertito into the bathroom, the same one we used with Raun. It provided us with a simple nondistracting environment . . . no dazzling wall pieces, no busy windows, no mesmerizing lights. The confined space also kept the child in close contact with us.

We sat opposite each other, our backs planted firmly against the wall. The little boy walked aimlessly around in circles. His body seemed clumsy as he tiptoed on the tile floor. Both his hands flapped vigorously. We began to note several distinctive particulars.

Robertito never looked directly at anyone or any thing, yet he obviously could see. When Suzi lifted an oatmeal cookie from her pocket and held it in front of him, he either did not see it or ignored it. Yet, when she brought it around to his side, he immediately turned and grabbed for it. Robertito absorbed much of his environment using peripheral vision. In that manner, he could easily watch his flapping hands at the side of his head.

Despite his preference for perceiving the world tangentially, we did notice that he looked directly at the cookie when he grabbed for it, though he maintained that focus only momentarily. In another instance, when Suzi sensed him preoccupied with the faint sound of a distant siren, she snapped her fingers right in front of his eyes. No response. Not even a flutter in his eyelids or eyeballs. Apparently, he had the power to blind himself, to shut off his vision in order to concentrate on his other senses.

Although generally unresponsive to most sounds, this little boy paid careful attention to soft, almost imperceptible, noises. We turned on the tape recorder which we had placed in the bathtub. The room filled with the melodic and lyrical piano music of Chopin's *Nocturnes*. Robertito moved his head from side to side. He made the strange clicking sound with his tongue. An awe-struck expression lit up his face. Something about his gaze reminded me of the peaceful, wide-eyed stare of a Tibetan monk.

We watched him be what he could be, do what he could do, and wondered about the doctors who once tied his hands to stop him from flapping, the psychologists who wrapped him in a rug and dragged him screaming across the floor, the behaviorists who wanted to slap his hand and finally his face because he did not conform to a specific tack. We thought of the physician who suggested electric shock treatment to correct all the "bizarre" and "intolerable" behavior. And so most everyone in little Robertito's world played judge and executioner.

They defined certain behavior as good and other behavior as bad. Using those distinctions as commandments, they then took the license to forcibly extinguish the so-called bad or inappropriate behaviors, as if Robertito was not, in fact, at two and three and four years of age doing the very best he could based on his abilities and limitations. To treat a dysfunctioning child, who already displays dramatic difficulties in relating to our world, in such an abusive and hostile fashion raises serious questions. But the issue is side-stepped by the professional, who does not examine his own methods in the face of "no progress," but simply dismisses the child as uneducable or incurable.

At no time did we intend to physically manipulate Robertito, either to stop or encourage any movement or response. The attitude of "to love is to be happy with" created the foundation from which we approached him. We had no conditions to which he must conform, no expectations which he had to fulfill. Most important, we would make no judgments about good or bad, appropriate or inappropriate. In effect, like all of us, this strange little boy did the best he could.

Respecting his dignity and his world, we decided if he could not join us, we would join him—build a bridge through the silence, if possible, and motivate him to want to be here, to want to participate. Thus, we would try to create an easy, beautiful, responsive and loving environment for him to enter.

In joining him, we did what he did. When he flapped his arms, we flapped our arms. When he made the clicking sound with his tongue, we made the same clicking sound with our tongues. He toe-walked; we toe-walked. He grunted; we grunted. With the exception of defecating in our pants, an activity he still maintained, we followed him, taking our cues as he presented them. Imitating him was not simply a strategy or pose; we were really there, moving in earnest, participating as a caring friend, trying to say, "Hey, Robertito, we're right here; we're with you and we love you." The session continued to the point of exhaustion. Eight hours later, a little after six o'clock, Suzi, Robertito and I emerged from the bathroom. The Sotos had already returned. They looked at us expectantly.

"Wait," I smiled, anticipating their questions. "We all had a very beautiful day together—in the bathroom. After observing for several hours, Suzi and I joined your son. We did everything that he did with a loving and accepting attitude."

Francisca took her child's hand and led him to the couch. *"Sienta-te. Sienta-te,"* she said firmly, yet affectionately. Then, turning to us, she asked, "Did he respond to you? And did he know you were there?"

"I know how much you want things for Robertito. We do, too," Suzi said. "At no time did he respond in a way we could understand. So we don't know if he was even aware of our presence." Suzi tapped her chest. "Somehow, deep inside, I know it counts. We have to trust that and allow what happens."

Francisca nodded her head, trying to camouflage her disappointment.

Roby began to speak rapidly as Jaime waved his hands to slow the burst of words. "We have met your lovely children. Bryn and Thea are quite beautiful and affectionate, Raun, well...Raun is unbelievable. I never thought he would be...be so, so normal. He introduced himself, sat on my lap, and asked to see Robertito. When I said you were with him in the bathroom, he shook his head like an old man and asked if Robertito was autistic."

Tears filled Suzi's eyes. "Wait," she said, "I want to get the kids. I know how much they wanted to meet Robertito." She called to them at the staircase. The sounds of little feet rumbled across the ceiling toward the stairs.

Bryn appeared first. "Oh, Robertito," she exclaimed, "you're so cute!" Thea and Raun followed. The children gathered around their strange new friend. They smiled and chatted with great excitement.

"Look at his fat cheeks," Raun shouted. "I just lov'em." Any child in the universe with chubby cheeks is automatically adopted by Raun as a special friend. Some children are excited by ice cream, others by toys...our son manages to be quite different most of the time. After a couple of minutes, Raun, visibly confused, turned to his mother. "Mama, why doesn't he talk to me? He never answers. When I tried to take his hand, he pulled away."

"Remember our talk, Raun," Suzi replied. "Robertito doesn't speak. Maybe one day he will, but right now he can't. He also doesn't like to be touched, but don't think it means he doesn't like you."

"Joanna and Brian didn't talk either," Raun declared, pondering his association. "Robertito's autistic like them!"

"Yes," I said. In a hushed voice, Jaime translated our conversation into Spanish.

Thea stood beside little Robertito and laughed warmly as she flapped her hands like him. It was her way of saying hello. For a moment, just a fraction of a second, he paused. It seemed as if, in that instant, Robertito actually looked directly at Thea.

As previously arranged, our visitors left for dinner and returned at eight o'clock. Raun had been put to bed. Sasha, with Bryn and Thea's help, guided Robertito into the den. The girls wanted to work with him; to join him in his world as they once did with their own brother.

As I stoked the fire, Suzi offered our visitors organic grape juice, turned and mellowed like a fine wine.

"Are you still with us, Jaime?" I asked jokingly of the Maestro.

"Yes, definitely, Señor Kaufman." This warm and unpretentious man seldom smiled.

I leaned forward, looked directly into Francisca's eyes, and asked, "How would you feel if your son never changed, if he could never do anything more than you see here today?" Jaime's eyes jumped back and forth, registering surprise at my question. Then, mimicking my tone, he translated it. Roby sighed. Francisca's face flushed; her eyes narrowed. An expression of great sadness and pain overwhelmed her face. Anger curled her lips. She fought her instinct to cry or scream or shout.

Again, as gently as possible, I asked the same question. Jaime hesitated, then repeated it. This time, Francisca gave in to the feeling and sobbed heavily. Roby held his wife, barely containing himself.

When she regained her composure, she faced me and said: "It would be awful, terrible. Don't you think so?" And so began our first Option dialogue.

"Well," I said, "What I think is not as important as what you think. It's your son, it's your pain. What is it about his being this way that is so awful, so terrible?"

"He can't do anything for himself."

"What do you mean?"

"He does not feed himself. He cannot dress himself. He is not toilet trained. He does not talk. I could go on and on."

"All right, what is it about all those things which he can't do that gets you so upset?"

"I want more for him," she said, crying again.

"I understand that, but wanting more for someone we love is different than being unhappy about not having more. What is it about all those things he can't do that upsets you so much?"

"Most children his age do many things. Although he's four, he's like an infant. People stare at Robertito, make fun of him. I can't stand it."

"Why?"

"He's not a freak. I don't want him treated that way."

"What do you mean?" I asked.

"The whispering. The pointed fingers. The laughter."

"What about that makes you unhappy?"

She glanced at Roby, who remained silent but obviously involved. "I ... I," she stuttered, "I'm afraid it will always be that way."

"Why do you believe that?"

"Because I don't see any changes," she answered. "Because he gets older and older without learning new things."

"Since your fear is about the future, why do you believe if, up till now, he has learned very little or even nothing, that it means it will always be that way?"

Francisca looked at me confused. "I don't know," she said. "I guess it doesn't have to mean it'll always be that way." She paused to rub her eyes. "Okay," she continued, grinning self-consciously, "but I'm still unhappy about the way Robertito is."

"What are you afraid would happen if you weren't unhappy about his condition?"

"Then, maybe, I wouldn't do anything about it."

"Are you saying by being unhappy, you stay in touch with wanting to change the situation?"

"Yes," she said.

Roby's face lit up, but as he raised his head to speak, I held my finger to my lips.

Directing myself back to his wife, I said: "Why do you believe you have to be unhappy in order to pursue what you want?"

"I don't," she answered, quite clear on that point. "But I guess I act like I do." She shook her head. "This is all very new for me."

"What is?" I asked.

"Well, if my son is sick and I am not unhappy, then maybe it would mean I did not care about him," she concluded.

"Okay," Suzi interjected. "Let me give you back your statement as a question. If your son is sick and you do not get unhappy, would that mean you don't care?"

"I don't know. I'm not sure any more," Francisca mumbled.

"What would you guess?" Suzi continued.

"The more I think about it, the sillier it is. Why do you have to be miserable when someone you love is sick? Sometimes you are so busy helping them, there is no time to feel sad . . . and yet, you still care. I know, I had that situation once with my mother when she was very sick." Francisca smiled fully for the first time since her arrival. She kept shaking her head up and down.

I apologized to Roby for my curious finger, but thanked him for holding his comment.

He had understood. "Bears," he said, "I want you to know that each time you asked a question, I tried to answer it for myself. Each time, I found my own thoughts in Francisca's answers. Often I have worried about whether this will go on forever. Now, I feel different."

We continued the dialogues until three in the morning. Roby further explored his fears about the future, his concerns about who would care for his son when he died. He uncovered the belief that if he wasn't afraid of these possibilities, he might not do as much as he could. When I asked him why he believed that, he answered that he didn't know. So I asked him what he would be afraid would happen if he no longer believed it. Immediately, he laughed. His answer was the same as before; the fear he might not do all he can. At that moment, as he came to understand how he frightened himself into moving, the belief and the fear disappeared. No, he assured himself, he did not have to scare himself to make sure he covered every base. In fact, he became aware the fear of the future had actually diverted him from fully attending to all that he could in the "now."

I quoted to him the words of a wall poster in a friend's office. It read: "I'm an old man now. I've worried about many things in my life, most of which never happened."

Francisca reviewed her thoughts and feelings about being responsible for Robertito's condition. When she could not give one concrete example illustrating how she might have caused his problem, she blamed it on heredity. Why did she believe that? She didn't know. What was she afraid would happen if she no longer believed it? Her answer surprised both her and her husband. If she no longer believed it, then she would have another child. And how would she feel about that? Bad. Why? Because she did not want to stop trying to help Robertito. Why did another child mean that? It didn't . . . necessarily. And so, piece by piece, she unraveled some of her fears.

At ten minutes to three, Roby suggested they leave. He carried his son to the car as I followed with his briefcase. Francisca, Suzi and Jaime joined us on the sidewalk.

"It has been a most enlightening evening," Jaime said, shaking my hand.

"Perhaps, later in the week, I will ask you some questions," I said. The others laughed as the Maestro smiled awkwardly.

Roby grabbed both Suzi's hand and my hand. His arms trembled as he said: *"Gracias. Muchas gracias."* Without warning, Suzi kissed him on the cheek. Obviously very touched, he turned quickly to hide his emotions and slid into the driver's seat. Suzi then hugged and kissed Francisca. Jaime stepped back, anticipating her next move. Sensing his discomfort, she threw him a kiss.

"Nine in the morning," I shouted as the car left the curb. Time was so short, so limited. We wanted to cram as much into this week as possible.

Suzi looked at me with a knowing smirk, then she consulted my wristwatch. "I know exactly what kind of crazy week this is going to be. Okay, superman, if you can do it, I can too."

TUESDAY—The Second Day

The Sotos arrived at nine o'clock. Jaime bowed when I opened the door. Before entering the house, Francisca and Roby, both red-eyed, began chattering simultaneously. The Maestro put up his hand like an umpire, slightly embarrassed to hush his employers. Francisca indicated Roby would speak.

"A very strange and wonderful thing occurred in the hotel this morning," he said. "Normally, when Robertito rises, he sits on the bed, flaps his hands or clicks his teeth. Always, he appears listless, confused, like he does not know what to do. He'll just stay in that position until someone comes for him. This morning was very different. He sat up in bed as usual, but his expression appeared more thoughtful than at most other times. He didn't flap or make sounds. With great determination, he slid off the bed and walked directly into the bathroom. And waited there ... in the bathroom!"

I nodded. Awed. Dazzled by the information. In the midst of Roby's narrative, another significant event occurred. Little Robertito had left us standing in the doorway while he toe-walked through the living room, down the hallway and into our bathroom. A connection established and reaffirmed.

Suzi beamed like a proud mother, her blue eyes ablaze. She waved to us as she jogged through the house to greet the waiting student. *"Buenos dias,* Robertito," she said cheerfully as she closed the door to our tile classroom.

Addressing Roby and Francisca I said, "We'd like both of you to observe today, one at a time. The only place possible is from the bathtub. With the glass doors closed, you won't be distracting. I put a stool in the tub so you can look over the top of the bath enclosure."

"I would like Francisca to go first," Roby insisted, tapping his wife on her shoulder to bestow her with what he considered an honor. We all agreed.

"One more thing," I added, looking at Jaime. "We decided if Robertito has some receptive language, some awareness of the words which have been used around him, it would be all in Spanish. So, in view of that possibility, Suzi and I decided to speak only in Spanish when we're with him. Can you give me a fast lesson, a list of familiar words or even short phrases?"

"Of course," the Maestro replied. "I will sit with the Sotos and we will write the words for you in both English and Spanish."

"Write big," I said. "I want to tack that paper up on the bathroom for both Suzi and me." Talking through Jaime had become much easier. He had learned to mirror the tone and inflections of our voices.

"Also," I continued, "Suzi knows some Spanish. She spoke to Robertito in Spanish yesterday. She's a natural with language. Me? Well, I'd want to review the pronunciation with you. I'm an enthusiastic student, but with a tin ear."

When they finished their list, we carefully reviewed the words and phrases together; *agua* (water), *la música* (music), *habla* (talk), *mira* (look), *jugo* (juice), *leche* (milk), *los ojos* (eyes), *las manos* (hands), *la boca* (mouth), *diga-me* (tell me), *un besita* (a little kiss), *aquí* (here), *pongala aquí* (put it here), *yo te amo* (I love you).

With Francisca positioned behind the glass doors, we began our day in the bathroom with her son. Suzi had already turned on the music and sat with him on the floor. They rocked together, from side to side. A peculiar smile dawned on Robertito's round face. If I wanted to jump beyond what I could definitely know, I might speculate that this little person appeared to be enjoying himself. One activity gave birth to the next. Whatever he did, we did.

At lunch time, Roby replaced his wife. Having been closeted in the bathtub for hours, her hair, her face and her shirt dripped with perspiration. Nevertheless, she left the room smiling.

Sasha slipped in food for Robertito. We fed him organic peanut butter and jelly on stone-ground wheat bread. Normally, he would feed himself with his hands sloppily, depositing food concurrently in his lap and on the floor. Since we wanted to develop eye contact, we fed him ourselves ... morsel by morsel. At first, we had to hold a piece of bread beside his flapping hand to draw his attention to us. Then we placed the food between our eyes, inches in front of our faces, and smiled. We also used soft, verbal cues to try to maintain his attention. Robertito grabbed the food awkwardly, moving his hands lethargically as if they were only vaguely attached to his body. *"Mira,"* Suzi said each time she held up another piece of food.

"Oh, Robertito, Robertito," she suddenly exclaimed. *"Yo te amo,* Robertito." Suzi whipped her head around, barely able to control her excitement. "Bears! Bears! He looked directly at me for a fraction of a second. He really did. I'm positive. Right at me!"

For the next several hours, we sensed Robertito observing us observe him. On one occasion when we flapped together, he stopped abruptly, leaving Suzi and me still shaking our arms. From his peripherial vision, he watched us with curiosity. We stopped flapping. Then, he shook his hands again. We followed. An incredible smile dawned on his face. He had it. I couldn't believe it, but he had it! And only in a day and a half. "How could it be moving so fast?" I thought to myself. "Ah," I chuckled, "fast and slow; they're only judgments and expectations."

We offered him puzzles and other simple toys which he discarded immediately. Suzi and I stroked his legs on and off during the entire day. Robertito moved away each time. Finally, toward evening, he allowed physical contact. I moved from stroking his legs to stroking his arms. Very, very slowly and gently, I eased my hands across his belly and around his back. The little man stopped flapping while being touched. Suddenly, he jumped to his feet and walked in circles again. We followed.

Dinner was also served on the bathroom floor. We had to first compete with his hand-flapping again until we drew his attention to the meal. I put each morsel of food between my eyes and smiled, repeating our luncheon ritual. He seemed more directed this time. On four occasions, he stared boldly at me, though only for a few seconds at a time. Real and spontaneous eye contact! These movements originated within him. They were beautiful and profound steps.

A child coming from himself, motivated from within, is significantly more powerful and effective in growing and in getting what he wants. If Robertito could ever climb the mountain, we knew he would have to do it himself . . . not as a function of anyone's commands, but as an expression of his own wanting.

After the Sotos returned from their dinner, Sasha and the children took Robertito into the den again. In the distance, we could hear Raun's enthusiastic voice: "I just love his cheeks. Thea, look! They're so cute, those fat cheeks." Jaime translated his words.

Clearing his throat and swallowing noisily, Roby faced me and asked: "Will you teach him how to eat with utensils?"

"Oh," I smiled, "in a way, Roby, we aren't trying to teach him anything specific at the moment. We want to create connections, build bridges. Eye contact is very essential. Children learn by copying, imitating. If Robertito does not look at us or hear us, then, of course, he will not learn how we move in the environment and how he can move in the environment." I paused, wanting them to digest everything . . . and to question everything if they wanted.

"Since it's so, so much more difficult for him to do that than the average child," I continued, "we have to take special care, create a special environment. For example, he's hypersensitive to sound. When he's bombarded, he closes his hearing down to protect himself. For you and me, a cough sounds like a cough. Perhaps, for your son, it sounds like an earthquake. So, we try to bring music and our words to him in a gentle, soft manner."

"Yes, yes," Francisca said. "I've noticed his tendency to flap his hands more or pull away when there are many people in a room with him. People make much noise."

"Also," Suzi interjected, "people are visually very bombarding."

"Things begin to fit," Roby said with great excitement. "Now that you have said that, I remember watching him look directly at a small red truck we once gave him. Also at a door knob. Also at the leg of our dining room table. But, usually, he would never look directly at a person. In fact, he is much more relaxed alone. He seems confused when a lot of people move around him; it's his most difficult time. I never realized that before."

"And what could you know from that?" I asked.

Roby nodded. "That if we want to make contact or teach him something, it's best to do it without a lot of people around . . . one-to-one like we are doing here. Now I really understand about the bathroom."

"Beautiful," I commented. "Your observations, ultimately, are more important than ours. Roby, Francisca—it's you who will be putting this together. In a couple of days, you'll be on your own. You'll be watching for cues and deciding how to respond. You said you wanted to work with Robertito all day, every day. Okay. Your attitude is still the key because if you're loving and accepting, you'll also be a better observer. When we have expectations or need things to happen, we're distracted by our goals, by our fears. Being here moment to moment is essential."

"Look at all the professionals who told you Robertito was unresponsive," Suzi said. "Yet we've noticed many small statements . . . with his eyes, with his varied responses to being touched, with the imitation games. It's incredible, but some people discard such tiny bits of information as insignificant. But we know, if you're sensitive to all those cues, big and small, you create opportunities to make contact in a meaningful way."

"He's very into eating," I added. "You can use it . . . use everything! Anything! I'm not talking about bribing or conditioning. Each morsel of food can set the stage for possible eye contact. Our smile, our warmth is just a way to say hello. He doesn't have to perform to eat. Yet when he takes the food, he might look past it and find our faces. And in that moment, we can be there saying something with our eyes, our expressions, our voices."

"Suppose he doesn't look?" Francisca asked.

"Then we wait," I suggested. "It makes all the difference in the world if we let it come from him. There's quite a distance to travel before we would try to teach him specific things like eating with forks and spoons."

"Yes, I see," Roby said. "You are talking about being there with him and for him."

"Even more than that. We're talking about going with him," I emphasized. "First: acceptance, contact, joining his world. Second: with our attitude and the responsive environment, we want to draw him out . . . have him be motivated to try. Then, and only then, would he be ready to really learn many different things. And there's a bonus. If he's motivated, in touch, finally watching us, then he'll learn much by himself."

"In a way," Suzi said, touching Francisca's hand, "it's trusting the child. And trusting yourself to trust the child."

"But he has very definite...ah, how, ah, can I say it properly?" Roby stuttered.

"It doesn't matter how you say it," I assured him.

"Well, he has specific handicaps. The on-and-off hearing."

"I don't know if that's a handicap," I said, "as much as it's a way to take care of himself. He can certainly hear and see."

"What about memory?" Roby asked. "He can't remember from one moment to the next. Every day he looks at his hand like he's seeing it for the first time."

"I've noticed that, too," I said. "Especially with food, which we know he likes. He follows the food ferociously until it goes out of sight—behind my hand, in my pocket. Once it's out of sight, he doesn't pursue it as if he can't remember it or retain it without having it in front of him. It's a kind of memory dysfunction."

"There's nothing we can do for that," Roby concluded.

"Let's look at it in terms of motivation. Research illustrates that doctors will often predict that two people with identical brain damage resulting from strokes will never be able to talk or walk because the centers in the brain which control those functions have been destroyed. Yet, a year later, one stroke victim is speaking and moving about easily; the other is still mute and bedridden. When you ask for an explanation, the doctors say: 'Well, it's will-to-live.' In effect, the person who learned to speak and move again had to find new pathways in his brain, create new connections amid the debris. Since it required an incredible thrust, the person had to be highly motivated. And there's the key. Call it 'will-to-live' or motivation, but that's the power and energy we give ourselves to do what others might label as impossible. And that's what I'd love to see Robertito do. But you can't give him the spark. You can only be there, like a midwife, helping him find it within himself."

"Do you think he will find it?" Francisca asked.

"We can't really know that," I said. "We can only stay in touch with what we want for Robertito, for ourselves, and then do what we can to get what we want. Part of acceptance is allowing him to come our way or not come our way. Which leads me to a question. Francisca, how would you feel if your son never changed, never learned more than he knows at this moment?"

Jaime peered at me, his head cocked slightly to the side.

"Maestro?" I called.

"Ah, Señor Kaufman. I wondered why you were going back to that question."

"I'm not, Jaime, I'm going forward to that question," I said. Jaime became very pensive, then translated my words.

The Sotos looked at each other. Roby sighed. Francisca turned to me and said: "Still, it is a difficult question."

"Why?" I asked.

Her face became flushed. Her eyes reddened instantly. Tears flowed down her cheeks.

"What are you unhappy about?"

"Being a mother was something I wanted more than anything, more than anything else in the world. To love a child and have him love me. It's not..." Francisca stopped herself. She glanced at her husband, touched her fingertips to his face and said: "I know it's the same for him, too. We try to love Robertito and he rejects us."

"Do you believe that?"

"Isn't it obvious?" she said.

"How do you see it as obvious?" I asked.

"If I go to hug him and kiss him, he moves away."

"Why do you believe moving away means rejecting?"

"That's a good question," Roby interjected, leaning forward on the edge of his chair. "I think I always believed that's what his moving away meant. But if he's oversensitive, he could be protecting himself... like with the hearing. So when I call him, the switch isn't even turned on. Then, of course, he would not respond. And maybe, in some way, he's frightened." He rubbed his forehead nervously. "I guess I was so busy being hurt about being rejected, I never questioned why."

"And now?" I asked.

"And now," Roby said, "there are other possibilities. I can see it differently."

"Let me ask the question again. Do you believe moving away means rejecting?"

"I don't think I do any more," he answered.

"'Don't think' sounds like you're not sure."

Roby smirked self-consciously. "I guess I'm still deciding."

"About what?"

"About what this all means. If Robertito is doing what he can to take care of himself, that would be more than just okay with me. I would want him to be able to do that for himself." A huge grin radiated his face.

"What are you smiling about?" Suzi asked.

"Oh, I guess, at how you assume things without ever questioning them. Somehow, I thought Robertito's action meant something about me... like if I were a better father, he'd let me touch him."

"Do you still believe that?"

"No," Roby affirmed.

"And you, Francisca?" Suzi asked.

"I can see how Robertito is trying to take care of himself... in the only way he knows how. I can accept that. It doesn't have to mean we're not good parents. But, oh Suzi, you know. I want to hug my son. I want to hold him close. I want him to hold me close."

"I know how much you want those things. I was once there, too," Suzi said gently. "But being unhappy about not having them is different than wanting them. What is it about not having that exchange of affection that's so painful?"

"I feel so empty."

"What do you mean?" Suzi asked.

"Like something is missing. There's supposed to be more."

"In what way?" I asked.

"Between a child and its mother," Francisca said, "There is a whole relationship which does not exist between Robertito and me. There should be so much more."

"Why do you believe that?"

"That's why I had a child."

"I understand what you wanted in having a child. But why do you believe there's supposed to be any more than there is right now with Robertito?"

"Because I want it!" she insisted.

"Why does wanting it mean it's supposed to happen?"

"I don't know. I don't know," Francisca said, shaking her head from side to side. "When I think about it, it sounds foolish. What is, is . . . but I still want so much more."

"That's what you want. But how do you feel about 'what is' right now?" I asked.

"Okay," she said with a touch of hesitation. "I feel clearer. You can really drive yourself crazy trying to make your life fit your dreams. I see that now."

"That's what we mean when we talk about expectations, shoulds and supposed to's," I added. "We get into needing things to be a certain way in order for us to be happy. If they're not, we're miserable. And so, while we look anxiously for what we don't have, we frequently miss what we do have."

"I'm proof of that," Francisca grinned, pointing to herself. "I have barely allowed myself to be excited about what's happened in these past two days because I'm still so concerned about Robertito being toilet-trained, feeding himself, talking. All the normal things a child is supposed to do."

Francisca stood up and turned away from us.

"What's the matter," Roby said, jumping to his feet.

"I'm alright," she said. "I just realized something. In a way, I've never really loved Robertito for what he is; I've always loved him for what I hoped he would become, what I thought every little boy should become."

"That's not true," Roby insisted. "You've loved him and given him so much."

"Yes, I know, Roby, in a way that's true. I have given him everything I could. Tried to touch him, sing to him, talk to him, teach him and . . . and even discipline him. But maybe now, I can give him even more by accepting him, loving him as he is."

WEDNESDAY—The Third Day

The Sotos arrived at exactly nine o'clock. Before anyone could be seated, Francisca started talking very rapidly. Jaime put both hands up, trying to slow the avalanche of words. Suddenly, she started crying. Roby held her, then spoke quietly to Jaime who turned to us.

"Señor Soto asks me to explain to you what happened last night in the car. Robertito and his mother sat in the back seat, which is usual. Always, the child pulls his arms into his body and falls asleep wrapped up in himself. Last night, quite specifically, he did something he has never done before. Never! Robertito edged across the seat until he sat right next to Francisca. Then, several seconds later, he rested his hand on his mother's arm, leaned his head against her shoulder and fell asleep." Jaime, our dignified and very formal interpreter, drew a handkerchief from his breast pocket and put it to his eyes.

We all stood there. Together. In silence. Smiling through moist eyes for the mother who had waited four years for such a gesture from her child. Francisca hugged Suzi, then put her arms tightly around me. Her son walked easily across the room and headed for the land of toilets and tubs. Suzi kissed Jaime, then followed our student. The Maestro beamed.

"I don't understand," Francisca began. "You and Suzi have been working with Robertito and yet, he is different with us."

"Because you're different with him, Francisca," I said. "By working on yourself, you've been working with him. Each night, you've looked at some of your unhappiness and the beliefs which caused them. Every time you've changed a belief, you've changed your attitude and your feelings about yourself and your son. Your eyes, your smile, the touch of your hand, your body language—it all has begun to change. Remember, we're not talking about poses or strategy. When we're more accepting, Robertito knows. When we show him he can move us, he takes more risks."

"I don't know whether we're fully accepting yet," Roby admitted.

"Wherever you are now, your attitude has obviously made a difference already. We can explore it more tonight. Today, we'd like both of you to start working with your son. Okay?"

Roby and Francisca nodded their heads enthusiastically.

"You'll start right after lunch."

Eye contact with Robertito had improved dramatically. From time to time, he would look directly at us, sometimes for as long as eight to ten seconds. We noticed he stopped and started flapping more often in an effort to control us. He smiled much more easily. Though he still watched us peripherally most of the time, he seemed to understand we were there for him; without demands, without conditions. When Suzi out-flapped him, shaking her hands faster than him, Robertito burst out laughing. They both giggled for several minutes.

Roby and Francisca took over the session in the afternoon. Suzi and I worked with them alternately. By early evening, we stood sweating behind the glass doors of the bathtub.

Robertito's spontaneous eye contact increased significantly all day. Francisca fed him dinner eye-to-eye. But we segmented half the meal for an experiment. Roby placed pieces of vegetables in all different parts of the room. Robertito watched carefully, then reached for the food as his father deposited it. One time, Roby put some carrots on a ledge too high for his son to see. At first, Robertito just stood immobile. The blank stare returned to his eyes. Then, very slowly, very methodically, he raised his arm and felt along the inside of the ledge. Within seconds, he stuffed the food into his mouth. A mind-boggling feat for this little boy. We could actually watch him develop before our eyes, actually witness his unfolding from moment to moment. His flowering made the movement with our son, Raun, suddenly seem like slow motion. It took eight weeks or seven hundred hours until we had developed observable eye contact. It took many months until Raun could retain objects in his mind without concretely seeing them.

Our excitement consumed us. We decided to try to make the interaction between Robertito and his parents slightly more sophisticated. Roby placed plastic containers of juice and water in different parts of the room, out of his son's reach, but clearly within his line of vision. Robertito stood below the medicine cabinet and scratched on the mirror. He looked frantically at the can of yellow liquid beyond his reach.

"Jugo. Jugo. Jugo," his father repeated. *"Digame, Robertito. Jugo."* Allowing five seconds for any kind

of response, he gave his mute son the juice. These games continued throughout the remainder of the day.

As Robertito became more attentive, wanting more from us and his parents, we tried to place ourselves in positions of use. Each time he indicated his desire for food, by grabbing or even by standing and looking at the object, we came to his assistance immediately.

In the last moments of the session, Francisca introduced a simple stacking toy designed for six-month-old infants. Each time her son knocked it down, she rebuilt it. Just as we left the bathroom, Robertito bent down and placed one block on top of another. The roar of our applause and cheering chased him from the room.

After dinner, we continued the dialogues with Roby and Francisca. They explored more of their discomforts, unearthed more of their beliefs. We dealt with their questions about their own abilities to continue the program in Mexico. As they became more accepting and trusting of themselves, they began to realize they could have the answers if they allowed themselves to freely look.

* * *

THURSDAY—The Fourth Day

The morning session with Robertito signaled another movement. The Sotos accented physical contact, but not as a designed strategy. It evolved naturally during the first minutes they spent together. Roby imitated and tickled his son. Francisca hummed and stroked him while he stood stiffly like a figure cast in bronze. Then, quite casually, as if he had done it a thousand times, Robertito suddenly plopped into his mother's lap. Her mouth opened wide in delight. When she embraced him instinctively, he pulled away and jumped to his feet. Five minutes later, he dropped into her lap again. This time he remained seated for several minutes. Francisca handed her son insert cups. He flapped the colorful plastic toys by the side of his head, then dropped them to the floor. They repeated this exchange many times. We noticed Robertito's increased agility with his hands, though he still moved them with considerable awkwardness.

Roby presented lunch to his son in the same fashion as the previous dinner. He fed half to him eye-to-eye and placed the remaining food around the room. Little Robertito did not follow his father. Instead, he grabbed the juice container off the floor and held it. He put it to his mouth, but the cover cheated him of a drink. Roby moved to seize the can, but stopped himself and waited. His son walked up to him, dropping the container right in front of his feet. Roby gave him a drink quickly. Unwilling to assume Robertito knew what he did, they duplicated the situation with the water container. The little boy picked up the can and, this time, literally dropped it on his father's shoes.

After lunch we coerced Jaime to take a position in the bathtub. He declined at first, but the outcry from all of us persuaded him. The Maestro leaned against the tile wall, watching the child he had grown to love.

Continual talking to Robertito about what we did and naming every item we touched formed an important aspect of the program. We suggested that Roby and Francisca shorten words and language forms. *Jugo* would become *ju. La musica* would become *moo.* In other areas, such as expressions of love or excitement, they maintained the full richness of speech.

During early afternoon, we had a change of guard at our home. Sasha returned to the city and Elise, a dear and loving friend, joined to help. Her bubbling, new-age, astrology-oriented vision added another specialness to the texture of moods and energy at the house. Until our crew returned from school, she positioned herself outside the bathroom door. Later, she shared with us her endeavor to envision the room filled with white light so that Robertito might see an even clearer path.

We spent our last full evening together with the Sotos trying to lay to rest any remaining beliefs which caused them to be uncomfortable or disturbed about their son or themselves. Francisca discussed a problematic relationship she had with a dear friend. In the midst of a dialogue, she apologized for dealing with material she thought irrelevant to her son and our common purpose.

"Everything in our life is relevant, pertinent," I suggested. "How often has a person expressed anger toward someone they loved as an outlet for the anger they actually felt in another frustrating situation. And so, the frustrating situation or other problematic relationships affect other aspects of our lives. We're not compartmentalized, split into neat little sections. So, as we don't have set mechanics for helping Robertito, neither do we have set subjects for helping ourselves."

FRIDAY—The Fifth Day

Although we used our last day to continue observing and exploring, we reviewed and embraced the events of the past week. The visible movement had been dramatic. The totally withdrawn and inwardly focused little boy now sat on our laps and giggled in our faces. The child who never pursued anything or expressed his wants now found hidden objects and brought containers of juice and water to people in order to solicit their assistance. The staring, hand-flapping Robertito deviated from his well-entrenched patterns to hold cups and stack blocks. Though he continued to retain old behaviors, his commitment to self-stimulating activities, such as hand-flapping and rocking, had dwindled dramatically. He had taken giant steps to cross the bridge, to meet us in a way that he had never done before in his life.

In this day's session, Francisca began by handing the insertion cups to her son. He turned them in front of his eyes, then tossed them across the room. Smiling, she gathered the plastic containers and inserted one into the other. Robertito, flapping slightly, watched from the corner of his eye. Quite often, he looked directly at his mother. She gave him the cups again. Robertito dropped them to the floor. They continued this exchange for almost twenty minutes with Francisca talking and demonstrating how one cup fits into another.

Roby served lunch in the usual manner; some pieces offered and others hidden around the room. They positioned the liquids within Robertito's easy reach. Their son brought the juice can to his father. *"Digame,* Robertito. *Ju. Ju,"* Roby repeated as he filled the glass. The little boy sat on the floor and rocked from side to side after the meal. Roby joined him. They both smiled . . . at each other.

Although the conversations were kept hushed and subdued, we noticed Robertito's growing tolerance for louder sounds. He also made a definite statement about his interest in music by fingering the tape recorder until Francisca switched it on.

We ended the session in mid-afternoon and gathered in the living room. Bryn arrived minutes later from school. She kissed everyone in the room. Jaime blushed, flattered by her affection. Thea and Raun entered the house noisily. Within seconds, our son ran to Robertito and stroked his cheeks gently. Laughter bubbled throughout the room in response to Raun's infectious giggle.

Although Jaime still translated the conversation, we all talked together easily, intimately. With Thea on my lap, with Raun touching Robertito, with Bryn sitting ladylike beside Roby, with Suzi smiling warmly at Francisca, we had become, for these moments, a loving family of people sharing and enjoying one another.

After playing a game of "thumbs" with my son, I ushered the children into the den beside the kitchen. Bryn and Thea took charge of Robertito authoritatively. Returning to the living room, I smiled at Roby and Francisca, who busily composed an elaborate list, complete with numbers and indentations. Reflections of a college outline.

"Why the list?" I asked.

"So we make sure we remember," Roby asserted.

"What is there to remember?"

Roby laughed. "Bears, are you serious?"

"Uh-huh."

"All the games we have established with Robertito, things to watch for, cues to catalog."

"Is that all?" I asked.

"Yes, that is all," Roby replied.

"How come you don't have to make lists of all the things we explored during our long evening sessions?"

"Those are part of us," he answered.

"Are you saying what we did with Robertito isn't part of you?" I questioned.

Grinning broadly, he said, "I . . . I guess so."

"Do you believe that?"

"No, I don't," He said. "Everything we've done here has become part of us." Roby put his pencil down.

"Roby, you can still make your list. I only wanted to clarify why you did it. Sometimes we can observe ourselves doing precisely the same behavior . . . one time from unhappiness, another time from our good feelings."

I took Suzi's hand and looked into her bright eyes,

then turned back to Roby and Francisca. "The reason I raised the questions about the list is because I want both of you to know you are your own best expert on yourself and your situation. Don't see the list as a guide to the future; at best, it's only a record of the past. If Suzi and I suggested turning left and, tomorrow, it seemed apparent to you to turn right, then trust yourself and turn right."

"There aren't any rules of conduct," Suzi interjected. "Only your choices, your decisions. And you can know better than anyone else, including us, what there is for you to do."

"I'd like to pose one more question, specifically to you, Francisca," I said. "It's one I've asked you almost every day. How would you feel if Robertito never changed from the way he is today, never learned anything more?"

She smiled broadly. "Bears, when you asked me that on the first day I met you, I became so upset, so angry, I wanted to run out of your house and never, never come back. How could I have traveled over three thousand miles to be asked such a crazy question? I thought there was only one possible answer—that, of course, I had to feel terrible if he didn't improve." A long, relaxed sigh echoed from her throat. "Now I can say it would be okay. I never realized by not accepting Robertito as he is, I was disapproving of him."

"It's like saying to a person it's not okay to be who you are; you must be something else to be acceptable," Suzi commented.

"Yes, I understand," Francisca said. "Although I want more for Robertito and we will work for more, I can see my son clearer now and can enjoy him now—really enjoy him. Oh, God, I feel so much easier with myself." Her face glowed; her eyes emanated a peacefulness which had never been apparent before.

Bryn charged into the living room wide-eyed. She

held her index finger in front of her lips, hushing our conversation, and motioned for us to follow quickly. We gathered at the kitchen door. A bottle of juice balanced precariously near the edge of the counter. On tiptoes, little Robertito stretched his arms as high as possible, but missed his mark. A strange, throaty sound oozed from him. And then it became apparent. *"Ju. Ju. Ju."* Francisca laughed and cried as she quickly poured the juice into a plastic glass.

Raun pulled on Suzi's pants. "Mama, can I have juice, too?"

"I'll give him some," Thea offered.

When we turned to re-enter the living room, I saw Roby sitting by himself, his face flushed. Francisca sat beside him quietly, then talked softly to Jaime. "Francisca," he said, "believes Roby would like to be alone." The Sotos rose from the couch.

"Tell them to stay. We'll be in the other room." I asked Elise and the children to keep Robertito in the kitchen, while Suzi and I sat in the den. A man's muffled sobbing filtered through the walls.

Within the next hour, Robertito used two more words in order to communicate his wants.

Later, we reassembled in the living room. Roby and the Maestro completed a rather intense conversation. Jaime directed his words toward me.

"Señor Soto would like to say something, but he is concerned you might get insulted."

I laughed. "Tell him I doubt it. If I get insulted, I do that to myself. And since I don't want to feel uncomfortable or upset, there's no risk. Let him say what he would like."

Jaime spoke again for Roby. "The Sotos would like to pay you. They have calculated that you have worked with them and their son for almost eighty hours during the past week. They realize you and Suzi had to stop many other things in order to do this. They wish to compensate you for teaching them."

Leaning forward, I put my hands on top of Robertito and Francisca's hands. I searched their sensitive faces. "First, I'm not insulted. I understand your intentions. If we wanted to be paid, I would have told you that in the beginning. We chose to be here, to help. I don't know if we could always do this, but we wanted to do it now. We've been enriched by knowing you, your son, and witnessing his movement. It has been a very beautiful week, a very complete week. Your joy stands as our payment."

Roby nodded, acknowledging my words. Francisca's eyes sparkled. Caring thought passed from person to person in the silence. Suddenly, the blaring horn of a taxi invaded the room. Jaime excused himself, stepping outside to ask the driver to wait. Roby checked his passports and plane tickets.

Suzi fought back tears as she hugged Roby, Francisca and little Robertito. I embraced each of them as did our children. Then I turned to Jaime, refusing to say my goodbye to him with a formal handshake. As I reached to hug him, he reached to hug me. We patted each other on the back and laughed.

"Señor Kaufman, I am slow at changing, but this has been a great learning experience for me. On the day we met, you asked me to call you Bears. I am ready now."

"Peace, Jaime," I smiled.

"And to you, Bears. Adios," he said. Then the Maestro embraced Suzi.

"I have no more words," Roby whispered. "My feelings are too strong for my words." He bowed his head and led his family down the walk to the waiting car.

THE BOOK OF DAVID

Beside the road, where the loose gravel hugged the curb, an old man with a full gray beard bicycled up a gentle slope. A white handkerchief, wrapped tightly around his head and folded in the front into a triangle, absorbed the perspiration dripping from his hairline. His face, though deeply lined and parched like old leather, had a playful, magical air. His bright eyes twinkled. Halting his ten-speed bicycle before the curb, he dismounted and lifted it easily over the ten-inch cement obstacle. Once back on the bike, the old man pedaled down the walk, turning into the courtyard of a small aparment building.

After he maneuvered the front wheel into an appropriate stand, he proceeded to perform a series of deep knee bends. Completing the calisthenic, he clasped his hands over his head, stretched to the left and to the right, grunting loudly each time he tilted the upper portion of his torso to form a right angle with his hips and legs. His red-and-black checked shirt loosened out of his pants, exposed taut skin to the open air. He promptly pushed the garment back behind his waistband and tightened the belt. After blowing his nose loudly, he arched his body forward and touched his palms to the ground. Then he stood erect like a valiant old soldier, pointed his face toward the sky and performed a rhythmic breathing exercise. A quick set of jumping-jacks sapped his waning energy.

Though Charles "Scoot" Hogan had passed his seventy-third birthday, his thin, athletic, limber body responded easily to each movement.

A long, yellow school bus paused at the sidewalk and discharged some children. They immediately scattered in all directions. One little boy, wearing a soiled polo shirt and dungarees rolled up to his knees, ran past the old man toward the building's entrance. When he saw Scoot, he stopped dead in his tracks. David Seaton took eight giant steps backwards, putting his hands out to the side as if to balance. He reversed his briefcase to match his blue baseball cap already backwards on his head.

"What'a we got here?" Scoot said, purposely overreacting like a demented scientist in a grade-B movie. "Humm . . . a boy with hair instead of a face and a backside instead of a front side." Pivoting on his toes, David twirled around and smiled. "Oh Lord!" the old man exclaimed in mock surprise. "It's you! Well, well, could'a fooled me, yes sir! Some act, ya have, for a seven-year-old person."

"Seven and a half," corrected David.

"Yes, yes. Seven and a half it is," the old man said with a gravelly chuckle. "How's ma fella?"

"Fine. Did you finish your exercises?"

"Just about," he answered loud and clear as he performed one last series of deep knee bends. "Davey, if ya got your health, ya got it all."

"Would you like to see some of my drawings?"

The old man nodded, genuinely excited about the sharing.

David withdrew several drawings from his small briefcase. He unfolded a large one, displaying it on the lawn. The collection revealed brightly colored animals at a zoo.

"Well, well! I'll be. Seems like we have an artist cookin' on McHenry Street. Yes sir...a genuine artist."

"You really like it, Scoot?" David asked.

"Sure do; mighty fine, mighty fine, I tell you. Just remember, every artist, every ballplayer, every bicyclist, every everybody started somewhere. You got the makin's, Davey. And I should know; after all, I twirled a pencil or two in my time."

The old man removed the cloth from his head and smiled at his young companion. "See this? Keeps the sweat out of my eyes—a little trick I knew long before all those fancy joggers with their fancy duds and headbands. How'd ya do in the try-outs?"

The little boy lowered his head, biting his upper lip. Sensing the answer, Scoot continued: "Well, no matter. Some of us is good, some of us is better than good. Don't mean a thing, Mr. Longface David Seaton." The boy managed a smile. "That's a darn sight better. Yes sir, darn sight better." The old man pulled out a piece of gum from his pocket. "Got this special for ya. Checked it all out; says here it's sugarless. Wouldn't want'a give ya something which knocks holes in those young teeth of yours."

"Thanks, Scoot," David said as he threw the gum into his mouth. The old man tapped him affectionately on the head.

"Can I help you lock up the bike?" the boy asked.

"Funny you should ask. Just in the nick of time, you

are. Help is what I need," Scoot said. Winding the chain through the tires and the frame, he hooked two loops together. David inserted the lock and snapped it closed with a quick flick of his hand.

"Fine job, young man. Every time I watch you do that, I'm more and more surprised 'bout how fast ya manage it. C'mon, take a bow—champ!" David stood up and threw his hands over his head like a prize-fighter. He bowed to an imaginary audience, enjoying the charade.

The two entered the building hand-in-hand. They rode the elevator to the same floor, but went to different apartments on the opposite sides of the hall.

"Scoot, can I come over in a little while?" David asked.

"Sure thing. An old man like me sure does appreciate having a visitor. Ol' Larry L. and Maggie will be waitin' for ya too. Any time, ya hear, just pay us a visit." As he finished the last word, he disappeared into his apartment.

After ringing the bell once, then twice, without a response, David started to kick the bottom of the door while holding the button continually depressed. He added the clamor of a pounding fist to the dissonant symphony. Suddenly, the door whipped open.

"Jesus Christ, David. I was in the bathroom. You don't have to be so damn inconsiderate. Now get inside. And put your hat on straight!" As he moved across the threshold, he kicked the door again with all his might. Janice Seaton slapped her son across the face.

Ten minutes later, David reopened the front door. His mother grabbed him. "Now listen here, young man; you just can't decide to go out. I'm your mother. Now where do you think you're going?"

"Just across the hall to visit Scoot."

Lowering her voice, his mother said, "David, why don't you play with some friends your own age?"

"I don't have any friends."

"You don't try. What about Tommy on the second floor or Darren on the third? If you spend your time with some old man, you'll never make friends."

"But Scoot is my friend."

"You know damn well that's not what I'm talking about," she continued. "I'm going to speak to your father about this. It's time we do something."

Ignoring her words, he walked across the hall and knocked on the old man's door which had been left slightly ajar. "Come in, come in ... been expectin'ya," said a wispy voice.

David slipped into the old man's apartment. His mother shook her head from side to side as she watched her son pull the door closed behind him.

"Careful, careful," Scoot said to David. "That new wire is for a special tunnel I'm building for Ol' Larry L." The old man smiled, tipping his head at his pet lizard who stood motionless in the gigantic enclosure spanning one entire wall of the living room. "When I'm finished, he'll be able to crawl all the way to the window and sun himself on the ledge if he likes." Wire by wire, Scoot fastened different sections of mesh into one continuous piece.

In the center of the room, a large floor-to-ceiling cage housed Maggie, a huge black-and-orange myna bird. "Sit down, sit down," the bird squawked, repeating himself like his master.

"Not now, Maggie," David replied much in the same fashion he would talk with anyone.

"Sit down, sit down," Maggie repeated.

"Shush, shush!" Scoot commanded.

"Shush, shush, scoot, toot. Sit down, sit down." The lizard began to move, diverting the bird's attention.

"Finally, some peace and quiet," the old man muttered. "Davey, go into the kitchen ... you'll find something just for you."

Anticipating the surprise, the little boy raced into the other room to find two chocolate-chip cookies waiting for him. Slipping into a chair, he ate them, then returned to the living room.

"Boy, they were real good."

"Only the best for a friend, Davey. All natural too. Can't be too careful these days. Ya want to live long like me? Well, eat only what's natural for ya. All that paint in the food is no damn good for anyone, man or lizard."

"Mom says people who don't shop in the supermarket with everyone else are queer."

The old man whipped his head around, slightly offended. Confronted by David's innocent expression, he smiled and said: "Well, let's see. What I think your mom meant is that those people are different. But ya know, Davey, we're all different. Take Larry L. When I bought him at the Fairweather Pet Shop, there weren't another like him. See those big green dots on his back . . . well, no other lizard anyone's ever seen had green dots on his back. And Maggie here, well, guess ya could say she's queer as a three-dollar bill. Only one leg, but ya see how she stands and takes good care of herself."

David stared at the bird's single leg. He always thought something had to be very strange about Maggie, but never wanted to ask. "You think if I had one leg," he asked, "I could stand like that?"

"Don't know," the old man answered quickly. "Nobody could ever know till it happens. Too much fussin' 'bout tomorrow, Davey. Ya got two feet today. That's all that counts, I tell ya."

"Could I help you now?" David asked, fascinated by the ease with which Scoot manipulated the tools.

"Sure can. Don't ask what it is with you, always arrivin' when I need help. Get over here, c'mon. Okay now, watch me, then you do it with those pinchers."

After several abortive attempts, the old man guided the little boy's hands until he bent the wire. The two worked side by side for fifteen minutes.

The door bell rang. "Yes, who's there?" Scoot shouted without changing position or interrupting his work.

"Mr. Hogan, it's Mrs. Seaton. Is my son still in there?"

"Sure is!"

"Please send him home immediately."

The silence in the room enveloped them. Scoot looked at David, whose face twitched with anger. "Hey, Davey ma man, what's that I see?"

"I want to stay here," the young boy insisted.

"Well, there are different times for different things. We had a nice visit, you and I. You'll come again. Nothing to pout about. I'm sure Larry L. and Maggie would tell ya the same if they could."

David nodded, then managed to squeeze out a half-smile as he left. Scoot hummed as he continued to work alone.

* * *

"It's ridiculous," Janice Seaton said adamantly. Her long hair, conspicuously colored red, fell in front of her face, partially camouflaging her high cheekbones and angular chin. Snapping her head to the side, she whipped the loose strand back over her shoulder. Her fingers fiddled with the strap from her pocket book; her green eyes stared at the wall, never focusing directly on me as she talked.

"Those idiots in school tell me I have a problem and 'I' have to correct it. They stood there, like some sort of firing squad. Just ridiculous. David's guidance counselor, Mr. Ceddar with his flat head and dumb crewcut ... you'd think someone's been hiding him in a closet for the last twenty years. And Mr. Griffen, the principal, always scratching his chin and shaking his head like God Almighty. Miss Dean, his teacher, is so uptight I get stomach cramps just thinking about her. And the queer ass of them all, Miss Templer, the school psychologist. She was so nervous I thought she'd get diarrhea in the middle of the meeting. They all just ran at the mouth, blabbering like they had nothing to do with it—the poor innocent dears! Well, let me tell you, before he went to that school, David was a lovely boy. No kicking in the doors and lighting fires. Now, he's not even civil to anyone. He's the kind of kid only a mother could love and even that's getting pretty difficult. I don't know what happened." Bending her head down, she massaged the corners of her eyes with her fingers.

"God knows I tried," Janice continued. "After Doug left me, I had no one to help. Just David and me. It's hard to be a woman with a child all alone." She jumped from her seat and walked to the window. As she pulled at the collar of her sweater, she cursed the garment. Suddenly, she spun around and faced me directly for the first time. "Look, I'm here for David, not for me."

"Is there any difference? You two are kind of a team," I said. "How you feel, how you see things will affect how you are with him. If you're more comfortable, happier, clearer, you'll be doing something for David in a very direct way."

"Yeh, that sounds nice, but I'm not the one with the problems. He is. We could talk from now to doomsday; that isn't going to change him. Really, this whole business is terribly frustrating."

"In what way?" I asked.

"You had to see their smug looks at the school, like I was some sort of low life. They didn't come out and say it. Too sharp for that. But it was between the lines. 'Hey, lady, you screwed up your kid.' Damn them!"

"What about the meeting upsets you?"

Janice returned to the chair, crossing her legs almost violently. "I did a pretty damn good job. We've been on our own for the last five years. No one can tell me I didn't provide or take care of my son. No way. I did all I could."

"Then why does what they say upset you?"

"Who the hell are they to talk to me like that? Why don't they look in their own classrooms? If Miss Dean was my teacher, I'd probably go nuts too. Shit on them!" Janice rubbed her forehead, then folded her arms militantly across her chest. Her hands trembled.

"Given they talked to you in the way they did, said all the things they said...what about their words makes you so unhappy?"

"I don't know. My mind's blank. A total blank." She made a clicking sound with her tongue, then sighed.

"Well, if you guessed at an answer, what would it be?" I asked.

"Maybe they're right, the bastards," she said. Her eyes filled with tears. Her face became flushed. She jumped off the chair and stood by the window again. "Not that it's all my fault. I really tried, me, being alone with the kid. All his damn father did was deliver presents once a month and take his bows. Sure, daddy was a real high. Mommy was Scrooge. You think that's easy? Listen, I'm not complaining. I get my check each week. It's just that David...well, he acts like he doesn't like me." She cringed.

"What about that makes you unhappy?"

"If he doesn't like me, it must mean something."

"What might that be?"

"I don't know," she said. "Maybe it does show it's my fault...I mean in some small way."

"How?"

"Last week, when the jerk set the art supplies in the back of his classroom on fire, he came home and actually bragged about it. They want to throw him out of school and he brags about it, puts on this hero act."

"What about that bothers you?"

"Everything. If my son acts that way, it doesn't say much for the values I've given him."

"What do you mean?"

"Hey," Janice said, her face tightening. "What is this, the Spanish Inquisition?"

I smiled. "Sometimes, questions help us find out what we feel and know. You don't have to answer them, if you don't want to."

She relaxed her jaw muscles. "No. It's okay. What did you ask me last?"

"What do you remember?"

"The question about what it means," she said. "David should be a good boy, not cause all this trouble. He's only seven, just a baby— a *baby!* I got an apartment in a good building; the kids in the neighborhood are nice, really fine children from good families. Yet, he doesn't play with them. Worse than that, he'd rather be with this decrepit old man than with children his own age. The kid's so strange sometimes. Like I don't know him. Maybe I did screw up. Somewhere, somehow, I must've failed." She exhaled a deep sigh. "Do we have to go on?"

"Why don't you want to go on?"

"If I answer your question, that would be going on," she said. A forced laugh erupted from her throat. "That stupid I'm not, thank you." Janice opened the door and said: "Give me a couple of minutes." She walked out onto the porch. As she watched some squirrels scurry up a nearby tree, her stern, almost harsh, expression melted into a soft smile. Her eyes glistened. She relaxed her body against the railing. Several minutes later, she came back into the room. The muscles in her face tensed. She pressed her teeth together, then released them, creating a rippling motion on the sides of her jaw.

"I kept thinking I wanted to leave," she continued, "but every time I decided to go, the next minute, I decided to stay here. I guess the stay decision won out."

"Why did you want to leave?"

"Well, ah . . . don't make a big deal out of this, but I guess, I'm kind of afraid."

"Of what, Janice?"

"Of finding out something I don't want to."

"What do you mean?"

"Well," she said clearing her dry throat, "here I am talking about how maybe I failed. Yesterday, I didn't think like that. It's scary."

"Why?"

Tears flooded her eyes. The color drained from her face. "I have to be strong. When Doug first left, I went to pieces. They thought I was going to have a nervous breakdown. The doctor put me on tranquilizers, while my mother looked after David. I remember one day, when I came to visit him, I burst out crying. Must've scared the shit out of him. He just pushed away from me and ran to his grandmother. After that, I said to myself—'no more.' I was going to be strong, be a good mother." Janice sighed. "I'm afraid to be weak again."

"What do you mean by weak?"

"Fall apart, like I did. Not be able to handle it. Maybe, if I talk too much, maybe . . ."

"Maybe what, Janice?"

"Maybe I'll bring it on again," she said.

"Do you believe that?"

"No, not really. I'm different now, I really am. But somehow, I'm still scared."

"About what?"

"That I won't be a good mother or that I'm not now. Sometimes it's all so confusing. I try, honest I do."

"What are you afraid would happen if you weren't scared about not being a good mother?" I asked.

"Then I'd really screw up."

"What do you mean?"

"Well, you know, every time I get that way, I do something. Like last week, right after I got real uptight about thinking I didn't spend enough time with David, I took him to the movies and then the pancake house."

"So are you saying that by being scared and uptight, you remember to do things with your son?"

"Yes, I guess so."

"Why do you believe you have to be scared and uptight to remember to do those things?"

"Sounds kind of jerky, doesn't it? I guess that's the way I've always done things. Not just with David. When I was in high school, I always used to get nervous before tests, worrying about doing badly. Real crazy, if you know what I mean. Then I'd study and study and sure enough, I'd be so nervous when the time came, I could barely think. And I did pretty lousy on some of those tests. So it all went for naught. Maybe that's what I'm doing with David, huh?"

"What do you think?"

"It sounds like the same thing. Boy, I never learned. Like pressing buttons. Every time I get crazy, I do something."

"What are you afraid would happen if you didn't get 'crazy?'"

"Then I wouldn't think about it and wouldn't do anything. But you know what, I've done plenty of things without being that way."

"Then do you still believe you have to be that way to be a good mother?"

"No, not any more. Every time I felt that way, I didn't know whether I was coming or going. Kinda feels that way with David." She paused and nodded her head. "I never really looked at what I was doing until just now. Wow! You live and learn." A pause. "Uh, also, I have this thing about I have to pay for whatever I get.

So if I worry, I'm paying my dues, so to speak—and then everything will be okay."

"Do you believe that?"

"I don't know any more. It doesn't make sense to me."

"Well, if it doesn't make sense to you and, as in your example about worrying for tests, it doesn't get you what you want, then, do you want to still believe it?"

"No," she grinned for a second, then locked her face into a stern expression. Relaxing slightly, she said; "Okay, I really see the point—being scared doesn't get me to be a good mother, just gets me to take my son places once in a while and be nuts the rest of the time. But that still doesn't change the fact—I turned out to be the terrible mother, just like I dreaded."

"What do you mean when you call yourself a terrible mother?"

"It's becoming very obvious to everyone. How much proof do I need? My son's a terror at school, getting into trouble all the time."

"And what do you believe that means about you?"

"Hey, I'm better than I used to be. Before, if David fell and cut himself, I thought that meant I blew it. His father, on one of his monthly visits, saw a lump on David's head. He screamed at me, saying I couldn't even take care of my own kid properly. And I believed him. I was supposed to be there every minute. Could you imagine that? Now it all sounds so crazy, but then, it was real. Everything meant the worst was happening. After a while, just being with David became scary." Janice rubbed her hands together. "I guess that's why I scream and hit him." She started to cry. "I always tell myself he deserved it, God help me. If I didn't say that, I'd smash my hands off for doing it. My—my parents never, never hit me. Never! But I had to do it to make him behave."

"Janice, does the screaming and hitting get you what you want?"

"No. Just the opposite. I think I knew that even then, when it first started," she said wiping her eyes.

"Then why did or do you do it?"

"I get so angry at him, so damn furious!"

"What about?"

"It's the same circle. When he's bad, I think I'm not doing a good job."

"What do you mean?"

"Something is missing that I should have given him. When I was in grade school, I was a pretty good student right from the beginning, even with my worrying. As soon as David entered first grade, he couldn't make it. Damn!"

"What about that makes you so uncomfortable?"

"He was such a bright baby. Talking at nine months. I expected so much."

"What do you mean?"

"I thought he would be a great student, that he would do fantastic."

"Why are you unhappy that he didn't?"

"That is a good question," she said smiling weakly. Again, she stood stiffly by the window. "I'm back to the same place. It means, somehow, I'm not a good mother. Christ, I sound so repetitious. I keep saying the same thing over and over again. Aren't you a little bored with me?"

"Why do you ask?"

"I can't believe how you can sit there, so calmly, and listen to all this shit." She returned to her seat. "I guess if you can, so can I," she said, her voice sharp and loud. "I don't remember exactly what the question was."

"Well," I suggested, "why don't you answer the question you do remember."

"The bit about David being a poor student . . . which doesn't mean, by the way, that he's not smart. Sometimes, he's sharp as a razor—figured out how to use a slide rule by himself. Anyway, a parent's supposed to help a kid want to learn. You show them how you feel, how you see it. I did everything, but David has no interest in school or learning."

"Does a child always do what you say or feel what you feel?" I asked.

"No, of course not."

"When they decide to do something that's different than you asked or wanted, did you do that or did they do that?"

Janice didn't answer immediately. "I guess they do that. It's like that saying—you can lead a horse to water, but you can't make him drink." She allowed a half-smile, still holding some of her facial muscles rigid.

"What are you smiling about?" I asked.

"Suddenly, I don't feel so guilty."

"Does that mean you still feel a little guilty?"

"I guess."

"About what?"

"Maybe I missed something back then," she said.

"And if you did, how would you feel?"

"Guilty. Unhappy."

"Why?"

"Because I didn't want to miss anything."

"When you say guilty, do you mean you're unhappy now that you might have missed something in the past?"

"Yes."

"Why, Janice?"

"I'm suddenly not sure."

"What are you afraid would happen if you didn't feel guilty?"

"Then maybe I'd miss it again."

"Are you saying by being uncomfortable about the past, you take care of the present better?"

"Uh-huh. I guess so. Sounds a bit dumb. It's the same thing I did to make sure I'm the good mother."

"Do you believe you have to do that?"

"Well, that's what I've done," she said, shaking her head.

"But do you believe it now?"

"No, I don't think so."

"Could you stay alert, do all that you can do even if you didn't feel guilty?"

"Sure. That seems possible now. I never looked at myself this way before. It's not so bad." she paused, shifted her body to face me and said; "But if I'm not unhappy about David's problems, then . . ."

"Then what?"

"Then maybe I don't care. How could a mother see a child having all these problems and not be concerned?"

"Is unhappy and concerned the same thing for you?"

She smiled again, still withheld but allowing more of her face to express her feelings. "There's quite a difference!"

"Okay, do you have to be unhappy about David's situation in order to be concerned?"

"No. That's really amazing. But there's something more," she said. "One more big thing. It always feels like he's driving me crazy, like he's in control . . . pressing my buttons."

"How?"

"Take something which just strings me out. He knows I don't like him to reverse his baseball hat on his head. It might be stupid, but I don't like it. Yet, every time he sees me, he flips it around just to upset me. I don't understand why he does it."

"Janice, you and I could speculate on his motives, but it would be only guessing. He does what he does for his own reasons. What we can explore here is why, when he turns his hat around, does it annoy you?"

"Because he does it on spite; he knows exactly what he's doing."

"Let's assume what you think is so. He's doing it for spite. Why is that so upsetting?"

"Because it's not okay for him to do that."

"Why not?"

Her hands clenched into fists. "I expect him to respect me."

"What does that mean?"

"Do what I say!"

"What do you think it means if he doesn't?"

"That he doesn't care. If he loved me, he'd do what I ask."

"Why do you believe that?"

"That's just so," she affirmed.

"Have you ever not done what someone asked and still loved them?"

A smile rippled across her face. "All the time. I don't do what my mother says I should do with David, yet I love her. The same goes for my dad and my friend, Annie. I see what you mean."

"Perhaps, Janice, what might be nice to recognize is that you're seeing what you mean. You've given yourself these answers and you're deciding, each moment, what to do with them."

"It's weird, but it's almost like I knew it all the time. I guess David's being spiteful doesn't have to mean he doesn't love me. That's so clear . . . wow, before, well, it's unbelievable."

"What is?"

"Every time he turned his hat, I thought, well, there he goes again, saying he doesn't care. And you know what that meant . . . Christ, I was a shitty mother. I feel so much lighter. How the hell am I going to remember all this?"

"Why does it matter?"

"Because I want to remember." She paused almost

a full minute before speaking. "You know, I could feel my stomach tightening like a vise. Almost did my fear trip again. Stopped right in the middle." Janice beamed; her first full smile since we began. "I'll remember because I want to."

"Okay," I said, nodding my head. "I'll see David on Tuesday. Then, if you'd like, we can talk more next week."

"The time flew," she acknowledged as she rose from the chair. Straightening her pants, she asked self-consciously: "Can I tell you something else?"

"Sure," I replied.

"We've talked about my problems. But this couldn't have been a picnic for David either. Remember, I told you about him being a poor student and all that. Well, he got a C on his first test. You know what I did? I yelled at him for not working hard enough, like he was supposed to get an A for me. I didn't say one nice thing to him about it. That must've been hard on him. It's so much clearer now . . . before, it was such a blur."

She put her hand out to shake mine. The power of her grip and the vigor with which she pumped my arm surprised me. "Another thing," she said, standing in the doorway.

"Go ahead," I said, smiling at the lady who just an hour before didn't want to talk.

"We still didn't discuss how I should deal with David."

"There's no 'should,' Janice, unless you put one there. You said you're clearer now, not as frightened about some of the things we've discussed. Nobody could know more about how to do it for David than you."

She snapped her head to the side again, tossing the hair out of her face. "Funny, but yesterday, if you said that, you could have been talking in Chinese. I wouldn't have understood a word you said." Janice Seaton laughed. "You know something strange, for the first

time in a long time, I'm really excited about seeing my
son."

* * *

The heavy rain rapped against the window panes,
competing with the drone of the teacher's voice as she
lectured to her second grade class about early American history. Though her words painted pictures of
horsedrawn wagons moving across colorful landscapes,
little faces peered blankly out of the window while little
hands doodled images on clean, white pads.

Estelle Dean knew she had lost them an hour ago.
For several years she had fought for changes in the
curriculum, lobbying for "her" children as if life and
breath were at stake. After ten years, she had given
up the old dream and settled into the monotony of covering a range of material which she disliked and which
bored her. At first, she had tried to inject the materials
with a special life, using skits, drawings, records, even
group activities such as dances and songs from the era.
But each year, her students, equally bored, would stare
emptily at her or let their vacant eyes drift aimlessly
around the room, intuitively aware that their teacher
had switched herself onto automatic pilot just to get
through it. Twice in the past, Miss Dean, as the children called her, had seriously contemplated quitting.
In each instance, she explored other avenues to use her
skills and talents, ultimately finding no viable alternative. She continued teaching by default, confronting,
each morning, the nagging temptation to run, but refusing to cower to an impulse which carried the label
of failure with it.

Her tongue, dry and pasty, slapped against the inside of her mouth as she strung one sentence after
another like an endless stream of water tumbling from
a broken faucet. One little girl bit her nails furiously,

compulsively, totally engrossed in working her teeth
expertly around the tip of each finger. Another chewed
on her pencil as she watched the little hamster pace
his cage at the front of the classroom. Two students
whispered to each other near the back of the room,
their hushed words muffled by rustling feet and the
noise of bodies continually shifting positions. A rather
husky little boy colored the wings of a paper airplane
one of the squadron of seven he neatly assembled on
his desk. One girl's eyelids floated at half-mast as she
stared hypnotically at the blackboard while rocking
back and forth at her desk.

Although Miss Dean stopped talking, her students
didn't seem to notice. She surveyed the class from behind the book and considered screaming to shock them,
to wake them from their lulled stupor. Something in
her class's casual unconcerned manner felt like an insult, as if her very existence was of no consequence to
them. The gurgling in her stomach distracted her for
a moment. Then she felt her eyes drawn to a particular
seat in the room. David Seaton shot tiny pieces of paper
down the third row with an improvised sling-shot he
had constructed with two pencils and a rubberband.
His natural flamboyance had attracted the attention
of a small, but highly attentive audience among his
peers.

Estelle Dean insisted she could handle a disruptive
child during a quick inner dialogue. But David felt
more like competition; aloof, arrogant and strong-
willed from the very first moment she encountered him,
an ultimate affront to her ability to reach her own
students. At first, she tried to dismiss her initial judgments, blaming his previous reputation as a troublemaker for her assessment.

Although she had been curt and defensive, feeling
victimized by having this child placed in her class, she

believed her coolness could not have effected, certainly not have triggered, David's actions on that first day. He had obdurately refused to sit in his assigned seat in the back of the room, one she had chosen in order to segment him from the more serious students. He protested her instructions by standing at the side of the room. Miss Dean politely, but emphatically, lectured him about her own refusal to tolerate the kind of behavior he had exhibited in his previous class. Later, he participated in a pushing fight with two other students and crowned his annoying antics with several vulgar statements whispered to his classmates. Their laughter infuriated her more than his words. Somehow, she knew he had won, but assured herself it would be only a momentary victory.

She declared war. The slightest provocation brought a swift, hard response. If he talked out of turn, he lost his right to participate verbally with his classmates for the entire day. If he made a disturbance of any sort, he was sent immediately to the principal's office. Break him quickly! But as the weeks became months, her effort and energy seemingly fueled his disruptive behavior.

David's actions not only inhibited her in dealing with the other students, but often diverted her attention from the rest of the class. He had no right to cheat them of her time, she thought, no right at all to disturb the other students with his ridiculous behavior. Her younger brother used to perform similar actions, creating a constant bombardment of noise and aggressive behavior to draw the attention of her parents away from her. And it had worked. She had fought him then as she fought David now, assuring herself such behavior would not work in her class. And yet it did. Damn him, she muttered under her breath, twenty-two students had as much right as this one child.

Though Colin Adams also shot spit-balls across the room, she ignored him, her eyes and total attention consumed by David.

"David Seaton, stand up! Now! This very instant!" she shouted.

David looked around at his classmates, some of whom giggled. He remained seated. As Miss Dean rose from her chair, the entire class turned around to watch David. He still remained seated, though his eyes darted back and forth betraying his own discomfort.

"Young man, I told you to get up."

"Why?" David asked, fully aware of the reason for her attention.

"I'm not going to say it again! I want you to get up." Slowly, she moved down the aisle. Her face flushed as she clenched her right hand.

"It's not fair. I wasn't the only one shooting papers."

"I said get up."

As she approached him, he slid out of his seat and jumped into a chair two rows over. The room filled with sprinklings of laughter.

"I'm not playing a game, David," she said, trying to control her anger, knowing if she said what she felt he would have won, cracked her shell like her brother had done so many times before.

Suddenly, David rose and stood at attention like a cadet at a military academy. Another bubbling of laughter filled the room again.

"I will not let you continue to disrupt this class. Do you hear me?" she said. David did not respond. "You've been nothing but trouble since the beginning of the term. Nothing but trouble. We have a lot of material to cover. If you cared about your classmates, you wouldn't be doing these things. Stand in the back of the room, in the corner. If you do or say anything, out . . . out you go, no but's, if's or maybe's. Do you understand?"

"Can I take my book with me?" David asked.

"No, young man. You should have thought of that before you started shooting those papers into everyone's face."

"I didn't shoot them into anyone's face."

She could feel her blood pressure rise. In another era, perhaps during the turn of the century, she might have justly slapped him across the face. "There's one in every class," she muttered to herself.

"Don't argue with me, just get to the back of the room." David walked to the rear of the class. "That's not good enough. Stand in the corner." He edged into the corner.

"David Seaton, class, doesn't care about any of you. All he cares about is himself. You might think he's funny, but don't be fooled. He's very sad, very sad indeed."

Several of her favorite students, whom she had seated in the front seats of each row, made faces at David. Estelle felt vindicated by their response.

As she continued to discuss the design and activities in an early American town, she kept staring at the little boy in the rear corner. One more thing, just one more thing and out he goes, she thought. And good riddance. Suddenly, she felt embarrassed. You're acting like a fool, she counseled herself, trying to focus on the lesson.

The class was noticeably more alert since her confrontation with David. Everyone paid attention for at least five minutes; then the little minds began to slip away again. David hated Miss Dean more than Frieda Carrol, his teacher from the first grade. He had started that year working quite diligently until those first test scores. Then, his mother and Mrs. Carrol accused him of not trying hard enough and not working up to his potential. His teacher said this was particularly evident during reading lessons, when he never paid attention. On several occasions, in front of the class, Mrs. Carrol told David she might change her mind about him. Perhaps he really couldn't do the work. Perhaps it was just too difficult for him. She liked David, but her primitive brand of reverse psychology backfired. David tried even less and quickly began to exhibit unruly behavior. Mrs. Carrol hesitantly noted for the records that David Seaton represented a serious discipline problem.

David became restless standing in one place. He shifted his weight from one leg to another while making a series of comical faces for the benefit of his observant teacher. Finally, tiring of that game, he closed his eyes. The drone of Miss Dean's voice became distant, a monotone hum which reminded him of the air conditioner in his bedroom window. Several minutes passed before he looked up at his teacher again. She appeared completely absorbed in the lesson. Slowly, ever so slowly, he inched his way toward the window, hoping to see some intriguing event outside which would occupy his thoughts.

"What do you thing you're doing?" Estelle Dean said, sporting a self-satisfied smile.

"Just finding a comfortable place to stand," he answered, striking an innocent "Who, me?" pose.

"Just finding a comfortable place to stand," she mimicked him. "Well, isn't that just wonderful? You forget quickly why you're there, don't you? Just find a 'comfortable' place back in the corner or I'll send you to Mr. Griffen's office and you know what that'll mean!"

He moved back to his original position. His last excursion to Mr. Griffen's office resulted in an intense telephone conversation during which the school official insisted his mother come immediately to remove her son from school. The principal threatened suspension. Yet, for David, the most disturbing repercussion was his mother's constant badgering about the necessity for leaving work and losing half-a-day's pay in order to salvage the situation. Determined now to avoid her involvement, he stood motionless, conforming to his teacher's wishes.

More restless than before, he slid his hands into his pocket. His fingers touched the matchbook he had taken from the kitchen table during breakfast. He had almost forgotten. David surveyed the room carefully. Once convinced that no one noticed his presence any longer, he withdrew the book, dislodged a match and struck it against the black flint paper. The flare of the ignition startled him. His gasp attracted the teacher's attention.

"My God, David Seaton, what are you doing?" she exclaimed.

He immediately threw the matchbook and ignited match down on the floor beside him. It landed on a pile of artwork beside several cans of paint and other art supplies. Within seconds, a can of paint remover exploded into flames.

"Oh Lord!" Miss Dean screeched. "Now children, everyone get up and leave the room! Now! C'mon! Quickly! Let's go. Janet and Paul, don't run. There's no need to run. Victor, go to the principal's office and tell him what's happened."

As she spoke, she broke the small glass window of the fire alarm near her desk and pulled the handle. Little mechanical hammers slammed mercilessly on large iron bells throughout the school. Groans and moans met the deafening sound as students and teachers alike responded sluggishly to what they anticipated as another unannounced fire drill.

David just stood there, amazed at the turn of events while he watched the flames consume one painting after another. He tried to stamp his foot on the burning paper in an effort to extinguish the fire.

"David!" Estelle Dean screamed. She felt her body

lunge forward, her arms stretch in an instinctive gesture to use the molecules of air to propel her to the back of the room. Images of burning flesh almost blinded her as she ran between the rows of desks.

She grabbed her student's arm, dragging him away from the fire. "David, what are you doing? You've caused enough trouble. Stop fighting me, damn it—let's go!"

Tears blurred his vision. Deaf to Miss Dean's words, numb to the tugging on his arm as she pulled him across the room, he kept stamping his foot on the floor, seizing on the fantasy that somehow the activity of his leg would eradicate the fire and the entire incident simultaneously. At that moment, the principal, accompanied by his group of assistants, sprinted into the room and smothered the fire quickly with portable fire extinguishers. A mountain of foam blanketed the art supplies.

Mr. Griffen, barely containing his anger, grabbed David's arm and escorted him out of the classroom. "There'll be hell to pay for this, young man."

* * *

Janice Seaton accompanied her son to the bottom of the hill. The two figures stopped; their animated faces confronted one another. Finally, David separated from his mother and began to climb the stairs alone. Janice waved to me from below, shrugged her shoulders, then walked away.

The little boy negotiated the steps easily, never once looking at me as I leaned against the railing of the small deck, obviously awaiting his arrival. His blue jeans had been carefully pressed, a sharp crease lined the front of each leg. His polo shirt, imprinted with a gigantic brown mushroom, outlined his small, round pot belly. The baseball hat, turned backwards, looked like a bowl sitting on top of his head.

In the midst of his ascent, David paused, then carefully backed down several steps and halted again. He looked up at me, waiting for a comment. My silence seemed to surprise him. Without ceremony, he proceeded to climb, completing the short journey to my one-room house on top of the hill. Bounding up the last few stairs two at a time, he deposited himself directly in front of me. Standing at attention, he talked more to my belt buckle than to my face.

"Hello," he said in a froggish little voice. "I'm David Seaton."

"Hello, David, I'm Bears."

His eyes registered his suspicion as they searched my face. "That's a dumb name," he responded.

I smiled. "Come in, if you'd like." He followed me through the glass sliding door. I sat on the small couch, indicating for him to sit opposite me. He did not respond; instead, he stood stiffly in the corner of the room.

"Are you going to shoot me?" he asked.

I looked at him with curiosity, grinning warmly from ear to ear. "What do you think?"

"I don't see a gun," he observed in a flat tone. Pivoting on his heels, he turned around and sat in the corner on the floor. "I want to sit here."

"Whatever you'd like," I said.

"I didn't want to come," he announced.

"Why not?"

"There's nothing wrong with me," he declared, twisting his shoelaces with his fingers.

"Why do you think coming here means something is wrong with you?"

"That's what Mr. Griffen said and so did my teacher. So did Mama."

"Do you believe them?"

"You ask, um, silly questions," he said with a grin splashed across his face.

"Sometimes, David, questions help us learn all different kinds of things about ourselves. Why did the question sound silly to you?"

"I thought, uh, all big people are supposed to know what they're talking about." Sarcasm edged his words.

"Well, if they're comfortable and clear, that might be so. I guess you could say the same about little people, children—if they're comfortable and clear, they'd know what they were talking about too."

David laughed. "You mean I could know as much as you?"

"What do you think?"

"Maybe," he said, obviously enjoying the notion. "Are you trying to trick me or something?"

"How?"

"Well, you talk in a funny way. I mean, uh, you talk to me nice."

"I talk to you like I'd talk to anyone who came here. A big person, a small person, an in-between person—it doesn't matter. We're all doing the best we can. What do you think?"

"There you go again, talking nice."

"What do you mean when you say I talk nice to you?" I asked.

He rose from the floor and walked over to the couch without seating himself.

"Well, like most people, big people like Miss Dean, Mr. Griffen, Mama—they're always telling me things like I'm stupid. No one really ever asks me—um, asks me what I know. Like with this, a big thing that happened in school—" Breaking off abruptly, turned away.

"What big thing?"

"Did you see my mother?" he asked, ignoring the question.

"Yes, David. Why do you ask?"

"'Cause, since last week, she seems, you know, funny."

"What do you mean?"

"Uh, like she lets me wear my hat backwards. That's a big thing for Mama. She used to always scream at me about my hat. But, last time, she said if it's that important to me, it was alright with her."

"How did you feel about that?"

"Okay," he said, his lips betraying a slight smile. "You know, I felt so funny when she said it that I put my hat straight. Could we play tic-tac-toe? I'd feel better if we played for a little while."

"Sure," I replied. "If you want to."

"Don't just let me win," he counseled. "That's what Uncle Jerry does all the time. He treats me like a baby."

"I'll give it my all," I assured him.

David sat on the couch enthusiastically. I handed him a pencil and blank paper, which he filled immediately with criss-crossing lines. The first game ended in a stalemate, as did the second and the third. He seemed confused with the outcome, as if he had expected me not to keep my word and purposely lose the game in a fashion not unlike his uncle's

"You go first this time," he said. When I won the game, he threw his pencil on the floor, walked back to his corner and began pounding his fists on the floor.

"What are you feeling, David?"

"I don't want to talk!"

Though he contorted his face, his expression seemed devoid of real anger. The pounding continued for several minutes. I sat beside him and banged my fists in a similar fashion. David looked at me in disbelief, then he paused from his activity. I paused as well. When he continued, I continued. He peered at me from the corner of his eyes. Jumping to his feet, he said, "You're crazy," then sat down on the couch, occupying my seat, and folded his arms across his chest.

"Why do you think I'm crazy?" I asked as I seated myself opposite him.

He blushed "C'mon."

"I really don't know your reasons for calling me crazy."

"That's what they call me when I do it."

"Ah, I see. And do you believe that means you're crazy?"

"If I say no, what'll happen?" he said.

"It's okay with me whatever your answer is. It doesn't matter what I think—what matters is what you think."

David stared at me amazed. "I don't believe them. I hate them. Miss Dean, Mr. Griffen, Aunt Eve, Karen, everyone except Scoot."

"Why do you hate them?"

"'Cause they don't like me."

"What about their not liking you makes you unhappy?"

"I want to be liked," he said emphatically.

"Sure, but that doesn't explain why you'd be unhappy if you weren't."

"'Cause, 'cause nobody really gives me a chance."

"What do you mean, David?"

"Well, last week, Aunt Eve, Mama, Uncle Jerry were going to the movies. I wanted to go. Some of my friends saw the picture—it was okay for kids. Mama said I didn't know, uh, how to act, always causing trouble and all that. I promised I wouldn't but she didn't believe me. Neither did Aunt Eve or Uncle Jerry . . . I could tell. And . . ."

"And then what happened?"

"I . . . well, I yelled and banged my fists on the table." He began to cry. "Causing trouble just like they said I would."

"Why did you do that?"

"It didn't matter. They already told me I was bad."

"I understand; but why, when they said you were bad, did you do what you did?"

"To get back."

"What do you mean?"

His little hands formed into fists. "Well, I wanted them to be unhappy like me."

"Why?"

"So they'd take me."

"And did they?"

"No."

"What are you afraid would happen if you didn't yell and bang?"

"They'd never take me."

"Why is that?" I asked.

"'Cause then they'd, uh, they wouldn't know I really wanted to go."

"Why do you believe that?"

"I don't know. You think I could just tell them?"

"What do you think?"

"I don't know. When I do, um, those other things, I never get to go. But if I didn't, it wouldn't matter."

"Do you believe that?"

He grinned. "I guess you don't have to scream for something to matter. Like with Scoot—when I wanted to visit him, I just asked. Most of the time he says yes, but sometimes he says no. He knows it matters to me."

"How do you feel, David?"

"Okay," he smiled. "Can I come back?"

"Sure, if you'd like. We still have some time now."

David rose from his seat and stood next to the window, looking out for his mother.

"Bears, you know, uh, it's not much fun when people always think you're bad."

"What about it is not much fun?"

"Nobody gives me a chance. When Miss Dean put me in the last row, I knew she wanted me away from the other kids 'cause Mrs. Carrol, my first grade teacher, told her things."

"What kind of 'things?'"

"You know, that I make trouble."

"And how do you feel about that?"

He turned away from me, tucking his hands into his pockets. Silence. Suddenly, the room filled with the choking sound of a little boy crying. I waited until he finished before asking him the next question.

"Why does Mrs. Carrol saying you cause trouble make you so unhappy?"

"I don't want to cause so many problems. I just can't help it."

"What do you mean?"

"I just do it."

"I know it feels like that. Why don't you give me an example and show me what you mean?"

Sitting back down on the couch, he fumbled with the pencil. "Yesterday, Miss Dean put me in the back of the room for talking—but Allen and Margie were also talking; but she didn't do anything to them. It wasn't fair. So I called her an ass."

"Is that what you mean by causing a problem, doing something that you feel just happens?"

"Yes."

"Why did you call her an ass?"

"'Cause she is."

"Why?"

"She always picks on me, punishes me when nothing happens to the other kids."

"Let's assume what you say is correct. Why does that upset you?"

"'Cause I don't want to be picked on. That's why I called her an ass."

"Ah. Are you saying you call her an ass so she won't pick on you any more?"

He looked at me and smiled. "Uh-huh," he admitted.

"Then does it just happen, like you can't help it or do you do those 'things' for a reason?"

"I guess there's a reason," he concluded. A big smile dawned on his face.

"What are you smiling about?"

"Mama always says I have no control. Every time something like that happens, I think, yup, it's true, I have no control. But I do, I really do. Does that mean I'm terrible . . . you know—that I do it on purpose?"

"What do you think?" I asked.

"I don't feel terrible."

"Okay. Maybe, David, now that you see when you you called Miss Dean an ass, you did it for a reason . . . like trying to upset her so she'd stop—maybe now you can ask yourself, does it get you what you want?"

He shook his head from side to side, biting his upper lip thoughtfully.

"I guess you could also ask yourself if there's a better way."

He nodded. "Oh, there's my mother," he said peering out the window. "Bears, can I come back?"

"Sure."

In a very peculiar gesture, David walked up to me and put out his hand hesitantly. I shook it heartily. Looking up at my rather large hulk, he said: "Someday, we'll be the same size."

"In many ways, David, we're both already the same size."

*   *   *

Janice twirled her hair in ringlets; her foot tapped out a nervous drum beat; her eyelids fluttered each time she looked directly at me. Suddenly, her tense expression melted into a warm smile.

"I know it's going to sound impossible," she began, "but David has changed already. Only one session and

135

I see a real difference. Not that everything is smooth, but nice things have happened. You know what that crazy kid did—I told him it was okay to wear his hat backwards and sure enough, later in the day, he wore it forward like I like it. He felt so soft, Bears, and that's not the word I thought I'd ever find myself using in describing my son. He, he stopped fighting me. We stopped fighting each other." She laughed awkwardly. "I guess, maybe, I've changed too. I can't say things are hunky-dory, but they got better this week. There's one thing, well, uh, more than one—but there's something that really bothers me."

"What?" I asked.

"The old man."

"What old man?"

"The one David goes to almost every afternoon. It's not natural, an old man spending all that time with the kid."

"Why isn't that natural?"

"People play, I mean, spend time with people their own age."

"That might be what most people do, but why would it be unnatural to spend time with people of different ages?"

"Okay, it's not unnatural in itself—it's just that he wants to be with that old man so much of the time."

"What about that makes you uncomfortable?"

"Because, well, that's unnatural," she said.

"Why do you believe that?"

"It's not normal for a kid to be with an old man instead of children his own age."

"Why not? What's not normal about it?"

"I don't know what's not normal about it. The more I listen to myself, the more absurd I sound. It really isn't as weird as I thought. I'm getting all confused."

"About what?"

"It's like I think I know why I feel certain ways, but when I really look, I don't have any reasons—in fact, the reasons I do things seem so senseless. All this kind of talk is so new to me. I guess if David had a grandfather across the hall who wanted to play with him all the time, I wouldn't think that was so weird. It could be great, I guess."

"Well, if it's no longer weird and is possibly even great, is there anything else about the relationship which bothers you?"

"Yeh!" Janice declared. "I want him to play with children his own age."

"Wanting him to play with children his own age is different from being upset with him playing with an elderly man. What about that still upsets you?"

"The man himself—this Mr. Hogan. He has a ridiculous nickname—Scoot. Normal people have dogs and cats for pets, right? Right! This weirdo—there I go again with that word—this gentleman has a lizard and a talking bird, and would you believe it, the bird's not even a parrot—a parrot would be too normal. The whole scene just turns me off."

"What about it turns you off?"

"I make sure I'm home from work when David gets home from school . . . I had to take a cut in salary to do it. I don't mind; I'm not complaining, but—and here's the killer—when he gets home, he doesn't say two words to me, just runs across the hall to Scoot's apartment. It's really upsetting." Janice flipped her head, throwing her hair over her shoulder in a quick easy movement.

"What's upsetting about it?"

"I don't know," she said. Her eyes were moist.

"Well, if you guessed at any answer, what would it be?"

"It shows me he doesn't like me. He prefers some

stranger to his own mother." Tears came; smearing her mascara into dark, vertical tracks extending from her eyes to her chin.

"Why does that make you unhappy?"

"I don't know. I want to be a good mother, really, I do."

"Why do you believe David's friendship with Scoot means you're not a good mother?"

"As you ask me, I really don't believe it means that. I guess it just means there's something about Mr. Hogan which David finds . . . uh, attractive. I'll be damned if I know what it is. Somehow, I'm still a little angry about it."

"What are you afraid would happen if you weren't angry about his relationship with Scoot?"

"Then I wouldn't do anything about it."

"Are you saying your anger keeps you focused on wanting to do something about what you see?"

"Yes," she said. "There I go again. Kind of silly, isn't it?"

"It's what you do to take care of yourself—based on what you believe," I interjected. "But now, you can ask, do you believe you have to be angry in order to do that?"

"No. Everywhere I turn, I'm driving myself nuts. Guess I never thought there was another way, if you know what I mean?"

I nodded.

"Bears, it's changing—bit by bit, I see it different, different than before. Really I do. I don't have to be angry about it. It seems so simple, almost too simple. After driving myself crazy for almost thirty years, you'd think it'd be more difficult to change things. Well, well, just listen to me. One thing solved, another comes up. Still haven't solved the problem since I don't know what to do."

"What do you want to do?"

She laughed. "Don't tell me it's that easy. Okay, I'll give it a whirl. Maybe, if I planned something with David, took him to the movies or make paintings with him, drawing and that kind of stuff, then he might want to stay home with me. Make it fun for him. And maybe, just maybe, like that insane baseball hat, if I stopped fighting him about Scoot, he wouldn't fight back by going there all the time. So I'm a genius now." She smiled theatrically, then her faced flushed.

"What are you feeling?" I asked.

"A little uncomfortable."

"What about?"

"The old man. He's a weirdo for sure, but he's kind of nice, especially to David. Every time I've talked to him, I'm always nasty. Yet, you know what? The man still stays friendly with my kid. Got to give it to him. Even my bitchiness didn't scare him off. Jesus, I don't know why I do things like that."

"Why don't you take this opportunity and ask yourself?"

"Okay—Janice, deary," she began as she mimicked my voice, "why did you do that to poor old Mr. Hogan? Because, I wanted to chase him away," she replied, purposely exaggerating her New York accent. "But, it didn't work, did it Janice?" she said, her voice soft and mellow. "Nope, it didn't work. After all is said and done, it really didn't feel good treating him like that . . . kind of shitting on him just because I couldn't handle it—uh, pardon my Russian."

"What's uncomfortable about that awareness?"

"It doesn't exactly prove I'm a nice person."

"Why is that?"

"Nice people don't do that to other people or haven't you noticed?"

"What do you mean?"

"Bears, you know what I mean!"

"Sometimes two people will say the same thing, use

the very same words, but mean something different."

"Okay," she said, "I'm convinced. It's like—well, if you're feeling okay and being nice, you'd be nice to everyone. Ah!" she exclaimed, opening her eyes wide.

"Ah-what?"

"I can't exactly say I've been feeling okay, so how do I expect to be so nice? But you know, somewhere, deep down inside, I still feel a little crummy about how I treated him."

"Why?"

"I don't know." she answered, squirming in her seat. She adjusted her skirt carefully, then tapped her fingers on her thighs. "Guilt is a funny thing."

"How is it funny?"

"It doesn't go away that fast."

"What are you afraid would happen if you didn't feel guilty?"

"Then I'd be uncaring, insensitive."

"Do you believe that?"

"Yes. No. Yes-no, yes-no. I don't know any more. Don't they say the worst kind of criminal is one who doesn't feel bad afterwards?"

"What do you think that means?"

"Well, if they don't feel bad, then they didn't care, then they'll just do it again 'cause it didn't matter."

"Is that what you're saying you believe would happen if you didn't feel guilty about Scoot?"

"It's just wild. Yes, that's what I'm saying—but, no, definitely no, guilt aside, I'm not going to be that way with him any more."

"Okay, then do you believe you have to feel guilty in order to treat him nicely, in order to be caring and sensitive?"

"No." Shaking her head, she sighed. "How come I thought this would be so painful, talking about all this? You know what? I feel pretty decent. I don't feel at all confused. Like last week, I kept thinking about what

I said during our session. I really knew, for the first time, really clearly, that what Doug and my mother said about me being a bad mother, upset me only because I believed they were right. But they're not. I won't let them be right. I know that now. They could talk from now to doomsday, but I'm not buying it."

The remainder of the session revolved around her difficulties with being a single woman with a child. Janice discussed how she would often conceal David's existence in an effort, at least initially, not to frighten away various male friends. In questioning her own motives, she realized that in any prospective involvement, if the man didn't like children or want them, she would not allow herself to become serious— in effect, she would not want that kind of relationship. She delighted in seeing that her own child could be a quick and natural filter, alerting her to the character and wants of the men she met. Janice also verbalized her intuition that David, in fact, had to know about her charade since she sent him, all too often, to a neighbor's when being picked up for a date.

"Funny," she observed, "while I worked on this thing about me, talking about it for at least half this session, I kept thinking, 'Hey, Janice, what are you doing? You're here to help David.' Like I cheated or something. But even this has affected my son. I could see him thinking I was embarrassed about him or something just as dumb. Wow! I guess everything I do or feel involves David—somewhere, somehow."

* * *

The school bus backfired, sputtering as it lurched to a halt. The accordian doors stuck together momentarily, then belched open to clear a narrow exit for the onslaught of children who pushed each other off the steps and raced across the manicured lawns to the building's entrance. David lagged behind, scrutinizing the bicycle stand for Scoot's ten-speed racer. He spotted the familiar black frame elegantly pin-striped in white like a nineteen-fifty hot rod. A thick, silver lock held the heavy chains in place. He slapped his briefcase, annoyed he had missed the afternoon ritual with his friend, but excited the old man was home.

Charging up the stairs, he arrived on the third floor breathless and slightly dizzy, a panting tribute to his little legs which carried him skyward at a rate faster than the elevators. Once he regained his equilibrium, he skipped to his front door and rang the bell. He turned his baseball hat to face backward; paused, reconsidered his gesture, then turned the hat back to the front again. A smile dawned on his face. His mother opened the door, surprised at his ear-to-ear grin.

"Hi," he said, running through the house to dispose of his books.

"Hey," Janice called, "I thought it would be nice if we went into the old town; we could get some ice cream and walk around for awhile."

David, a confirmed ice cream addict, peered around the corner in the hallway. His eyebrows curled suspiciously as he stared at his mother. "Really? Do you mean it?"

"Would I make an offer and not mean it?"

"Would you?" David asked.

"No," she said. "Listen, young man, it's one of the best deals in town. And, how about a kiss?"

He kissed his mother easily. "Could we do it tomorrow?"

"Well, I don't know what'll be tomorrow. Let's go today, right now if you'd like."

"You see," David began, "Scoot, um, and I—we were going to finish Larry L.'s tunnel to the window. I can't let him down. I'm his helper."

Janice looked away as she filled the room with a

noisy sigh. Though somewhat annoyed and disappointed, she marveled at her general comfort with her son's declaration. "David, do what you want."

"Could we go tomorrow?" he asked.

"We'll see," she said, unwilling to commit herself, wondering if she had allowed herself to become an easy mark, the loser in an undeclared competition between her and the old man across the hall. "Well," she said, surprised with the apparent warmth of her own voice, "you have a nice time helping your friend. I'll see you for dinner."

Without looking at her, David slipped out the door and entered the old man's apartment.

"Waitin' for ya, scout. Last section goes right into place today and then ol' Larry L. can take his naps in the sunshine. Yes sir, a mighty satisfying event for a lizard." Scoot waved to the sixteen-inch reptile, which cocked its head, then swept its long tapered tail along the sand as if acknowledging the old man's words. "Today is the day. Sit ya self down, laddy . . . ya arrived just in time, ya did."

David sat next to Scoot, picked up his pair of pliers and helped twist the last section of wire mesh together. Scoot nodded approvingly at his young friend's handiwork. "Davey, many a man would be proud to have a son like you. Yes sir! Those are mighty fine hands ya got."

"And what about my head?" David asked.

"What'd ya think, you'd have fine hands but not have a fine head? Come now, laddy, they go together like the rain and clouds—thought you'd know that for sure, I did."

David smiled at his friend, then pointed to the last connecting wire he pushed into place. "Finished! Hurrah, it's done. Can we put it up now?"

"Sure thing. But first, we need some fuel for us workers," the old man said, taking David's hand. They walked into the kitchen. Two small glasses of milk and a plate of chocolate chip cookies awaited them on the table. They ate together in silence, often exchanging smiles as they munched on the thick round wafers.

Back in the living room, they held the long wire section against the wall. Scoot laughed when he realized they had made it several inches too long. "So much for ma ruler." With a marker, he carefully indicated the extra length. "Okay. Off it goes." He handed David a wire cutter and indicated for him to begin.

The boy cut along the marked line very carefully, snipping each individual wire of the mesh, one at a time. Scoot watched, nodded his approval, then rose to his feet saying, "Time to lower the ol' curtain and let Miss Big Mouth into the world." His nimble fingers untied the six square knots which held the canvas cover up around the bird cage. The grey material dropped to the floor.

"Scoot, scoot, toot, toot," Maggie barked, her single leg balancing her large black-and-orange body on a dowel suspended by wire from the ceiling. Her chattering vibrated the stick, yet her body remained secure on its thin, bony pillar.

"C'mon, ma lady, give an old man a break—how 'bout some peace and quiet from ya for me and ma pal, Davey."

"Ma pal, Davey. Shut up, shut up," the bird responded, twisting its head toward the lizard's cage. "Maggie, Maggie, Scoot, toot."

"How come it's always so silly . . . saying its own name all the time?" David asked.

"Kinda says what it hears. Repeats. Maggie doesn't think like me and you, no sir, but I'd put a dollar on her to outsmart most people I've known. And that's not just bird talk, son."

"Bird talk son, bird talk son."

"Pay no mind to the critter, Davey; she's a darn sight

wiser than her words, a darn sight."

Scoot admired the section as David clipped the last piece of wire. He lifted it easily up against the wall, placing it snugly into position. A perfect fit. The two workers smiled at each other.

"I did it good, didn't I?" David asked. His gentle mentor patted him on the shoulder affectionately and winked his response.

The front door buzzer sounded like a fog horn in the room. "Yes, yes, who's there?" Scoot shouted.

"Mr. Hogan, it's me—Mrs. Seaton, Davey's mother."

"Mama," David yelled, "I just got here, we're still not finished."

"I thought you might need some help."

David looked at the old man amazed.

"Let's set it down here. Sure could use another hand." As Scoot opened the door, he smiled easily at Janice, his small eyes peering at his visitor from beneath the gathered flesh tucked into the creases of his eyelids. His mouth curled a friendly hello. "Arrived just in the nick of time, ma dear woman." Taking her hand firmly, he guided her into the living room. David gaped at his mother.

"Hi, Davey," she chimed, trying to appear as nonchalant as possible. Her fingers tugged nervously at the sleeves of her blouse.

"Uh, hi, Mama," he said.

"Glad you two have been introduced," the old man laughed. "When people know each other, they make a better team." Janice's eyes jumped back and forth from the old man to her son. "When I was a bit young," he continued, "not too long ago, mind ya, but before either of ya set foot on this good earth, I spent some time at sea." He chuckled. "If ya could call the Charles River in Boston the sea. In those days, nobody could beat the *Taylor Dan* crew because we knew each other like brothers. Number one long boat racing team for three years runnin'. When we rowed—all twelve of us—you'd think one person with twenty-four arms moved that boat down the river. What a sight, I can tell ya. Us cuttin' water." He shook his head, his wrinkled face dramatizing the inner vision. "What a blessed sight!"

Suddenly aware of his rambling, the old man surveyed his audience self-consciously.

"Well, enough of ma bendin' ya ear. There's work to be done." He positioned his two assistants on either side of the mesh tunnel. They lifted the long, narrow section up against the wall. Scoot tacked in some rails as David hooked the loose pieces of wire together. Janice kept the tunnel steady, bracing it with her shoulder.

Once it was secure, Scoot removed the barrier at the end of the existing cage, giving the animal access to the tunnel. "C'mon now," he said to Larry L., "don't be frightened. The sun's been awaitin' for ya all day." A soft, melodic humming came from the old man's throat. As the reptile's short, stubby legs moved its elongated body across the base of the new extension, Scoot nodded thoughtfully, like an ancient seaman witnessing the changing of the tides. David jumped up and down, applauding the animal.

"All God's creatures, Mrs. Seaton, each one's special like my friend Larry L . . . like my friend and number one helper, Davey boy." He put his arm around the youngster's shoulder as he watched the lizard reach the sunshine which warmed the window ledge. His gravelly voice filled the room with the same throaty lullaby he had hummed before.

Janice watched Scoot and her son, awed by the reverence they accorded the lizard and by the obvious respect and love they gave each other. Just as she sighed, something brushed against her leg. She shifted her eyes in time to watch her son's tiny fingers wrap themselves snugly around her hand.

*   *   *

He kissed his mother, then hurdled up the stairs, two by two. Janice waved to me, her face decorated with an easy smile.

Her son approached me without hesitation, as if to communicate his power by peering directly into my eyes.

"Hello, Big Bear," he said, ironically finding the expression which my own children oftentimes used in addressing me.

"Hi, David."

When he dropped to the floor, I sat on the other end of the rug and faced him. I pulled my legs under my body in a half-lotus position. David did the exact same thing with his legs, making a specific point of mimicking me. When I smiled, he smiled. When I scratched my chin, he scratched his chin.

"We are all here for one another," I said. "Me for you and you for me."

Several minutes elasped without either of us speaking. Finally he said, "Are you going to shoot me?" He giggled, delighted by his own comment. Stretching toward the table, he reached for a blank page, which he proceeded to fold into a sleek paper airplane. He aimed the winged missile at me, using his thumb and index finger as his launching pad. I caught it in mid-air. "Wow—can I try?" he asked, impressed with my feat. I threw the plane gingerly back to him. His little hand grabbed it in flight. "Ah!" he exclaimed, amazed by his own ability.

"Anything you want to work on today?" I asked.

"Besides paper airplanes," he said.

"Or, including paper airplanes."

David fiddled with his fingers for a minute without speaking. "Mom came over to Scoot's and helped us put the lizard's tunnel on the wall. She was so nice."

"And how do you feel about that?"

"Well, I kinda like her more now. She doesn't treat me like Uncle Jerry and Miss Dean and Mr. Griffen and the lunchroom monitor and—" A smile interrupted his recital. "The real problem is Miss Dean, my teacher."

"In what way?"

"Remember when we talked? I told you how I make trouble to get things and how it really didn't work. Well, I tried to be nice and, and it didn't work either. She didn't listen to me."

"What do you mean?"

"Tommy and Jeff had a spitball fight while foureyes wrote a math problem on the blackboard."

"Who's four-eyes?" I asked.

"Oh, that's Miss Dean," he said, slightly embarrassed. "You see she has these thick old glasses and sometimes it looks like she has foureyes." He paused, giving me time to comment, possibly anticipating a reprimand. My silence became his cue to continue. "Well, while they had their spitball fight, Jeff hit Lisa Cromley in the back of the head by accident. She's the class cry-baby . . . so guess what she did? Miss Dean ran down the aisle, pulled me out of my chair and told me to stand in the back corner again. I told her I didn't shoot the spitball. She just pointed. Her face got all red. After class, I told her again I didn't do it. Honest, Bears, I didn't yell, or bang the desk or curse. I was nice, really nice, but she didn't care. I hate her."

"Why, David?"

"'Cause she's still blaming me even though I didn't do it, even though I acted real nice."

"What is it about her blaming you that gets you so upset?"

"It's not fair."

"What do you mean?"

"I want to make her stop always thinking it's me. But how can I do that if she doesn't believe me?"

"How do you think?"

"I thought by just being good, staying out of trouble. But it's not that easy. Suppose she doesn't know, suppose she never knows?"

"Then, how would you feel?"

"I don't want to be good if she doesn't ever know it."

"Why not?"

"'Cause, uh, then I, I just will get blamed anyway. What's the use?" His voice cracked as he spoke. "I don't like getting into trouble. Nobody trusts me, not like Ann-Marie or Mark Stein. When those matches started a fire, everyone said I did it on purpose. But I didn't, I swear I didn't. I got scared, I just threw them down." His shoulders quivered as he began to cry.

"What are you unhappy about?"

"That they don't believe me, nobody believes me."

"What is it about their not believing you which makes you so unhappy?"

"I don't know what to do, Bears. Mama has changed, but Miss Dean, she's the same."

"Let's suppose, as you say, she is the same. Why does that make you so unhappy?"

David pulled his feet from beneath him, extending them straight out until the soles of his shoes touched mine. "She'll always think I'm bad," he replied.

"Okay, and if what you say came true, what would be so upsetting about it?"

"Then maybe it'll mean I'm really bad—after all, she's the teacher. And then, I'll get into more and more trouble."

"Why do you believe if Miss Dean saw you as bad, it would mean you are bad?"

"I don't know," David said, shaking his head.

"Does Miss Dean see you as bad right now?"

"Yes, I think so."

"Okay—do you believe her right now, do you think you're a bad person?"

He shook his head vehemently.

"Then why do you believe if she thought that tomorrow, you might then agree with her?"

David shrugged his shoulders. "I guess if she keeps saying it and saying it, maybe...."

"Maybe what?"

"Maybe I'd think it was true."

"Do you believe that?" I asked.

"Well, not really."

"David, what are you afraid would happen if whatever Miss Dean said didn't matter?"

"Then, I think I'd be good...all for nothing. She wouldn't pay any attention to me and probably the kids wouldn't either."

"But is that the kind of attention you want?"

"No. I guess not. But then why should I be good?"

"It's not a matter of what you 'should' be, but what you want to be."

He grinned weakly and turned away.

"What is it?"

"When Mama is nice and I'm nice to Mama, I like it better."

"Then how do you want to be?"

"Like when I'm with Scoot. But he treats me good. Miss Dean doesn't care about me."

"And how do you feel about that?"

"Okay, as long as she doesn't pick on me."

"And how would you feel if she picked on you?"

"Angry at her?"

"Why?" I asked.

"I don't know. Well, 'cause I feel I've been stupid, being nice to her and all that stuff and she just puts me in the corner."

"What about that's disturbing?"

"I don't want to be in the corner," David declared.

"I know that, but what's disturbing being in the corner?"

"The other kids."

"What about the other kids?"

"They'll think I'm bad even if I'm not."

"Why would that make you unhappy."

"Because I'd like them to like me, just a little."

"Do you think that if you're put in the corner, they won't like you?"

"Some of them won't—but those kids don't matter. I guess if I'm nice to them, they'll like me." David smiled, then whipped the joy from his face with a serious expression. "But what about Miss Dean?"

"What about her?" I asked.

"What should I do?"

"David, what do you want to do?"

"I guess I'll try to be nice. It's really not so hard. Like when I'm with Scoot, I'm always nice and it's easy." His wide-eyed grin registered his surprise at his own words. "Wow, I used to think being good was hard. You know, when I do those things and I get into trouble, I act brave and all that, but most of the time I'm really scared. Uh, could I talk about something else?"

"Whatever you want," I replied.

"Bears, would you talk to my mother, um, about tests and marks and stuff like that. I could do better, but I wish she'd just leave me alone for awhile."

"David, why don't you talk to her yourself?"

"Me?"

"Uh-huh."

"But she won't listen."

"Why do you believe that?"

"She never used to listen."

"That was 'used to'—what about now?"

The boy looked sheepishly at me and curled his bottom lip behind his front teeth. "I guess I could try."

"And if she doesn't listen, how will you feel?"

"Could I try again?"

"What do you think?"

"I'd try again until she listened." He laughed. "And I'm going to really talk to her. I'm not going to bang my fists and stuff."

David raised the issue that the other children did not want to play with him. As we explored his peer group relationships, he realized that he, himself, had shied away from his classmates, afraid they would inevitably see him as a bad person and not like him. When asked why he believed he was a bad person, he faltered, finding no answer except the words of others. Did he believe them? No. Each time he reviewed it, his answers became clearer and clearer. He was not a bad person, he thought, only angry, and he decided he wasn't even angry any longer.

As he turned to leave, David asked, "Can I come back?"

"Sure. But I wonder why you always ask that question before you leave."

"To make sure. I guess I'm not used to people wanting to see me again, except for Scoot and, and maybe now ... Mama."

*   *   *

David returned for three more sessions, though his mother participated in more than double that number. Janice worked through her attitude and beliefs about herself and her parents, particularly the devastating effect she allowed her mother's judgment to have on her. Not only did she continue to explore the difficulties in her relationship with her son, but often acted swiftly on her discoveries.

After admitting to David her previous discomforts about dating, she asked him to be present and, indeed, very visible when a man called for her. Most of her male friends had no difficulty feeling an affection for the boy who greeted them at the door rather conspicuously. Scoot, once a taboo personage in the Seaton house, became a regular dinner guest, at least twice a week.

It took about a month until Janice drummed up the confidence to actually approach Miss Dean. They spent an afternoon together in a coffee shop near the school. At first, her son's teacher challenged all of Janice's statements, refusing to modify her vision of David. She insisted she had tried to show him more acceptable avenues in which to express himself, but he continued to disrupt the class in total disregard of her and the welfare of his classmates. A controlled anger edged her words. Had she noticed any differences in the past month? No, no differences. Then again, perhaps—just a bit, she thought, contradicting her first answer. Although Janice doubted the accuracy of Miss Dean's perception, she continued to probe, searching for the keys to unlock her position. When Estelle Dean accused her of bad parenting, she did not defend herself. Instead, Janice talked about how both she and her son would try to change for everyone's sake.

Her gut response to the meeting wasn't hopeful, until, three days later, David flew into the house after school with a dramatic announcement. Miss Dean, without explanation, changed his seat, placing him at the head of the third row, a position usually reserved for her most advanced students.

Within the next three-month period, David Seaton moved from the remedial reading section to the advanced placement group. A's and B's replaced C's and D's which had frequently occupied the upper left-hand portion of his test papers.

Another month passed before he telephoned.

"Hello," I said, picking up the receiver.

"Hi, Big Bear," he said. "It's David Seaton— you remember me?"

"Sure do, David. How's the man in the first seat of the third row?"

"You do remember," he exclaimed, giggling through his words. "That's me alright, still in the first seat. Bears, can I come visit you?"

"That's still your question, huh? Well my answer is the same. Yes, by all means, come visit. I'd love it."

I rocked leisurely in the hammock, waiting for my young friend on Saturday morning. The sound of several voices drew my attention. As I looked down the hill, I noted David's arrival. He appeared taller, thinner, generally more mature. No baseball hat capped his head. An old man, carrying a brown box, stood beside him. An easy, playful smile softened the deep crevices chiseled in his face. A little girl with blond pig-tails hung on to Janice's arm. They moved, en masse, up the path. David negotiated the first few stairs in a gentlemanly fashion, then sprinted up the hillside.

Shaking his hand, I said, "Hey, Davey, you're looking real fine. Your eyes tell me you know so much more than when I last saw you. That's wonderful."

Turning to the elderly man, I smiled. "And you must be the famous Scoot, keeper of lizards, myna birds and special little boys."

"Haven't gotten myself a bear just yet, like Davey boy here," he said. We shared an old, very familiar smile.

"Must be my day," I said to the little girl still waiting to be introduced. "I get a chance to meet you. I'm Bears; what's your name?"

Hesitantly, she shook my hand; "I'm Lisa Cromley."

"Glad to meet you, Lisa Cromley." The name sounded so incredibly familiar. David's quick slingshot pantomime complete with head-holding and tearful finish reminded me of the little girl once caught in the midst of a spitball fight in Miss Dean's class. "Ah yes. You're the young lady from Miss Dean's class." She looked at David, obviously excited to be so distinctly remembered.

Eyes met eyes. No one spoke for a period of time. "Go ahead," Janice urged her son.

"Well, um, Bears, uh, we made something special for you ... all of us. I guess it's my present, but everyone helped."

Scoot put the box on the ground and unveiled a small handmade replica of my little one-room house. Inside, a miniature boy, complete with a blue baseball hat on backwards, faced a rather huge bear. Both the boy and the bear sat opposite each other in a half-Lotus position. David's report card was pasted on the roof; three A's, two B's and one C. The inscription beside it read: "I'm not smart, I'm just happy ... thank you, David Seaton."

THE BOOK OF JONATHAN

"Green faces, and not just your garden variety. Bumps, like moles, all over their foreheads and cheeks. Something like dried vomit or a super case of acne, disgusting and interesting at the same time. Oh, yes," he said, rubbing his temple as if to bring the image into clearer focus. "Their heads are cone shaped. And they have arms like little children: thin, small, deformed, I guess, at least by our standards." Using his fingers like a comb, he swept his sandy-brown hair away from the front of his face, pressing the unkempt sides down over his ears. Electric-blue eyes traced the lines in his hands, then bounced from beam to beam, finding parallels between his fingers and the exposed, rib-caged structure of the room.

He poured some tea into a metal cup. Rust had formed by the handle. "The absolutely weirdest thing is that they didn't talk to me regular, you know, like we're doing now. They kind of stared at me and then, deep inside my head, I knew they were speaking to me. Hey, now wait a minute—you're not laughing at me, are you?"

"No, Jonathan—do I look like I'm laughing?"

"Not really, but that doesn't mean a thing. Damn," he hissed, jumping to his feet, "if you were laughing at me, I'd throw you the fuck out of here, right out ... you hear me?" He screamed his last words, head turned upwards, addressing the vaulted ceiling like a Shakespearean actor trying to project to the last row in the balcony. "They said Mars—bull. I knew they weren't from Mars. Probably Saturn, though, for awhile, I thought Pluto."

Suddenly, he smiled and charged at me, stopping with his face only five inches from mine. His skin seemed elastic as he cringed his eyebrows by the bridge of his nose and extended his jaw outward. "Arf, arf, arf," he barked. He glared at me, waiting for a reaction. I smiled warmly. "Hey, you're supposed to laugh. Don't you get it, Pluto the planet, Pluto the dog. Jesus, what am I wasting my time for?"

Jonathan stood on his toes between two beams, then ran his hands along the rough, hand-hewn planks respectfully. Without warning, he slammed his fist into one of the boards. The deafening sound ricocheted off the angled ceilings, echoing in every corner of the long, narrow, empty room. "You can't even count on this, not really," he said in a voice surprisingly mellow. "Been here for a hundred and fifty years, but one match— *poof*."

His expression grew ponderous. "Their leader, the big one, kind of outlined in neon—no kidding. He said they'd get me next time ... next time would be the last time." His breath quickened. Turning away, he grabbed a brown paper bag from a small makeshift table constructed sloppily from old bricks. "Want some peanuts?" he asked.

"No," I shook my head, "no thank you."

"You'll excuse me then, I have to take a shit. Oops, don't want to offend anyone with real talk," he said sarcastically. He drew in a deep breath and closed his eyes. "I'm sorry." His voice quivered. "I just can't seem to be nice to anyone. Will you be here when I finish?"

"Yes."

His face contorted with anger. "Very definite-sounding, aren't you? My father's definite-sounding too. Well, suppose I want you to go. This is my ... my castle, after all. My sister invited you here, not me!"

"You could ask me to leave," I suggested, wanting him to recognize his authority over me in this room.

"You could ask me to leave," he mimicked in a shrill falsetto voice. "But I'm not," he declared. "If I was an old man, with no hair and no teeth, they'd just call this senility without all this bother ... but, but I'm not an old man." The door to the bathroom slammed shut.

Two months ago, Jonathan had celebrated his sixteenth birthday. Although he was once heralded as a brilliant student, his grades dropped dramatically during his freshman year of high school. Julie, his older sister, had watched him graduate from marijuana to speed and acid. Her parents tried desperately to intercede, but the more they argued and punished their son, the more he seemed to slip beyond their advice and control.

Two years of therapy had not influenced the situation appreciably, except, Julie noted, for the incessant use of the term "paranoid schizophrenia" in describing Jon behind closed doors. She believed her mother preferred to envision him as sick, like having the flu or even cancer, in order to make his problem more manageable for her; perhaps she did so also to reduce her own concern about being responsible. His father, Mr. Morrow, in contrast, dismissed psychiatric terms as educated mumbo-jumbo, and an easy excuse handed on a silver platter to all those unwilling to participate and pull their fair share of the load. He saw himself as having been too easy, too supportive, too accommodating when he first realized his son's growing involvement with drugs. When he altered his perspective, deciding to treat the situation as a discipline problem, his relationship with his son completely disintegrated, leaving him furious at both himself and Jonathan.

Finally, the worst had happened, according to Julie. One morning Jonathan did not come to breakfast. The tea kettle was missing. Mr. Morrow shouted up the staircase several times, as did his wife, participating in a ritual he deplored. By the end of the meal, their son's continued absence generated considerable concern, enough to send them, along with Julie, searching for this delinquent family member. They quickly discovered that he had not slept in his bed. As they went from room to room, they heard a creaking noise in the attic. Mr. Morrow yanked open the door and charged upstairs.

Near the fireplace, which had not been operated in half a century, Jonathan lay curled up in his quilt on the floor. A portable hot plate, which they had used on camping trips, sat on the ancient mantel, the missing copper tea kettle perched on top. Two empty plates and a portable radio rested on the brick table built hastily during the night. A large, wide-brimmed hat hung from a nail embedded in the massive stone chimney which soared up through the middle of the floor and extended well beyond the roof. Although it was currently an attic, the house's original builder had polished the interior wood with a dark red stain and floored the room in oak, creating unknowingly or knowingly, an aura not unlike that of a primitive church; the massive hearth served as an altar, accented by the extreme pitch of the exposed roof-line.

"What the hell is this all about?" his father screamed,

jarring his son from a sound sleep. Mrs. Morrow put her hand on her husband's shoulder in an effort to sedate his anger. "Well, god damn it, I'm talking to you!"

Jonathan sat up and looked at his father blankly. "I'm going to live up here."

"We'll damn well see about that. Now bring the tea kettle downstairs and you'd better move, buddy, or you'll miss the bus to school."

"I'm not going to school."

"I said get up and go downstairs, *now*." Jonathan did not move. Mr. Morrow grabbed him by the arm and dragged him across the floor.

"Daddy," Julie protested.

Embarrassed, he dropped his son's arm and stormed out of the attic.

"Jon, how could you do this?" his mother said as she left.

Julie sat down next to her brother. "What are you doing?" No response. "You can tell me. Have I ever done anything against you?"

He turned around wide-eyed, a strange grin plastered on his face. Julie became frightened, but tried not to show it. "I can't leave," he said. "If I leave, they'll get me."

"Who?"

He pulled away. "I can't tell you."

"Yes you can. C'mon, Jon, tell me."

He shook his head, refusing to talk.

"Okay, do your shit, but don't come crawling to me when you need a friend."

That evening, Julie returned to the attic. The entrance had been bolted closed. She knocked quietly. No answer. "Jon, will you open up? It's me." She pounded on the narrow wood door.

The click of the metal catch startled her. He opened the door just a crack in order to scrutinize the staircase.

Once satisfied he had only this single visitor, he admitted his sister grumblingly, then bolted the door behind her.

Julie stared at the lock, confused, not remembering any such device on the inside of the attic door.

"Don't look so confused, sis," he smirked proudly. "I lifted it from my bedroom."

"Why did you do that?"

"I don't want them to get me."

"Don't worry," Julie responded, "Daddy said he's just going to let you rot up here. If you can't act civil, he doesn't want anything to do with you. Hey, don't you think it's enough? I don't know what your point is, but you sure made it." She found herself laughing.

"What the fuck is so funny?" he demanded.

"You and I, silly, sitting here in this attic. Are you coming down?"

He shook his head.

"Okay, can't say I didn't try. See you!" she said, snubbing her nose and acting very flippantly.

He let her go out without any comment. Metal slammed against metal. Jonathan had rebolted the door. Then he crawled under his blanket, pulling his knees up to his stomach in a fetal position, curling his hands in front of his chest like an infant. As he looked around the room, frightened and alone, his body began to tremble.

The next morning, Jonathan did not come to the table. The tea kettle had not been returned. Julie and her parents ate in silence. When her father rose from the table to leave, she stopped him. "Daddy, this is crazy. Are we just going to make believe he died?"

"We went through this last night. I'm willing to help him in any way I can, provided he comes a little bit in my direction first. All he has to do is give a little."

"He probably feels the same way about you," she countered.

"Listen, young lady, I don't care what he feels at this point. Where is it written that a father should allow himself to be abused by his son? Tell me, where is it written?" Before he left the room, Mr. Morrow footnoted his thoughts by muttering under his breath.

"Mom, how about you?" Julie asked.

"How about me?" she said, annoyed by her daughter's question.

"Aren't you going to do anything?"

"Your father so happens to be right. It's always Jon this and Jon that. If he's going to live in this world, he's going to have to learn to deal with the people in it."

"Suppose he can't," she said, biting her lip.

"What's that supposed to mean?"

"Nothing," Julie answered.

"Are you hiding something from me?"

"No, Mom, but maybe he's scared. People don't act like themselves when they're scared."

"Oh, suddenly we're blessed with a philosopher in the family. Your brother has nothing to be afraid of," Mrs. Morrow insisted.

"Nothing, except himself," Julie whispered loudly enough to be heard. Her mother swallowed uncomfortably, denying a response. But the thought, nevertheless, haunted her.

The following evening, Julie tip-toed up the attic stairs after her parents went to bed. She knocked quietly on the door and called her brother's name.

The bolt slid open. Jonathan looked more haggard than on the previous day. His eyes seemed bulged and fixed. He moved sluggishly away from the door without greeting his sister, intent on a Beethoven symphony that played on the radio. Standing atop his little brick table, he conducted an imaginary orchestra, pale and drawn as if he had rehearsed all night.

"Jon, how long do you intend to keep this up?"

"I don't know," he answered, waving his arms in a curiously convincing manner. "Almost professional, almost real" were the words Julie would use later to describe her brother's ability to conduct non-existent musicians in an empty attic. "As long as they're trying to get me," Jonathan continued, "I can't leave. Give me a minute, I'm almost finished with the fourth movement." When the symphony ended, he bowed to the applause on the radio, then dropped to the floor breathless.

"Who, Jon . . . who's trying to get you?"

"I can't tell you."

"Why not?"

"You'll tell them."

"I won't, I promise."

"Julie, you can't tell them, you can't," he said desperately, purposely avoiding her eyes. "They'll think I'm crazy. One phone call to Dr. Wright and they'll put me in some hospital with all those crazies."

"I won't say anything. I give you my word," she insisted.

"They're creatures."

"What kind of creatures?" she asked, trying to subdue her frustration with his limited answers.

"They're not from here."

"I don't understand, Jon. Are they people you don't know . . . like from the police?"

"I'm trying to tell you, they're not people, they're creatures . . . from another planet."

Julie's mouth dropped open; she was jolted by her brother's comment. The cold, flat intensity of his voice frightened her. If he had made up the story, his joke succeeded in off-balancing her. If he had meant it, she believed he had to be losing his mind.

"Okay, now, tell me the truth," she asked, forcing a smile.

"Get out of here. I told you the truth, you ass."

"Okay, okay! I believe you," she lied, wanting to maintain contact, afraid to leave him alone.

"No. Interview over. That's all for today. I want to be alone. I've got to think." He ushered her out of the door and bolted it behind her. A couple of seconds later he opened the door again, but she was gone. "Julie," he called in a hushed whisper. "Julie, please come back. I'll be nice, Julie, I promise. Please. Please, Julie."

She stood in the hallway, out of sight, listening to her brother's pleas. Twice she decided to go back, but each time she found herself unable to move. The snap of the bolt released her from her frozen position, yet she walked away from the attic rather than toward it.

Two weeks elapsed since that night until my first visit with Jonathan. During this time, the Morrows called Dr. Wright, who, as predicted, suggested a limited incarceration in an appropriate hospital. Julie interceded, fully aware her brother would battle anyone who attempted to separate him from the attic.

I walked the length of the floor, exploring the polished beams and the stained glass inset on the wall facing the street. Jonathan remained in the bathroom. Finally, the toilet was flushed. Another ten minutes passed until he came out. His hair, obviously wet, had been brushed flat against his head. He had tucked his shirt carefully into his jeans, looking significantly more studious than before.

"You're still here," he said, pretending to be surprised. He inflated his chest like a prize-fighter trying to out-psych his opponent. "Listen, if we talk—and I haven't decided about that yet—I'm not going to bullshit you. I need a system, a working perspective. My sister told me about your lectures and your books. I guess I'm supposed to be impressed." He put his hand up in the air. "Please, I'll try again. What do you think about my visitors?"

"What visitors?" I asked.

"You know, the men with the green faces." He waited anxiously for my response.

"Jon," I said, "to tell you what I think would only be giving you my ideas, my visions. What matters for you is what you think and what you come to know."

"Then that's what I want to talk about. Green faces."

"What about green faces?"

"They scare the shit out of me, to be perfectly honest."

"What about them frightens you?"

"They make believe they have my best interest at heart; you know, if I go along, they give me the 'everything-will-be-fine' song-and-dance routine. But I know. They can't be trusted."

"What do you mean?"

"They tease you, lure you in, then, *wap*, they give you what you least expect. You see, that's why I can't leave. If I go outside, they'll get me and then—"

"And then what, Jonathan?"

"I'll lose control. You know what it's like having someone else just take you over, pull the strings like you're some sort of a doll. I'm halfway there already."

"How do you see that?" I questioned.

"All the drugs. You do know about the drugs, don't you?"

I shook my head. "Your sister said very little, giving me only the briefest sketch of the situation."

He stared at me suspiciously, then decided to accept my basic ignorance. "Well, well, two more points for Julie—she's really scoring tonight." He looked at me directly, his eyes soft for the first time. 'She's really special, you know." He turned away and slammed his hand on the mantel. "It's so complicated." Jonathan put his hand up again, then paced the room twice before continuing.

"In the last two years, I've taken enough speed and acid to cause brain damage," he asserted. "I know, I researched it. Sometimes I had bad trips, really bad ones. Then weeks, sometimes even months later, the same lousy experience would happen again, just like I'm still on acid, but I'm not. You know what I mean?"

"Why don't you give me an example?"

"Well, about a year and a half ago, Ricky, my friend, and I dropped some cubes. They were supposed to be light doses. Well, I think if Ricky hadn't been there with me, that light dose would have buried me, put me under. I laid on the couch, waiting for something to happen. Then, I felt myself getting smaller and smaller, all curled up against the soft pillows. It was a weird sensation, but not really uncomfortable. Finally, I got so small, I couldn't have been more than a fraction of an inch high. The couch seemed enormous, maybe two hundred feet long. Ricky's living room looked like the inside of an airplane hangar. I was just digging my smallness when I heard this noise, a squeaking, chattery sound. At the other end of the room, I saw a rat, but not just a regular rat. Since I had shrunk, the rat looked like a huge, hairy mountain.

"Then, suddenly, I realized the rat was crawling across the room, getting closer and closer. I knew he had come for me. This white, foamy stuff was all over his teeth. I started to scream. I think by that time Ricky was half out of his mind, but he sat next to me and kept telling me there wasn't any rat. When I believed him, it disappeared, but when I thought he lied, I could see it again, bigger each time." He exhaled a nervous sigh. "Somehow, I got through the night. Now ... I could be sitting in class or walking home and I get this rush, like it's happening over and over again—me, small, on this enormous couch with this giant rat crawling toward me." He stopped talking. His hands trembled.

"What are you feeling?"

"I almost did it. The rat almost came again."

"Why did you stop it?"

"Christ, that's obvious, isn't it?"

"Let me share something with you that we could do together if you'd like. Dreams, daydreams, fantasies, all those kinds of experiences are constantly analyzed and reanalyzed by a variety of people who ascribe different meanings to different activities. Often, they interpret a dream in terms of symbols. Well, we don't do that. We've found the most meaningful part of the dream is the next minute after it stops. Since it's our dream or our trip, we stop it when we want to for specific and knowable reasons. Sometimes, it's meaningful to recreate the dream or fantasy, take it up to the point where it stopped and continue. It's easy and you don't have to be in a special state to do it. That's why I thought it might be useful to you to let the experience come ... perhaps, take it beyond the point you stopped during your acid trip. It's up to you."

"I don't want to do it," he said emphatically. "Anyway, we keep getting off the subject. I think the men from Saturn want to possess me."

"Why?"

"I don't know."

"If you guess," I suggested, "what would your answer be?"

"Use me as an experiment," he said. "Huh, I never thought about that before. That's it, I'd be experimented on."

"How?"

"With drugs, of course," he declared, talking as he paced slowly around the fireplace. "And I know about drugs, boy, do I know about drugs. For awhile it was fine, sometimes really great except for those horrible couple of experiences. It got to be so much a part of my life that I don't think I did anything straight. All those trips to the refrigerator. All those lectures I never heard, stoned out of my head. You know what, it's like

I've been gone for two years, a zombie, an empty pot-head, either too far down or too far up to be there, half-alive like an idiot."

"What do you mean by idiot?"

"Stupid. How could I have been so incredibly stupid and burn away my brain? I hate myself for doing it."

"Why?"

"'Cause even when I dropped acid, somewhere I knew."

"What did you know, Jonathan?"

"That I was blowing myself away at the same time. That I couldn't handle it, just like the bastard said."

"What bastard?"

"My dear father. He calls me a shit before anything happens. You know what that bastard once did—I always remember it like it just happened. I came home at mid-session during the eighth grade with a note from the gym teacher saying I missed too many classes. Mr. Ziff threatened to give me an incomplete, the whole bit. I was doing great in all my other subjects, I just couldn't make it with this teacher. Well, you'd think the incomplete was the only thing happening all year. My dear respectable father hit me and not just one time. He kept saying I'd better shape up—this was a bad sign, a cop-out. He said he knew I couldn't make it, couldn't handle it. The bastard!"

"What about thinking about him gets you so angry?"

"He kept saying that. When I broke my bike on the first day I got it, Jesus, did he scream. The kickstand didn't work right and when the bike fell, the cable for the gears ripped. You'd think I just robbed a bank or murdered someone. Boy, did he harp on telling me how I disappointed him. Another sign, he said, of my copping out. Everything became such a pain." Jonathan shuddered.

"Why did you shudder?" I asked.

"I can feel it right now. The ultimate fuck-up. You

know, when you walk around half scared all the time and someone offers you a joint and you puff your ass off and suddenly feel silly and good all over, you don't ask too many questions. It beats being uptight."

"Why were you uptight?"

"Always wondering when he'd accuse me next of being a shit and copping out. I never could feel comfortable."

"Why not?"

"I had to keep watching—otherwise, I'd fuck up all the time."

"Are you saying by feeling uncomfortable, you make sure you don't mess things up?"

Jonathan did not answer immediately. Then he blurted a response. "Yes, sure—yes!"

"Why do you believe you have to be uncomfortable in order to watch out for yourself?"

"Because...when you're not uncomfortable, you don't care." He cocked his head and furrowed his eyebrows peculiarly. "That doesn't sound so right."

"Why not?"

"I care about my music, but I'm not uptight about it. Strange, really strange."

"What's so strange?"

"First, I'm uncomfortable to make sure I don't cop out. Then I get so nervous, I smoke and drop acid." He laughed bitterly. "And that's the ultimate cop-out." He shook his head back and forth. "What a crazy scene! I guess I thought being uptight helped me handle it."

"And now?"

"It doesn't make any sense. I guess it never made any sense. Does that mean it'll change?"

"What do you think?"

"I guess I could take care of myself without being uptight. Okay," he said, allowing a quick smile to ripple across his face. "A point for your side. Ten points and it's your game."

"Not mine, Jon, but yours. There might be something else to note here—by your own words, you get yourself uncomfortable to take care of yourself, not to hurt yourself."

He eyed me cautiously, straining the muscles in his jaw. "I can see that, I really can. I guess I went overboard, got so uptight I needed the drugs to bring me down. Okay, that explains some of it . . . but not enough to make it okay by any stretch of the imagination."

"What about it is still not okay?"

"That I didn't know better."

"What about not knowing better upsets you?"

"Maybe it shows there's a loose wire, something out of joint . . . you know, a little batty."

"Do you believe that?"

"Yes. How else can you explain it?"

"If I explained it, I'd be giving you my version, which is not as important as you hearing your version. How would you explain that not knowing better, let's say about the drugs, means something is out of joint?"

"'Cause I didn't decide to take more and more drugs. After awhile, I couldn't help it."

"What do you mean?"

"Like something inside, something I didn't know about, didn't control, just took over and kept driving me and driving me. Each day, I'd say . . . this is the last time, enough, no more after today. And then the next day, I'd say the same thing, over and over and over again. Like a broken record. Yet, the next day, I'd smoke my ass off or down some pills. I couldn't help it."

"Why do you believe that?"

"It's not a matter of believing it, that's how I felt. I couldn't help myself."

"What do you mean by 'couldn't help yourself'?"

"Part of me didn't want to do it any more, but another part, even stronger, did . . . I guess." He stopped, confused. "Let me go back. I knew why I wanted to stop—so that seemed to be part of me. I knew why I took the stuff at the beginning, but I didn't know why I continued . . . it's like I didn't control that part of me."

"Why, if you weren't aware of a reason to continue, did you believe it meant you didn't control it?"

"I . . . I don't know," he said. "It just seemed that way."

"What are you afraid would happen if you didn't continue with the drugs?"

"I'd be—" His eyes teared as he stared at me. "You know what my first thought was? Without drugs, I'd have to do it. Put myself to the test."

"What test?"

"The not-copping-out test. Maybe he'd be right, maybe I couldn't handle it. God, that still seems scary."

"Why?"

"To know you can't make it, to really know you're a fuck-up."

"Let's suppose the worst came to pass for you, everything you feared—you couldn't handle it, couldn't make it . . . then how would you feel?"

He squeezed his eyes shut. "All of a sudden, that doesn't seem like the catastrophe I always thought it'd be. It would be done, finally done." Jonathan lifted his head, a sheepish smile creased his face. "Nobody can take away how good I am with my music, that's one thing. I know I can learn more, especially with reading. I love to read. So if I try and don't make it . . ."

"What do you mean by 'don't make it'?"

"You know, not getting the good grades, not being the boy wonder everyone said I was supposed to be. It's weird, it doesn't seem so scary now. In fact, I feel relieved."

"How come?"

"I'm usually so busy worrying about what he thinks. When I look at what I think, it feels okay." He rubbed his hands together while letting a stream of air pass audibly through his lips. "Spent so much time being scared I'd be an idiot, all I did was act like one."

"How do you feel?"

"Knocked on my ass. I never asked myself these kinds of questions. In therapy, all I do is ramble on and on. I never get too much of anything, except pain. You know, my mother always says what you don't know, won't hurt you—and I bought it totally. I kept thinking if I got close to knowing what was going on, it'd be terrible. What I thought it meant, it doesn't mean at all." He shook his head. "You know, Julie thinks I needed to talk to someone who I couldn't outsmart. Well, you sure turned me around."

"Do you think that's possible?"

"Sure. You got me to talk my ass off."

"Did 'I' do that for you or did 'you' do that for yourself?"

Jonathan smirked at the floor, avoiding my face. "Touché," he whispered.

"I'm going to go now," I said.

"What kind of shit is this? I thought I could talk about anything I wanted to."

"Oh, I thought that's what you did."

"Yeah, but what about those men from Saturn? I have to figure out a plan. You got to help me."

"Maybe we'll work on it next time. I'll be in touch with Julie. She'll let you know when I can come back. Probably in a few days, if I can arrange it." Jonathan knelt in front of the fireplace like a monk, then crawled silently under his blanket and turned away, facing the wall opposite me. "Goodbye, Jon," I said. He didn't answer.

Julie became our liaison. She also discussed with her parents my suggestion for a group meeting, possibly including the entire family—with or without Jon, depending on their inclination, though I seriously doubted whether they would be willing to participate in a discussion in the attic. Mr. and Mrs. Morrow declined. How about individual talks? No, not interested.

The Morrows felt they had extended themselves more than enough during the past several years. They were not willing to alter their position without some gesture from their son. "Jonathan has to do something himself to take care of his own problems," his father argued. "He's not an infant any longer. We're not going to pick up after him like nursemaids. He made his bed, now let him sleep in it."

Yet, as an accommodation to Julie, they agreed to let me spend more time with their son. In response to her daughter's insistence, Mrs. Morrow had finished one of my books and, recently, begun a second. She thought my approach was fascinating, wonderful, but not very realistic for dealing with situations such as her son's retreat to the attic. Anyway, she would be willing to wait and see.

The threat still remained. If Jonathan did not leave that attic soon, they would call Dr. Wright to handle the situation and if that meant having their son straitjacketed in order to get him to a psychiatric hospital, it would be done.

The following day, Julie and I spoke on the telephone.

"The earliest I can work it out would be Thursday," I said.

"But that's in three days." Her voice betrayed a controlled panic.

"I know. If I can do it sooner, I will. Why don't we deal with what I hear in your voice?"

"After you left last night," she said, "he seemed different, better, more in control, not as strange. But this morning, he looked like he lost it."

"Lost what?"

"His cool, his control on himself. He looked really

scared to be alone, but he still threw me out because I tried to get him to go downstairs. Maybe you should come tonight."

"I'm busy most of the evening, except, well, maybe later—but it would have to be around midnight. I don't mind, but I'm not sure your parents would want that."

"Tell me what I can do. I'm going to see him again later."

"You said he threw you out because you tried to get him to go downstairs. Remember when we talked about the attitude of 'to love is to be happy with'... it's a kind of accepting of someone, being there for them where they are, not where you'd like them to be. If you could really get into your brother's head right now, I think you'd discover that based on his fears, his beliefs, he is doing the best he can for himself. If he thought it would be good for himself, he would come down those stairs. For whatever reasons, he sees the attic as safer. Why would you want him to be in a place more frightening for him?"

"I wouldn't want that, Bears."

"Then, perhaps, if you just stayed with him in a loving and accepting way, you'd be giving him a special gift. Somehow, trying to push him is saying he's not doing good for himself. If he's not clear, he won't see your point. He'd probably just feel more alienated, more alone. If you can be where he is, that could be a beautiful experience for you both."

"Okay, for the moment, I'm inspired," Julie said. "But can I call you if I don't think it's working?"

"Sure. But try to remember that I'm not talking about a pose or the strategy of making believe you accept him. I'm talking about really being there and trusting yourself."

"I know. I know." Her breathing seemed more pronounced. "He's been difficult for everyone. I guess he can't help it."

"In a real way, he can," I said. "For Jon, at this moment, this is the best way he knows to take care of himself. If we can help him accept who he is, where he is and help him find out why he's so frightened, we give him an opportunity to find another way. There's nothing magical or mysterious about it. Since he has so many doubts about himself right now, if you don't accept him, he uses that as additional ammunition to prove to himself something's wrong with him."

"I think I understand," she affirmed. "Thanks, Bears."

Julie never called back that evening. I did not see her or her brother until three days later as originally arranged.

I stood in the narrow staircase for several minutes, knocking politely on the door as Jonathan paced back and forth on the other side, stalling, keeping the distance until that last moment when he might risk my leaving. He jerked the bolt open and peered out the door, his face partially hidden by the wide-rimmed leather hat I had seen hanging from the stone chimney. When he lifted his head, the light from the hall spotlighted his face. His lids seemed heavy, a darkness shadowed the skin beneath his eyes.

"Were you going to leave?" he asked. His mouth moved sluggishly, his lips pasty and thick.

"I had considered it," I said.

"Yes, but were you going to leave?"

"I don't think so," I smiled. His face assumed an almost-smile. "Well, do I get invited in?"

"Sure, sure," he muttered absentmindedly.

The table had been dismantled. The bricks had been reassembled to form a protective wall around the area in which he slept. Steam hissed from the mouth of the tea kettle. His clothes, wrinkled and soiled from four days of constant wear, hung sloppily on his body. He seemed weary, as if he had not slept for nights. A victim of battle fatigue in a war unannounced and unrecorded.

"I heard them again outside the door last night," he said.

"Who?"

"The ones with the green faces. They're just waiting for me to come down, to step outside that door and walk those stairs. Then zap! I'll disappear!" He paused for almost a minute, then continued. "At first it was okay up here, but now I'm getting caught between them."

"Between who?" I asked.

"Between those creatures out there and the rat in here. I've been trying to stay awake...if I'm awake, he can't get me. Oh, God, I know it's ridiculous, but I had to do something," he admitted, pointing at his miniature brick fortress. "Julie helped—she did." When he looked at me, his eyes glistened energetically though his face strained from near-exhaustion. "I know she...she thinks I'm crazy, but she sat here for hours doing her homework so I could sleep." He shook his head in disbelief. "She did that for me—no questions, just did it." Jonathan coughed several times. "Want some tea?"

"No, thank you," I said, aware of the existence of only one cup between us.

"It's real good, one of those herbal teas. That's it, shit, make some conversation," he said to himself in a scolding fashion. "Be social, well bred like the lunatics downstairs. The rat, Bears, it's coming closer and closer. I'm afraid it's going to get me. I keep stopping it, but..."

"But what?"

"But I'm getting more and more tired," he said. "I'm so fucking scared."

"About what?"

"About it getting me."

"What about that frightens you?"

"Everything, just everything," he said.

"Last time I came, I mentioned to you a way of dealing with dreams, fantasies and—"

"I remember," he shouted. "Keeps haunting me. I tried to let it go on, to continue, but somehow I couldn't. Not all alone, not by myself."

"Do you want to do it together?"

"Oh, Jesus, yes, but no."

"What's the 'no'?" I asked.

"Suppose it gets too horrible, too much for me to handle."

"You could always stop it," I suggested.

He stared at me, then buried his face in his hands. "You're serious, aren't you?"

"Yes—if you can trust yourself to go with it, Jon. Whatever you want."

"Then let's forget it, okay?"

"Fine."

"You really mean fine," he said, surprised.

"Sure. This is your expedition. You call the shots."

"I keep saying I want to talk about the creatures, but somehow I never get to it."

"What about the creatures?"

"I'm the target . . . why me?"

"What about that makes you upset?"

"It's so abstract, so random. What the fuck are those creatures doing in my life? My god damn life." He put his head into his hands and sighed. "When they're finished, the rest of my brain will be burnt away. I can't think any more."

"How come?"

"It doesn't get me anywhere. It's like having an internal obstacle course to fall and trip over. Oh, God!"

"What's the matter?"

"Back to the rat. Can't seem to keep my mind off it. When it happens, I can't decide whether it's in my head or outside of it." He paused and faced me, his eyes gripping mine. "Does it work? I mean if I go through it, will it be over finally?"

"Jonathan, most of our fears fall away when we understand why they're there. If we go through it, will it be over once and for all? I don't know. It's not up to me; it's your nightmare. No guarantees, but perhaps an opportunity."

"Maybe," he said hesitantly. "Maybe. I've got to go to the bathroom. Just a minute." He returned quickly. "Okay."

"Okay, what?"

"I want to continue the dream!"

He lay down on top of his blanket, leaning his head against the bottom rim of the fireplace. He cracked his knuckles methodically, one by one as he stared blankly at the wall. He removed the hat from his head and tossed it to the side.

"What do I do?" he questioned.

"Go through it, describe what you see, just begin," I suggested, sitting down beside him.

"But where?"

"Jon, wherever you want to."

He turned over on his side, curled his legs up toward his stomach and clasped his hands together just beneath his chin. "I'll start on the couch. I'm laying there." Jonathan drew a deep breath. 'Ricky and I took the stuff about an hour ago, but I can't be sure. I begin to feel light, almost dizzy. I let my eyes go out of focus. It's like drifting. My ears feel clogged. Everything seems far away. Wow, it's like liquid."

"What's like liquid?"

"The air. It's clear, but thick. My body feels strange—light and heavy at the same time. Now it begins; I'm floating downwards. I don't think I noticed it at first, but it's becoming more obvious." The muscles in his face became taut. "My body's shrinking, getting smaller and smaller. Must be the drug...everything's okay. It's okay. Please let it be okay, I kept saying to myself. But I'm still shrinking. I'll talk to Ricky, that'll make it stop. Ricky? Ricky? There he is. He's looking at me funny. 'Ricky, do I look smaller?' He's laughing, the idiot's laughing." Tiny beads of sweat gathered at Jonathan's hairline.

"I'm alone again. The couch. The room seems mammoth. And not just big. Everything is twisted, curved like in a fish-eye lens. Stay cool, it's only the drug. As I tried to relax, I called Ricky again. He didn't answer. Jesus, Ricky, where are you? I screamed, at least it felt like I screamed, but no sound came out of my mouth. It's not possible. I worked my jaw with my hands. Still no sounds. Just a rushing, like water from a faucet. Oh God, oh God."

"What's happening now, Jon?"

"I think I'm going to piss. Can't get up, the room's swirling. Jesus, I can't hold it in. I can't. Oh, shit," he groaned. "Damn, it's all over my legs. I'm soaked. What about the couch?" Jonathan moved his hands beneath him and felt the floor. "No—it's okay. Relax into it, you fink." He stopped talking.

"What's happening?"

"It's okay. It's a groove to be small, a real groove. The sound." He sat up and stared at a distant corner in the room. "Where the fuck's that sound coming from? Good, you're still here," he said.

"I can't sit up. My head's too heavy, too damn heavy. What the hell is that sound?" He angled his head, looking back into the same corner. His eyes bulged. "A rat. It's not possible. It's too big—shit, it's the size of a house." He peered at it intently. "It's a fucking rat. Why the hell am I so small? Oh, shit, it's moving, coming toward me. Ricky, Ricky, stay with me, c'mon, talk to me. Bears, are you there?"

"Yes, Jon, I'm right beside you."

"It's coming closer. Its teeth are enormous. My God, it's fucking ugly. I think it's going to kill me, no shit. It's going to kill me. I have to get out of here."

He threw the blanket off and stood up stiffly, trembling, his arms frozen by his sides.

"Where are you now?" I asked.

"I'm running. I didn't think I had it in me, but I got off the couch. It's behind me. I don't believe it, but I'm faster." He smirked.

"How do you feel now?"

"I can't keep it up, I'm getting tired. But I can't stop." Jon dropped to the floor. "I'm hiding now. It's dark, real dark. There's something soft in my face. Wait! Jesus, they're clothes. I must be in a closet—how the hell did I get here? The sound again. It's coming, getting closer." He moved his arms wildly as he rose to his feet. His labored breathing produced a heavy layer of sweat on his face. "I'm running again. It didn't work. He found me. There's no place to hide. Got to keep running. What? Oh, Jesus, the god damn rat is talking—I can hear it. It's calling my name. Keep moving, can't stop." Then Jonathan looked over his shoulder and moaned.

"What's there, Jon?"

"It's him. The rat is really him."

"Who?"

"My father. I knew it, I just knew it. Have to keep moving. I'm getting so tired. Oh, please, give me the energy. He's still after me. The rat. The rat." His voice became thin. "I can't stop now."

"What are you afraid would happen if you stopped?"

"He'll get me."

"Your father or the rat?"

Jonathan, panting furiously, began to laugh. "It doesn't matter. He's the rat—they have the same face." He swiveled his head again, checking behind him. "It's him, the bastard, it has to be him. I'm losing it, I'm losing it," he whispered breathlessly. "I can't run much more. My legs are numb. Please help me." He closed his eyes.

"I'm running down this street. It's like the one my aunt lives on in San Francisco. It just stops, a dead end in the middle of the air. I can't go any further, it's like a cliff over the fence. I'll climb it anyway. Please give me the strength to climb it. What am I doing—there's no place to go. He's getting closer. I can hear him. I can't move. What am I going to do? Please, what am I going to do?"

Suddenly, Jonathan turned around and screamed, his voice slicing through the room like a knife.

"What is it, Jonathan?"

"Me." He sobbed heavily. "It's me, me. It was me all the time."

"What's you?"

"The rat," he sobbed. "When I turned around this time, it wasn't my father any more, it was me."

"What about that upsets you so much?"

"The monster was me."

"What do you mean?"

"I'm afraid of what's inside me! Not a rat, not my father. What a disaster!"

"Why, Jon?"

"I could deal with my father. But how do I deal with this? The nightmare is me."

"What do you mean?"

"I'm crazy, sick," he asserted. "Remember, remember I said something must be out of joint. Well, this proves it."

"How?"

"I kept thinking it was the drugs. They did it. But Ricky and the others didn't go through the same horror show. Only me. There's something wrong with me."

"Why do you believe that?" I asked.

"Look what I did."

"That's what you did, but why does that prove something is wrong with you?"

"How else can you explain it?"

"Jon, why don't you take a shot at your own question?"

"I don't have an answer," he said, his voice strained and edged with anger.

"What are you afraid would happen if the scene with the rat was okay?"

"Then drugs would be okay."

"Why is that?"

"If it didn't matter what happened when I took drugs, then I'd just . . . no, that doesn't make any sense. We're back to the same thing as last time. I can't believe it. No. It couldn't be. Yes, I'm scaring myself so I don't do it again." He folded his arms in front of his chest. "I don't buy it, no way."

"What is it about what you said that you don't buy?" I asked.

"It's too easy. Oh, shit, what a dumb thing to say. Alright, alright . . . the more I think about it, maybe it's part of the answer. But there's got to be more. Like why the rat . . . why not an elephant or an alligator?" Jonathan's mouth dropped open.

"What is it?" I asked.

"The rat. Now I remember. Holy shit! One morning when I was about five, I went to the basement barefoot to find part of my erector set. Suddenly, I stepped on something lumpy and warm. I reached down to pick it up. When I looked at it, it was a rat. Blood dripped from its mouth. I threw it away and ran upstairs scared out of my mind. My father brought me right back down into the basement. He picked up the rat and dangled it by its tail right in front of my face. When I turned away crying, he forced me to look, saying the poison had killed it and it was good the rat died. I kept crying. I even made in my pants. He threw me onto the couch.

saying something about acting like a man, not a sissy."
Jonathan paused with a wide-eyed response to his own
words. "Hey, that's the couch, the same blue couch. It's
all there, everything."

"Historically, yes, but the way you remembered it
and kept it alive by using it, makes it part of the present, your present, not the past."

"I hated him for doing that to me."

"Why?"

"Because he said I wasn't good enough, wasn't man
enough." A whimpering sound came from his throat.

"What are you feeling?" I asked.

"That same lousy sensation in my gut. Exposed,
really exposed."

"What do you mean?"

"Just seeing another incident which shows there's
something wrong with me."

"Why do you believe that?"

"Because it's true. Most boys wouldn't have cried
like that."

"Do you believe that?" I asked.

He laughed. "I knew exactly what you'd ask next.
I kept thinking—that's what my father said. He taught
me to believe that."

"In a way, your father might have taught that belief
to you. But if you bought it, adopted it, gave it power
and lived by it as if it was true, then it's no longer your
father's belief, Jon, it's yours. And that's what you can
question. It doesn't matter when you learned it or who
taught it to you. Today, right now, do you believe most
boys would not have cried like you?"

"Maybe most of them wouldn't have ... but, I bet a
lot of kids would have cried."

"And what do you believe that might have meant
about those who did cry?"

"That they cried. That they were scared, I guess. I
could still see him dangling it in front of me like some

184

ridiculous trophy. Maybe if you did that to any kid, they'd react the same way." He bowed his head, shaking it back and forth. 'I always thought it meant I couldn't handle it, that my reaction was bad."

"And now?"

"I don't believe it's bad any more," he said emphatically.

"Do you still believe something is wrong with you?"

"I don't know if I could answer that one so clearly."

"Why not, Jon?"

He sighed. "My head feels thick, like mud. I understand more about what the rat was about and where it came from. But how do I know it won't come back?"

"Do you want it to come back?"

"No," he said, grinning weakly.

"Why the smile?" I asked.

"If you asked me that yesterday, I would have given you the same answer, but I would have felt different. It would have been a real uptight 'no.' Right now, it's just no. I don't feel afraid."

"Then if you don't want it to come back, will it?"

"I can't be absolutely sure."

"Well, if it comes back, how will that happen?"

"I don't understand your question," he said.

"Who brings the rat back again?"

"Me," he answered immediately, without hesitation. Then, he put his hand over his mouth as if to catch the words in mid-air.

"Okay, if you do it, then will you be doing it again in the future?"

He laughed again. "Jesus, everything gets so damn clear. It's absurd. Nope, it doesn't mean the same thing any more. I don't need that scene to stay away from drugs. I could stay away just because I want to." Jonathan retrieved the hat and placed it comically on his head. "Well, partner," he said with a thick western drawl, "we're gettin' 'em one by one."

I smiled easily. "I'll see you tomorrow, if I can."

"Hey, c'mon, you have to be kidding," Jonathan said. "We didn't even talk about the creatures."

"We can do that next time, if you'd like."

"If I'd like? I said I wanted to do that today, but you got me off the subject."

"I just asked questions. You chose your answers. Maybe that would be nice for you to see."

"What the fuck for?"

"Give me a second, okay?" I asked. He nodded his reply. 'Who brought the rat up?"

"Okay, So I did."

"And who remembered about the incident with your father?"

"C'mon, Bears, me of course."

"What can you know from that?"

"I talked about what I wanted to talk about, I guess," he smiled, unwilling to give his answer an absolute confirmation.

"You see your smile. It's really a beautiful smile," I observed. "It's a kind of letting go. When we learn about ourselves, we can do one of two things; be angry about what we don't know or celebrate what we do know. And if we find ourselves angry or annoyed, like with anything else, we can ask ourselves why? Jon, trust yourself. You'll get to it in your time, on your schedule. I'll see you tomorrow and confirm it with your sister, okay?"

He nodded his head slowly. "I have a lot to think about," he said as I left the attic.

That evening, Julie's voice seemed tense on the phone. 'Is tomorrow set?"

"Yes," I replied. "I tried to arrange it so I'd have a couple of hours. How are you doing?"

"I feel closer to Jon. We're been having some pretty heady conversations. I just try to accept him, like we discussed. He's opening up a little. But with my parents—nothing. He won't talk to them and they won't talk to him. It's ridiculous."

"Julie, you do what you can."

"But it's not always enough."

"If you're clear and it's what you want to do, then whatever you give is the best you have to give ... and that's all there is. Maybe not enough just means you wanted more."

"There's something else I didn't mention," she said. "I was going to tell you when you came tomorrow, but maybe I should do it now. They gave him a time limit. If he's not down from the attic by tomorrow night, they're calling Dr. Wright."

"We'll do the best we can. The most crucial person in this whole affair is not part of this current conversation. We can want what we want, but Jon has to decide for himself."

"But if he stays stubborn, they'll drag him out, I know they will. They'll put him in some hospital, lock him up like a criminal, and drug him."

"What are you saying, Julie?"

"I don't know what to do."

"You're doing what you can do," I said.

A long silence.

"Should we tell him about my father's decision? Maybe he'll do something crazy."

"Do you believe that?" I asked.

"No," she answered.

"Let me ask you something," I said. "If the tables were turned and you were up in that attic, would you want to know?"

"Yes. Yes, I would. But I don't know if I have the heart to break it to him ... could you do it?"

"Sure," I answered.

As I climbed the stairs to the attic for our next session, the door opened, revealing Jonathan boldly presenting himself without first going through his protective ritual of checking the stairway. He appeared noticeably less fatigued, though still battle-worn and unkempt.

"Hello," I said, entering the room.

He bolted the door, then poured a cup of tea which he handed to me. "Why are you looking at it so weird for? I washed the cup out first. Venereal disease isn't usually spread from teacup to teacup. I know," he said, shaking his head, "this is a poor beginning."

"How about it's neither poor nor rich, but simply another step along the way." I smiled at him as I sipped the Chamomile tea.

"No rat last night, Bears. Kind of missed him." Jonathan laughed. "My first decent night's sleep. You talk about celebrating, well, I can celebrate about that." He grinned oddly. "How about the creatures?"

"What about them?"

"I want to make them disappear . . . like my acid rat. I don't know how to do that since they're still out there, just waiting for me to come down." His hands trembled.

"What are you upset about?" I asked.

"You know they use drugs on people, all kinds of drugs. I promised I wouldn't use them any more, but they don't give a shit. They'll just shove them down my throat."

"Why would they do that?"

"For control. They want to blow away my will."

"What do you mean?"

"Listen, I almost lost it. I could have been some dumb junkie if I hadn't come up here." He turned away and walked to the other side of the room. "I said it, didn't I?"

"Said what, Jon?"

"What it's all about."

"Which is?"

Sitting down beside me on one of the bricks, he rubbed his hands together. "Remember I told you about how I kept deciding to stop." I nodded. "And how each time, I did it again and again. You see, in my school, wherever you turn, someone's trying to sell you drugs. In the lunchroom, in the locker room, by the side gate. It's wild; it's like a drug store. And every time I know it's there, I just buy. It's like some horrible magnet."

"Could you describe what you mean . . . step by step what happens?"

"Mark really deals big. I bought from him the last time. Ricky, Bill and I were sitting at the back table. Mark walks over, doing his 'I'm cool and independent' act. Then he plops his ass down right next to me. We have this big talk about nothing. That's like the introduction—it's a game. Then he whips out this bag from his jacket and shows us a whole assortment of shit. Bill shakes his head, but Ricky buys some qualudes. I could feel myself sweating. I got more and more anxious. Finally, I slapped my money into his hand." Jonathan exhaled uncomfortably.

"Why did you decide to do that?"

"I didn't, not really. I kept thinking what'll happen if I need them later."

"What do you mean . . . 'need them later'?"

"You know, to get loose, to get away from all the bullshit in the house . . . maybe all the bullshit inside, like the rat."

"Okay, then, from what you just said, does it just happen, your buying the drugs, or do you, in fact, have reasons?"

He placed his hands in front of his face almost as if he were praying. "I guess I do have reasons. How come everything seems so obvious now, when just a couple of weeks ago, this whole thing was mud?"

"You're letting yourself answer questions you might have been afraid to ask several weeks ago," I said. "Okay, so if you had reasons, do you then decide, for those reasons, to buy?"

"Yeah. I do."

"Then do you control it?"

"Uh-huh, I really see that, but something else also happens. I get so afraid I'm going to buy it, it seems easier to do it, just to get it over with."

"At least after I buy it, I don't feel so damn anxious. Crazy, isn't it?"

"Well, why do you get anxious when you think you're going to buy it?"

"Because I don't want to buy it," Jonathan said.

"Not wanting to buy drugs is very different from being anxious about buying it. Why are you anxious about buying it?"

"Because," he said, "I know I'll be weak and buy it."

"Why do you believe that?"

"If you could see a movie of me in front of the dealers, you'd know why I believe that. I can't say no."

"Why not?"

"I told you already. I get afraid I might need them later and won't have them."

"So you purchase them to have them later. What's going to happen later?"

"The whole bit in my house, the rat ... all that shit. It's like a crazy circle, isn't it? I used the rat to frighten me away from the drugs, then I needed the drugs to get rid of the rat." He laughed.

"Are you saying you're still uncomfortable about the rat?"

"No. I'm okay with that. I am."

"Then if you're okay with it, if you no longer need the rat to help you know you don't want drugs, why do you believe you'll still buy them?"

"Not for that reason any more, but, just maybe, because I've always done it."

"Why if you've always done it in the past, even hundreds of times, does it mean you'll decide to do it again tomorrow?"

"I don't know. It doesn't necessarily mean that, unless I guess I'm in the same head."

"Are you?"

Jonathan smiled broadly. "I guess not. I don't feel scared."

"Does that mean you still have some fear about it?"

"A little. When you asked me to describe what happened when I buy, I did really have reasons—I even surprised myself. Some aren't there any more. So it's changed. But I don't know if maybe there are still other reasons and then, maybe, I'll find myself buying again."

"Why do you believe that?"

"Well, look at me, I'm nervous all over again. That must mean something."

"What?"

"I don't know. But that's exactly how I get just before I buy."

"Why does that happen?" I asked.

"Because I don't want to buy and I think I'm going to anyway."

"Why do you think that?"

"Because I can't stand feeling this way—I might as well get it over with and buy the shit."

"What happens after you buy it?"

"I'm not as anxious."

"Then, are you saying by buying it you get rid of some of the anxiety?"

"Sounds nuts, but that's really it. After I do it, I feel better...like released. That's really incredible. Now I understand why it feels so automatic. Okay, but why did I get anxious in the first place? Wait, wait! I know the answer. Because I was uptight about what I thought I'd do. I don't want to do that any more and I'm not going to."

"How do you feel?" I asked.

"Amazed. I feel unhooked." He sighed and shook his

hands, flapping them as if to throw off energy. "I don't feel anxious. What a relief! There's something exciting about knowing that I really do control it. I never understood that before and when my father kept saying I'm responsible, I guess that always seemed like being cursed. It doesn't now."

For the next two hours, Jonathan explored his perception of himself as a student, trying to uncover the reasons for the incredible pressure he experienced. He described his father's near-obsession with seeing his son achieve superlative grades in school. Jonathan had to be the best at everything. An 'A' confirmed his self-worth, but anything less was an indictment. In the eighth grade, when he suddenly had difficulty with math and French, he began to assume it meant something irrevocable about his ineptitude. His father's growing anger supported this vision. As Jonathan's anxiety increased, his ability to concentrate and study dramatically decreased. In effect, he began to appear "stupid" or "inept," fulfilling his original fear about himself.

What about having difficulty learning made him unhappy? It meant he was being exposed. What did he mean? They would know he couldn't do it. And what about their 'knowing' disturbed him? It confirmed what he knew. What did he know? That he was faking it all along; he couldn't really do it; he was stupid. Why did he believe that? It's something he always thought he knew. As he laid bare his reasons, they seemed flimsy and unreal to him. As he discarded them, so too he discarded the belief which they supported. A mark of 'B' or even a failing grade did not have to mean anything about him globally...he decided it just meant something about the way he approached a specific subject or subjects. It no longer indicated something was wrong with him.

"But why did he have to be such a bastard?" Jonathan complained.

"Who?" I asked.

"My father. Always critical, never giving an inch. Why, damn it, why?"

"Unless you can talk to your dad and he could answer those questions, you can't do anything but speculate on his answers or his reasons. We could never actually know. But there is something beautiful you can do— explore and even change, if you want to, your own reactions to what he says and does. That's within your bounds to know and control. So, what I would ask you based on what you just said is—why are you so angry with him."

"He made me miserable."

"How did he do that?"

"We just went through it. He pushed and pushed and pushed. Drove me crazy."

"How did his pushing drive you crazy?"

"I know I had a part in it, okay? If I get crazy, I do that. Look at me right now. But he was always there being critical. The hitting. The shouting. Never spent one lousy minute telling me and my sister we did well, only what we did shitty."

"Okay, Jon, that's what he did...but what about that gets you angry?"

"It hurt."

"Why did it hurt?"

"Because I knew...if he gave a damn about us, we wouldn't always have to prove something. It's like I was okay if I got great marks, but if I didn't, I wasn't worth caring about."

"What do you mean?"

"When I came home with a great report card, he'd be nice to me. If the card was anything less than great, he'd scream and walk away and leave me by myself.

He'd only love me if I was great."

"Do you believe that?"

"Isn't that obvious?" he retorted.

"Are you saying you believe it?"

Jonathan looked at me out of the corners of his eyes. "I know what happens when I answer quickly. Let me think." He walked over to the mantel and turned on the hot plate. "Yeah! I believe if I wasn't great, he didn't love me. So his love was shit."

"Why do you believe that?"

"He'd get angry and he wouldn't talk to me—turn on and off like a faucet. He didn't love me, not really."

"How did his anger and not talking to you prove he didn't love you?"

"Well, I know from me—I'm like that, I'm, I'm . . ." he sighed and turned away. "You know, I did the same thing to Julie when she first came up here. I was so pissed, unfriendly—a real bitch, I even told her to leave. But, you know, I still loved her, I did. I was just acting crazy. I've been really doing a job on myself, haven't I?"

"What do you mean?"

"I always saw my old man as not caring about me and gave it back to him double. Maybe when he's pissed, he's like me, doing all sorts of shitty things like yelling at his kids. Okay, so maybe he does love me, so maybe he's been angry for the last ten years, but what about me?"

"What about you?"

"He should suffer like I did."

"Why, Jonathan?"

"So then he'd know how it hurt."

"Why would you want that?"

"Oh, I don't know any more," he said, visibly deflated. "Maybe, so he'd change."

"Do you think people change by making them miserable?"

He chuckled as he poured the tea. "No, not that I've noticed."

"We have an expression we use," I shared with him, "using misery to fight misery just adds to the misery."

"Yeah. I'm a good example of that. So what does it mean, I just forgive and forget?"

"What do you want to do?"

"Bears, if I did that, I'd be an idiot."

"Why do you believe that?"

"After all his bullshit, if I just . . . oh, I don't know, just hugged him or something, I'd be saying it didn't matter."

"Does it?"

"Now, no. But then it did, it did very much."

"So if you were caring now, would you be saying when it happened it didn't matter?"

"No, I guess not. I'd just be talking about now. But I'd want him to know, I'd want to tell him. And wait, not to beat him with it. I guess I've done enough of that for the past two years. Look what it got me," he said, spreading his arms out from his sides as he laughed. "It got me a first class ticket to the attic."

"How do you feel?"

"Stronger and stronger."

"It's eleven o'clock," I observed. "I'm going to leave now. I'll try to see you tomorrow. Also, there's something I wanted to tell you," I said, about to inform him of his father's ultimatum.

"Before you say anything, there's something I want to tell you."

"Go ahead," I said.

"The green creatures from Saturn that we never seem to discuss . . . they're not real, not in the way I said. Did you think they were real?"

"Do you mean did I think you believed they were real?"

"Uh-huh."

"I didn't try to . . . second guess you. If you believed they were real, then they were certainly important to talk about. And if you didn't and you purposely fabricated them, well, you did that for a reason and, so, it would still be important to talk about. What I'm saying is that it didn't make a difference. If you made up a daydream and it scared you, it would be as valid as anything else in your life to talk about."

"Do you want to know why I made them up?" he asked.

"If you'd like to tell me."

"At first, they were kind of a joke. Thought I'd scare the shit out of my parents so they'd leave me alone up here. Then I decided if I talked about them, I would have to know what I'm talking about. So I started to visualize them, see what they looked like, what they'd do. In a way, they came alive—I made them up so I wouldn't be able to leave the attic and almost believed it. But I don't need them any more. I feel stronger about everything now."

"How do you feel about having made them up?"

"Okay. For a while, I was kind of convinced I was crazy . . . so this was just another one of my crazy things. But somewhere, I knew it was a game. I thought about Dr. Wright saying anyone who'd make up such a game had to be crazy."

"And do you believe that?"

"No way. I'm about as crazy as you are," he declared with a smirk.

"That knowledge and fifty cents will get you on the subway."

We both laughed.

"Bears, I just thought of something else, right now while we were laughing."

"What?"

"I'm going down. Out of the attic. I don't need this place any more. It's like I've been to another planet and I'm ready to come back."

"Humm," I smiled. "Do you want to be announced downstairs?"

He grinned self-consciously. "Are my parents home?"

"I think so. When I leave, they're usually sitting around the kitchen table."

"Would you go first and wait for me downstairs? I mean you don't have to. I can make it on my own. But . . . but, I'd like you there. Not in the kitchen, but downstairs, somewheres."

"You're on," I agreed, turning to leave.

"One second," Jonathan said. "What did you want to tell me?"

"Oh, I guess it doesn't matter any more. I'll see you on the main floor."

Julie, her long hair pinned on top of her head, her body discernible beneath her worn, baggy overalls, waited for me in the living room. When I came downstairs, she immediately cornered me.

"How did he take it when you told him?" she asked urgently.

"You mean about the ultimatum?"

"Of course," she blurted.

"I never told him." Her mouth fell open at my words. "There's more, Julie. I didn't have to tell him. Just watch the hallway."

She clasped her hands over her mouth. "You're kidding," she said.

"Me . . . no. And your brother didn't sound like he was kidding either."

At that moment, the creaking steps became apparent. Julie hugged my arm as we waited together. The muffled drone of her parents talking in the kitchen also filled the room. The footsteps became louder, then they stopped suddenly. Julie started to move toward the stairs.

I tapped her shoulder. "Give him a chance," I whispered. "It meant something for him to come down by himself." She shook her head in agreement and cried.

The sound started again. He continued stepping down, finally reaching the hallway. The wall blocked our vision. Almost in mock pantomime, his large head appeared from around the corner. He looked awkward at first, then he smiled, delighted to see us. His raised hand asked us to remain in the living room. Jonathan proceeded across the hall into the kitchen. His parents' conversation stopped instantly.

Julie pulled me into the dining room so we could watch. Both Mr. and Mrs. Morrow stood up, shaken and surprised by their son's appearance. Jonathan looked down at his arms for a long, long time. He walked directly over to his father, who backed up a step. Then, in silence, Jonathan embraced the man, closed his eyes and patted his back. Mr. Morrow stood there stiffly, not quite knowing what to do. He finally touched his son's shoulders awkwardly. Jonathan nodded and smiled, then hugged his mother.

*   *   *

Several days later I received a phone call from Julie. "I told my father that Jon didn't even know about his ultimatum, that he came down because he wanted to, not because he was threatened. You know what, that really impressed him. We all had a discussion last night and my parents decided they'd like to have some group discussions with all of us and with you. Could we still do that?"

"Sure," I said.

"And I got to tell you one more thing you're not going to believe."

"Try me."

"Jonathan said he'd like to choose the place for our first group session. My father looked at him peculiarly and didn't say anything. Well, you know what that nut did, and he wasn't being bitchy or anything, he said he wanted us to meet in the attic. And I could have fallen off my chair when my father said yes."

THE BOOK OF JEANETTE

Tiny particles of dust danced in the shafts of sunlight filtering through the checkerboard of window panes that dotted the entire length of the wall. The bowed heads of children seated in neat little rows graced the room with a hushed ecclesiastical air. Only the occasional rustling of feet and the readjustment of a little body in a squeaking chair broke the silence.

The class had been segmented into four reading sections. As the students worked diligently, eight-year-old Jeannette Ling, like many of her companions assigned to the lowest reading group, used her index finger to guide her eyes from word to word and line to line. Suddenly, she paused and raised her hand, but the gesture was so timid, it failed to gain the teacher's attention. Several minutes passed. Jeanette raised her hand higher as she squirmed behind her desk.

"Yes," Mr. Garland said, finally acknowledging her.

"May I go to the bathroom?" she asked, her voice barely audible.

"You'll have to speak up."

"May I go to the bathroom?" The strength and urgency of her own voice startled her. She eyed her classmates with obvious discomfort.

"Of course, but this time I don't want you spending all that time in there. Do what you have to do and then come back immediately." A scattering of laughter rippled through the room. Her face flushed. Embarrassed, she remained seated. "Jeanette, I said you could go!"

She rose hesitantly to her feet, then quickly bolted from the room. In the bathroom, the little girl leaned against the wall beside an enclosed toilet and vomited, overwhelmed momentarily by stomach cramps and nausea. After she braced herself in the corner, she squeezed her eyes tightly shut and waited, hoping this not-uncommon experience would pass quickly.

Jeanette returned to the classroom twenty minutes later. As she slinked to her seat, Mr. Garland addressed her curtly. "Jeanette, come up here!"

She faced her teacher, angling her head to the side. Her fingers busily played with a loose thread from her blouse.

"Listen," he said in a soft voice, "you've been gone for twenty minutes. I assume nothing is wrong. Right? For God's sake, Jeanette, answer me. I'm not going to bite you. Is anything wrong?"

She shook her head.

"Okay then, if nothing is wrong, twenty minutes in the bathroom is just unacceptable. And I warned you before you left." Exhaling a sigh, he tapped her on the shoulder in a peculiar, yet affectionate, gesture. 'This is the last time. You've got to shape up. Now, go ahead, go back to your seat and finish today's reading assignment."

Though absorbed initially in her book, her interest

waned. Her eyes wandered from the pages and settled on a series of drawings pinned to the bulletin board mounted by the door.

"Jeanette," Mr. Garland barked, "are you finished already?"

She bowed her head quickly, burying her face in the book. Her almond-shaped eyes teared as she cocked her head slightly to the side, almost as if to avoid looking directly at the book. Long, black hair and bangs clipped at her eye-brows framed her small, delicate face. Her tiny nose, cherubic lips and smooth skin gave her doll-like appearance. Her fragile hands and thin arms further supported this illusion.

The ticking of her wrist-watch distracted her. She stared hypnotically at the spastic second hand sweeping the silver dial, then lifted her head again and gazed at the drawings on the wall, leaving her lesson conspicuously incomplete.

"Jeanette—and you too, Douglas, since both of you obviously have all the time in the world to look around the room—I guess you've finished the assignment. Now come up to the front of the room. Both of you. C'mon. Right now, let's go," he said in a hard-edged voice as he clapped his hands like a football coach. "We don't have all day." When they arrived at his desk, he faced both children to the class. "We'll start with you, Jeanette." He eyed her with a soft, yet firm expression. "Why did Timmy's grandfather leave in the middle of the night in chapter six?"

Jeanette stood there, her head bowed as she stared at the floor.

"Did you hear the question?" he snapped impatiently. She nodded. "Well, then, go ahead and tell the class the answer."

"I don't know," she whispered, never once lifting her head.

"What am I going to do with you? You didn't com-

plete the assignment again, yet you had plenty of time
to look at the walls." Angered, yet charmed by her
retiring manner, he instructed her to remain after
school.

During lunch hour, while her friends ate and chatted
incessantly, Jeanette withdrew her third grade reader
from a small, red briefcase and began studying. She
tried to ignore the noise and activity in the room which
continually distracted her. Turning away from her
classmates, she struggled to keep her eyes riveted to
the page.

The giggling of two girls at the opposite side of the
table drew her attention, though Jeanette never confronted them directly, always spying at them out of the
corner of her eyes. They whispered secrets to each other
as they pointed at her.

Dana, who sat next to Jeanette, grinned sarcastically at the two hecklers. "Just ignore them," she counseled her friend. "They're idiots. C'mon, Jeanette, you
want me to help you with the story?" She shook her
head, adamantly refusing Dana's assistance. "Mr. Garland will never know. I can tell you what happens in
two minutes . . . that's all it would take," Dana insisted.

"No, I'll be okay," she assured her friend.

"That's pretty dumb, Jeanette," Elaine volunteered
from across the table.

"Mind your own business," Dana retorted defen-
sively. "She wants to do it by herself." Taking Jeanette's hand, she guided her to a small empty bench
at the side of the room.

"You didn't have to do that," Jeanette said. "Thanks."

"Elaine's a jerk. I didn't want to sit there anyway.
You sure you don't want me to help?"

"Just tell me how to say this word."

For the next thirty minutes, Jeanette plowed through
the pages, asking Dana to explain some words, but
never fully accepting aid.

After class, Mr. Garland confronted her.

"Look, honey," he began parentally. "I don't know how to get you to pay more attention. I have to give you another failing mark for today's lesson. If I ask you to read a story, I'm not kidding. You know I'm going to ask questions afterwards." Jeanette stared at her hands as she rubbed her fingers together. Keenly aware of his own huge two-hundred-and-sixty pound hulk in comparison to her tiny, wispy figure, he softened his voice purposely and bent down to her eye level. She avoided his glance. "Maybe I ought to have a conference with your parents. What do you think?"

Mumbling, Jeanette said, "But I did read the story."

"Then how come you didn't know the answer to my question?" he snapped, less sympathetic in the face of what he viewed as an obvious lie. "Okay, I'll give you another chance right now. Just before the flood in the last chapter, why did Timmy run back to the barn?"

Although she had completed the book only three hours ago, the story seemed muddled and distant to her. Jeanette's eyelids fluttered nervously.

"Well—I'm waiting!"

"I can't re—remember." Her voice faltered.

"Young lady, when you talk to me, I expect you to at least look at me. My face isn't down there on the floor." She glanced up at him for two seconds, then turned away again. "Between all the time you've been absent and all the times you just daydream in class, you're in danger of being left back. Do you understand what I'm saying?"

Jeanette nodded, suppressing an impulse to cry. She wanted to tell Mr. Garland that she had really tried, but the words never surfaced. In the corridor, she leaned against the green tile walls and gaped at the book in her hand. She hunched her shoulders as if chilled, then let her reader drop to the floor. Without looking back, Jeanette ran toward the exit at the end of the hall

* * *

Though worn and weathered, the old buildings had a kind of dignity, huddled like aging athletes along the narrow street. A black sky blanketed Chinatown's restaurant alley. Neon glittered. Barking horns mixed easily with the laughter of children. Slipping past the hordes of people on Mott Street, I turned left in search of Joy Ling Tea Garden.

Chiang had described his niece, Jeanette, in great detail. As a doctor of medicine and an herbologist, he treated her often during her many bouts with illness. At first, he surmised the child had a weak constitution which he attempted to bolster with herbs, an enriched diet and various Eastern remedies. Frustrated by her lack of response, he performed an extensive battery of tests, trying to pinpoint a deficit in her immunological system. A perfect specimen. Clinically, the picture of health.

Nevertheless, the little girl fell victim to everything from pneumonia to stomach cramps. Each illness sapped her strength, turning her focus inward. With a loss of weight came a loss of energy. Her increasingly introverted nature became evident not only to her family, but also to her teacher at school. Though always a struggling student, Jeanette seemed more and more disinterested in learning. Her marginal grades had become unacceptable. The school officials speculated that perhaps the pressure of a bilingual environment confused her—speaking and thinking in English at school while using mostly Chinese at home. Perhaps, they conjectured, the heavy push for ethnic identity turned her away from working in class.

"What heavy push?" Chiang protested as he listened

to his sister and brother-in-law relate the contents of a recent parent-teacher meeting. He knew his niece lived in the same environment in which many other Chinese-American children had flourished. He shook his head adamantly, dismissing the commentary.

Concerned with her withdrawal or "retreat," as he characterized it, Chiang considered answers outside of his area of expertise. In his judgment, he told me, he believed she suffered from a "confusion of thought." He would arrange a meeting, promising a sumptuous meal and a year's supply of jasmine tea, all of which he knew I wouldn't refuse.

As I entered the crowded restaurant, a small, muscular Chinese man jogged down the center aisle, nodding to various patrons as he passed their tables. He grabbed my hand firmly, then pumped it vigorously like a prizefighter. A gracious smile swept across his face.

"Mr. Kaufman, you are very easy to identify. I'm Daniel Ling. Chiang's description was perfect, even his speculation about which jacket you might wear. Humm," he grunted touching the garment, "made from pieces of old dungarees ... very clever." Then he laughed, uncanny in his direct response to my wide-eyed expression. "Ah, most people are thrown by the accent ... good old American Midwest. I'm an uprooted Ohio boy, believe it or not—followed the fortune cookie to New York. As you can see, no fortune ... but a little fame." He laughed again, pointing to the flickering neon sign in the window. "At least my name is in lights."

Just as I started to speak, he interrupted my first word, saying: "Come. And don't mind me, I talk a lot." Even as we walked, he peered back over his shoulder, still speaking: "My grandfather had little patience for the English tongue. He'd always say people in America talk too much and then, with a long face, he'd look at me and wonder how a Chinese boy from such fine ancestry could be so busy saying nothing. Each day, in early morning, he'd have me write out the old Buddhist saying—'He who speaks does not know; he who knows does not speak.' Never made much of an impression on me."

"I see," I confirmed smiling.

"But," he continued, "at seventeen, I finally figured out what was wrong with the saying and rewrote it." He stopped and pointed to the framed piece on the wall containing beautifully stylized Chinese letters inscribed on rice paper. "I will translate Daniel Ling's version for you. It says: 'He who knows speaks in order to know better.'" We both laughed. I found myself applauding.

He ushered me into a secluded alcove in the back of the restaurant, segmented by a thin curtain from the noisy chatter and clanging silverware. Mr. Ling bowed slightly, with a studied reverence, as he acknowledged the woman and the little girl seated at the table. His manner seemed startlingly inconsistent with his initial monologue.

"Mr. Kaufman," he said, "this is Sue Ling, my wife, and our daughter, Jeanette."

"I'm glad to meet both of you," I said, captivated by Jeanette's doll-like face.

Sue Ling took her husband's arm. She addressed me warmly. 'We are most honored to have you as our guest. My brother says only very special things about you. We will leave you two alone now."

"Not totally alone," Mr. Ling added. "The waiter will come back and forth bringing food—specialties of the house. Do you want silver or wood?" he asked, comically pointing to a shelf filled with chop-sticks.

"Wood," I answered. Seemingly pleased with my reply, he exited, pulling the curtains shut. As I turned to the little girl, Daniel Ling peeked his head back through the drapery. He coughed, then grinned. "Excuse. Please. One last thing. I know you're a vegetarian, so there will be no meat anywhere, not even in the hot and sour soup. We made a special portion. And also, our daughter selected these dishes in your honor. Thank you." He hesitated a moment to look at his child. He winked at her, touched my arm gently and left.

Jeanette avoided looking at me directly. Her large eyes discreetly explored the area just around my shoulder, giving her an elegant and timeless air of humility.

"I'm Bears, a friend of your Uncle Chiang...but I guess you know that."

She nodded without glancing up from the table.

"Okay," I said, acknowledging her head movement. "Maybe we can talk about why we're having dinner together. How's that sound?" Jeanette didn't answer. Silence. She began to pick at her nails nervously.

"Do you want to say hello?" I asked.

"Hello," she said in a soft, timid voice.

"Great. Hello to you," I responded. "Funny, when you come into a new place, it's real nice to have people to talk to you. Do you feel the same way?" She nodded her answer. "Thought so. Your father can certainly make people feel right at home."

At that moment, the waiter delivered two giant bowls of soup. "Could I have some vinegar?" I asked. He fulfilled my request within seconds. "Do you want some in your soup, Jeanette?"

"No, thank you," she said.

We drank the soup in silence. I found myself picking at the strange pieces of food floating in my bowl, noting how different it seemed from the standard fare served at most Chinese restaurants. Peering out of the corner of my eye, I noticed Jeanette watching me, not directly, but allowing herself, from time to time, to glance at me and observe my culinary exploits.

"Fantastic soup...really fine!" I said, noting with surprise, that the thick broth filled her bowl. "Don't you want your soup?" Jeanette shook her head meekly; her thin fingers made circles on the white table cloth. Suddenly I burped. She giggled, thoroughly delighted. "Ah," I exclaimed theatrically, wanting to retain her participation, "so you think that's funny... well, I guess it is. In my house, I'm the second best burper."

"Who's the first?" she asked.

"My wife, Suzi. She has this big, deep voice and when she burps it sounds like someone playing the tuba. Do you know what a tuba is?" She nodded.

The waiter collected the bowls, then delivered hors d'oeuvres and a set of chopsticks for each of us. "Do you want some?" I asked. She glanced at me momentarily. When she dropped her chin, I interpreted the gesture as a "yes." I dished some breaded shrimp and crab meat onto our plates; then covered the fish with a special hot garlic sauce.

While I ate, I marveled at her dexterity with the chopsticks. They were like extensions of her hands. Though I had used them frequently for many years, learning to eat with wooden sticks as an adult is like learning a second language with which you can become proficient and comfortable, but, somehow, never have that perfect fit. Jeanette's nimble fingers moved without instruction; mine still required cues from my head.

"Can you eat with silverware as well as you eat with those?" I asked.

"Uh-huh," she replied, "it's easy."

"Sometimes, what's easy for one person is very difficult for another." Jeanette stopped eating; her eyes skidded across the top of the table, silently confirming my statement.

"If I ask you a question, would you answer?" I queried.

"Depends."

"Well, then I'll try. Why do you think we're having dinner together?"

"To talk."

"About what?"

"About me."

"And how do you feel about that?"

"Scared." She still maintained her distance by refusing to allow herself any sustained eye contact.

"What are you scared about?"

"If you think I'm stupid, will I get left back?"

"Ah," I sighed. "Let me tell you about me. I do lots of different things, like write books and play with children. I also talk to people, all kinds of people, big ones, little ones—it doesn't matter. Often, I ask questions. Lots of questions." I leaned forward, cocking my head to the side just inches above the table and smiled. No response. "Sometimes," I continued, "people learn all sorts of wonderful things about themselves when they answer the questions. And there are no right or wrong answers, no smart or dumb ones...there's just answers. We all do the best we can. I don't know your school or your teacher. I'm not here for them; I'm here for you. Whatever we talk about is between you and me. I won't tell anyone about what we discuss, unless you want me to, and unless you say so. Understand?" She nodded her head affirmatively.

The waiter intruded, visibly disappointed that we had not yet consumed the food. Jeanette watched me lift my chopsticks, then she began eating.

"Your parents are fantastic chefs, you know that?"

"Daddy's not a chef—I once asked him. He likes to be called the cook, boss and chief bottle-washer. But I think he likes being called the boss the best. My mother only works here sometimes."

"Oh, I see." I paused to smile as I envisioned her father listing his titles to his daughter. "Before, you said you were scared that I might think you were stupid. Why?"

She downed some shrimps before answering. "That's

what everyone thinks. I don't like people to think that."

"Why not?"

"Because it makes me sad."

"What about their thinking you're stupid makes you sad?"

"I've always been ... well, schoolwork is hard for me," she admitted, fidgeting with her chopsticks. "I don't know why. It's easier for the other kids. Now that I'm in the third grade, I seem to have more trouble. Mr. Garland says I don't try."

"And do you?"

"Yes ... sort of."

"What do you mean?"

"I always start by trying, but then ... I don't know, I can't concentrate."

"Why, what happens?"

"Like in reading, I get so nervous, I can't keep my eyes on the page."

"Why do you get so nervous?"

"Because I'll just try like every time before and not get it right." She put her hands over her face. Tears ran down between her fingers.

"What's the matter, Jeanette?"

"I think I'm going to be sick."

"How do you know?"

"I feel it, just like in school."

"Describe it to me, if you can."

"My stomach feels funny."

"Why do you think that means you're going to be sick?" I asked.

"That's what always happens."

"Do you want it to happen now?"

After an extended period of silence, she removed her hands from her face. "I wanted it to happen, but when you asked me, then I didn't want it any more."

"How do you feel?"

She touched her stomach surprised. "Okay."

"Why the surprise?"

"It just disappeared. That's funny. I just didn't want it any more and, boom, it disappeared."

"And what about getting sick? Does that seem to happen when you want it to?"

The color drained from Jeanette's face. She clutched her hands beneath her chin, holding herself close as a shiver rippled through her body.

"What are you feeling now?"

"I'm cold. I feel sick again."

"Why?"

"I just feel sick."

"What are you afraid would happen if you didn't feel sick?"

"Then we'd probably talk more!" Her eyes riveted to mine for the first time since the beginning of dinner.

"Are you saying by feeling sick you get out of having to talk more?"

She turned her head away, her lips sealed. I waited several minutes. The waiter arrived just as Jeanette started to cry. He backed out through the curtain without depositing the dishes. Within seconds, Daniel Ling looked in. I motioned for him to leave us alone. He left hesitantly.

"Jeanette, you don't have to stay here and talk. It's really okay if you want to leave. You decide and whatever you decide will be right for you."

She shook her head up and down, acknowledging my words. Her hands busily wiped the tears from her eyes. At no time did she attempt to move from her chair.

"Why are you crying?"

"I got upset about answering the question."

"Why is that?"

"Because I knew what my answer would be."

"Do you want to share it?"

213

"It's true, if I feel sick, then I won't be able to talk any more. It's just like school. I used to make believe I was sick so I could stay home. Then, sometimes, I'd really get a stomachache or a cold. Now if we have a big test and I keep thinking about it, I'll get sick."

"When you think about a test, what do you think?"

"That I'm scared. That I don't want to take it."

"And then, what's the very next thing you feel, the very next thing?"

"Like on Monday, right after I spent all day scared about the spelling test, I felt like coughing. Before I knew it, I had a sore throat. That's so weird. It sounds just like what I used to do."

"Which is?"

"Make believe. Except now, I guess it's not make believe any more—it really happens." Her eyes beamed, accenting her thoughtful expression. "Do you think that's possible?"

"What do you think?"

"You mean every time I got sick, I wanted to be sick?"

"Do you think so? I can't answer that for you," I said, "only you can."

Smiling, she said, "Yes, I guess it's possible, maybe not all the time, but some of the time. Then that means maybe I could stop it. Right? Well, I don't know how."

"Maybe, as you described, it's no different than deciding to become sick. Perhaps, you could as easily decide, or just remember, to stay healthy even if you don't want to go to school or talk to someone. What do you think?"

"I can do it," she said. "Just like before, when you asked me that question—I didn't want to be sick any more and the stomachache went away before I knew it. I can't believe it—I don't have to get sick all the time. It's really no fun getting out of school that way." She squinted her eyes, then touched her nose to the table. "But suppose I think about the next test and get scared again?"

"Let's suppose that—what would you get scared about?"

"I'll think about not knowing the answers to the test," she said.

"And why would that make you unhappy?"

"I don't like making all those mistakes. I really don't want to."

"Sure, I understand," I affirmed. "You don't want to make mistakes on a test. But why are you unhappy when you do?"

"Because I know it'll just keep happening again and again."

"Why do you believe that?"

"Because it happened so many times already."

"What happened?"

"I get so upset, I can't even see the pages any more."

"Why, if it happened many times in the past, do you believe it will happen again on the next test?"

"I don't know, I mean maybe it won't, I guess—but suppose it does?"

"What are you afraid would happen if you weren't worried and upset it'll happen again?"

"Well, if I didn't worry about it, then I might not study and then I won't do well."

"Ah, are you saying by worrying you'll study and do well?"

"Yes, but that's kinda dumb because I study sometimes, but I never do well when I'm scared."

"Do you think you could not worry and still want to do well?"

"Uh-huh," she said, doubtfully.

"Do I detect a question in your voice like you don't quite believe your own answer?"

She smirked.

"Okay, what's the doubt?" I asked.

"What if my work doesn't get any better?"

"Let's talk about that. How would you feel if it didn't?"

"I guess if I tried, at least I could feel okay about it. Before, I've always been too scared to try. You know, when I'm not afraid, like when I write on the bottom of my drawings, I can spell pretty okay—not great, but okay." Jeanette smiled broadly. "I guess not being scared makes a difference. Our talk is easy, Bears."

"Uh-huh—like eating with chopsticks. How do you feel?"

"Better. Much better. I'm glad I didn't get sick," she giggled. "Wait, I'll be back in a second." She slipped off the chair and disappeared into the kitchen. I heard her little voice speaking Chinese to someone. Moments later, she arrived with the waiter, who delivered two dishes, a fish concoction sautéed in mushrooms and broccoli and a tofu platter bathed in black bean sauce, scallions and garlic. After depositing an ample portion in each of our dishes, the waiter withdrew.

"Ready?" I held my wooden utensils in the air.

"Ready," she said, expertly pinching a cube of bean curd with her chopsticks. Though evidently more relaxed, she still seemed to avoid looking at me for any length of time.

Mr. Ling served the dessert: fruits and ices designed like a bouquet of flowers.

"The dinner was just sensational, Daniel Ling. You and your wife are to be complimented. But the special gift was to be honored by dining with your daughter." Jeanette peeked at her father from the corner of her eyes. "Would you mind," I continued, "if Jeanette and I went down the street to Mai Teh Bakery for a favorite of mine . . . a don-tat?" My fetish for these little hand-sized egg custards, wrapped in the delicate crusts, filled my voice with obvious enthusiasm. Mr. Ling approved, even requested that we bring two back, one for him and one for his wife.

Jeanette and I walked hand-in-hand, glancing at each other casually, our attention drawn by the bustling activity in the street. Pausing at one of the open vegetable stands, I bought some bok choy and an assortment of bananas, yellow and green.

"You like bananas?" I asked.

"Yes."

"Well, then, let me see," I said, searching through my package for a ripe one. "Ah, here it is—this one has your name on it, invisible, of course." I slipped the banana into the pocket of her sweater. Jeanette giggled, now a touch more willing to display her feelings.

We continued our journey, weaving through clusters of people talking, laughing, window-shopping as they moved leisurely along in the after-work "I'm-on-my-own-time" cadence.

Interlocking her narrow fingers with mine, Jeanette squeezed my hand as she walked stoically, her shoulders slightly rounded, her glance fixed on the ground. Two children skipped past us. They waved to my little friend, who barely responded. An old man, balancing on a cane behind the counter of a corner newspaper stand, called to Jeanette in Chinese. She answered immediately, her manner polite and reserved.

Mai Teh Bakery and Tea House has a series of tables along one wall, extending from the front door to the back of the shop. A Formica counter and stools occupied the other section of the store. By early evening, it's wall-to-wall people.

"Pick a table, any one you want," I said with a sweeping hand motion.

Without hesitating, she claimed the only one available. Her sweater and my jacket gave us formal possession of the chairs, enabling us to move slowly along the glass showcase, knowing, inevitably, even after teasing ourselves with an endless array of items, we would select the one-and-only don-tat for our consumption.

A bearded, middle-aged man apparently recognized Jeanette. He greeted her openly, warmly, smiling and nodding as he talked to her. She seemed to like him, yet, at the same time, she shied away. As their conversation ebbed, a young boy, wearing a white apron which dragged on the floor, delivered our order to the table.

Jeanette limited her intake to only one don-tat. She sipped her tea with a certain flair, suspending the cup between her small, tapered hands. As I downed my third don-tat, she excused herself and walked over to a poster loosely taped on the wall. Colored drawings of dancers dressed in elaborate costumes drew my attention. The bottom of the announcement contained columns of Chinese symbols.

Cocking her head in the same shy manner she did when first meeting me, Jeanette angled herself peculiarly in front of the advertisement. She adjusted her position in order to view the poster out of the corner of her eyes, rather than meeting it head on. Something in her pose seemed timid and evasive.

She raised her finger, first directing it toward the right side of the poster, then, in mid-stream, changing direction and bringing it to the first column on the left. If my memory served me, Chinese is read by beginning first on the left-hand side of the page, reading down, then proceeding toward the right—an exercise certainly compatible to English, which also dictates a left-to-right movement. Then why the hesitation?

"Hi," she said, returning to the table.

"I'll be back in a second," I said. At the front of the bakery, I asked the cashier for a large piece of paper and a pencil. He donated a pen and several small sheets from a waiter's pad. Returning to the table, I tapped

Jeanette's hand and said: "We're going to do an experiment. Here, take the pencil and write the following letters. Okay?"

She adjusted her position, setting herself at the edge of the chair.

"Ready? Fine. Here we go. Write the letter A, now M, L, T, C, now the letters R, D, Y, S, B." And so I went on. The more proficient she became in responding, the faster I recited the letters. Her reactions were almost instantaneous, but with some notable exceptions. Every time I called out the letters B, P, D, and S, she hesitated. On several occasions, she reversed the "b" and the "d", writing them backwards, but, realizing her error, quickly corrected them.

"Now we'll change the game slightly. I'll write the letters this time and you call out their names."

Though flattered with my continued attention, she, nevertheless, remarked: "Isn't this kind of silly? I'm in the third grade, not the first."

"Do you think I would forget a fact as important as that? This is an experiment, remember, not a reading lesson."

Each time I wrote a letter, she named it. Again, the smooth flow of her immediate responses had definite exceptions. Verbally, she mixed up labeling the "b" and the "d", also confused the "d" and the "p." The "z" and the "s" also presented some difficulties. For a child learning how to read, these were common errors, but for a little girl with three years experience in written language, such mix-ups raised a whole series of questions as yet unexplored.

We continued for several minutes; each time Jeanette tripped over the same letters. And the pattern of her eye contact duplicated the manner in which she approached the poster on the wall, which, in turn, was not unlike the way she looked at people. She cocked her head just slightly to the side, watching me write out of the side of her eye. Suddenly, she turned away, decisively ending our little game.

"What are you feeling?" I asked.

"See. I tried to tell you schoolwork is not easy for me."

"We weren't doing schoolwork, at least not exactly. Oh Jeanette, I think we've come upon something sensational." Her face lit up, responding immediately to my excitement. "Sometimes, people are so busy judging others, so busy saying what it means when someone does something, they don't allow themselves to really look and see. When you went to read the poster, you almost started on the wrong side. But since both Chinese and English start on the left, you wouldn't be confused ... unless, unless you had a problem in the way you saw the world. I'll try to explain. When we're very little, we start to develop preferences ... favorites— like using our left hand or our right hand. Which hand do you use?"

"Both."

"Do you write with both hands?"

"I used to. Now I write mostly with this hand ... my right, and I draw with this one, my left."

"That could be part of what I'm talking about. Back to those favorites. When we develop favorites, how we do things becomes more and more regular, almost automatic. Most people don't think about which hand to write with; they use their favorite without thinking about it. The same goes for how we use our eyes. We begin very early in life to favor patterns of looking at things—for example, we can examine things from left to right or the reverse or start from the top and move downward. Is this making sense?"

"Uh-huh," she said, "but could you go a little slower?"

"Sure," I smiled. "These favorites help us make sense

out of what we see and do. Now, sometimes, we don't decide on favorites."

"Is that like me?" Jeanette asked.

"It certainly looks like a real possibility. Now without a favorite, each time we look at something, we have to kind of decide which way to go, from the left to right or right to left. That all takes time and with certain things, like the letters 'd' and 'b,' it can become very, very confusing. That could affect reading and writing, making what's easy for someone else difficult for you. And it has nothing to do with a person's intelligence. Some people call it an 'LD' problem or learning disability because it makes learning harder." I tapped her nose. "But, Jeanette, it won't get you sick or make you believe you're stupid... like we talked about before, we do that to ourselves for very specific reasons."

"I know that now," she replied.

"It's just wonderful," I said.

"Why?"

"Because, today, we've learned many things. Even, perhaps, spotted an 'LD' problem."

"But why is that wonderful?" she asked.

"Because with simple exercises, you can change it; then you won't have a problem knowing from which side of the page to begin or which letter is which and maybe other things we haven't discussed will also become much easier. Will you do another experiment with me?"

"Yes—yes—please," she said.

"First face me. No, not like that—straighten your head." I positioned her head frontal with my hands. 'That's better. Close your eyes. Good. Now relax. I don't want you to open them until I finish eating this dontat." We both laughed. "You're cheating." She let her lids close again and waited. I washed the last piece of crust down with some tea, which had grown cold.

"Good," I continued. "When I say open your eyes, let them open slowly and tell me how many thumbs you see." I raised my right hand and extended my thumb into the air. "Now. Open your eyes and tell me how many thumbs you see."

"Two."

"Are you sure?"

"Yes, two thumbs."

"Okay, as I move my hand toward you, tell me if the two thumbs ever become one."

As my finger came closer to her face, she shouted: "Stop. Now they're one."

I put my thumb about three feet away and asked her to tell me what she saw.

"Two thumbs again."

"Okay. Listen carefully, I want you to try to make them into one thumb."

She laughed. "How can I do that?"

"Just concentrate, try to do it if you can."

A huge grin dawned on her face. "Yes, yes. I've done it, it's one thumb."

"Fantastic, just wonderful . . . you can do it," I said, reaching across the table and squeezing her face in my hands. "It's not all the answers, but it sure explains so much."

I discussed how I observed her second perceptual dysfunction and how the double images, like the lack of a left-right preference, would make reading and studying difficult. With simple exercises, and maybe eye glasses, the problem could be completely eradicated. Her schoolwork would become much, much easier. But her becoming sick, not talking to people or seeing herself as dumb—those questions of unhappiness had to do with her thoughts and beliefs about herself, which, like the eye difficulties, she could change if she wanted.

"I already know I've decided not to get sick any more,

at least not to get out of school. Could you teach me those exercises?"

"Probably, but there are people I know who are really terrific in this area. They can also check to see if there are any other seeing problems. I want to talk to your parents about it, okay?"

She nodded her head. "Do I have to tell them I used to make believe I was sick to get out of school?"

"There's nothing you 'have to' do, at least not for me. Like I mentioned at the beginning of our talk, it's your thoughts, your feelings ... you decide."

"Then I'll tell them," she said forcefully, "'cause I want them to know I'm going to get better and better."

After we returned to her family's restaurant, I waited outside the kitchen while Jeanette disappeared through the swinging doors in search of her parents. The alcove behind the cashier had filled with people waiting for tables. Silverware and "wood" danced on tables throughout the room. Individual voices and words merged into an irregular chant. The muted sound of a toilet flushing provided an ironic harmony. Frowns, dark eyes, smiles, wet lips formed a single, living tapestry.

Sue Ling touched my arm lightly. She bowed slightly and said: "Please forgive us, but this is our most busy hour. Jeanette says you would like to speak to us. My husband asks, if you would not be offended, to talk with him in the kitchen or, if you have time, we will talk later."

"We can chat in the kitchen. If you don't mind, I don't either."

I followed her through the metal doors to a large chamber hissing with activity. A ten-foot wall contained nothing but gas burners. Three chefs juggled food in ten different woks simultaneously. Two other men sorted and prepared vegetables. A young woman sautéed pieces of meat while an elderly man supplied the cooks with sliced fish. Hands and legs moved rapidly, yet the energy seemed relaxed, almost mellow. They kept their talking to a minimum, apparently communicating only to help each other coordinate the food preparation.

The chef in the center turned around and nodded. It was Daniel Ling, dressed appropriately in white. We exchanged smiles as he instructed his two assistants to finish the dishes steaming in the woks he tended. Gathering his wife and child, he motioned for me to join them at a corner table, which doubled as a massive cutting board.

"Everyone works so easily together," I observed, admiring the unstated camaraderie.

"In my kitchen," Daniel said, "we do not work—we merely move together for the same purpose." For a moment, he looked like a priest; reverent, mellow, knowing. Then he fractured the mood, grinning slyly and saying: "A McDonald's stand we ain't." Suddenly, he glanced intently at his wife. Again, his mood changed. "I hope my comedy will not be seen as disrespect."

"It isn't. I know you care about Jeanette very much. Your humor helps us get to the next conversation. May I begin?"

Daniel talked to his staff in a soft voice, then said, "Please go ahead."

"Jeanette and I have discovered many beautiful things today. I know she wants to share them with you. But before I go, I'd also like to share something with you. In a strange way, what I'm going to say will probably be most unexpected. Yet, when we're loving and accepting of a child and willing to move with them, we give ourselves and them opportunities to see new things." I turned to Jeanette. "Face your father. Okay, now close your eyes. Fine. Mr. Ling, would you please put your thumb up into the air. Perfect. Okay, Jeanette, open your eyes and tell your father what you see."

Her eyelids slowly exposed black irises. "I see two thumbs."

Both her parents looked at her suspiciously. "I don't understand," her father said.

"Wait," I advised, "in a moment, I think you will. Jeanette, are you sure you see two thumbs?" She nodded her head, her expression turning very serious. "Can you make the two thumbs into one?"

Twenty seconds later, she shouted: "I did it. I did it again."

"Close your eyes again and relax. Now I'd like you to look at your father in any way that's comfortable to you." After opening her eyes, she cocked her head slightly, turned away and looked at him on an angle, out of the corner of her eye.

"Please, please explain," her mother urged.

"Right now, I can't be positive, but I think your daughter is looking at your husband using only one eye. She sees a double image, like the two thumbs, because her eyes do not work together most of the time—only when she concentrates and makes a special effort can she clear her vision. So everything she has to do in school with her eyes, like reading, studying, measuring—all of that is very difficult because of her perceptual problem or, perhaps, perceptual problems." I explained to them the dynamics of a left-right preference and how that might also be affecting their daughter.

Daniel Ling made a fist and banged it on the table. Everyone in the kitchen turned around. I put my hand over his trembling fist and said: "Why the anger?"

"They kept telling us at school that she does not try; they kept saying she is a poor student and all the time she had trouble seeing. And I, her father, punished her many times for getting poor marks, believing she didn't care." His eyes filled with tears.

"Dad, it's okay. I will do better now."

Sue Ling hugged her daughter tightly.

"What about that gets you so angry?" I asked Jeanette's father, watching the pained expression on his face. Daniel ignored my question. "Do you want to talk?"

"What is there to talk about?"

"We can only know that once we talk," I said. "There's a beautiful Chinese saying which goes like this: 'He who knows, speaks in order to know better.'"

Daniel Ling smiled self-consciously. He peered down at his fist, then slowly opened his hand. "See, I let go of my anger. What is done, is done." His breath whistled out from between closed teeth.

"Attitude plays a crucial role in all this," I added. "Jeanette's attitude and beliefs about herself. Yours. Her teachers. We have an expression we use often: 'To love is to be happy with.' In regard to those little people who come into our lives, it means, to love our children is to be happy with them as they are. It's like giving what you want, doing what you can, the best you can, but, at the same time, accepting that they too are doing the best they can. So often, children slightly different from the norm are quickly labeled and judged. People, their own teachers, are so busy trying to change them, they never really look, observe or trust themselves to go with the child instead of against him. And when that happens, these kinds of problems can be easily overlooked, never even noticed."

"But she has had eye tests in school," her mother insisted. "They said she had excellent vision."

"Sure. That's why I asked her to relax and close her eyes. I didn't want her to strain and concentrate to see correctly. When she had her eyes checked, probably first they did each eye separately which presents no problems for her. Then, when they did them together, she must've worked very hard, pushing herself to focus on the letters printed on the chart. When she makes both eyes work together, her vision is probably excellent. But, you see, that's not the question. On an everyday basis, it's difficult for her to do that. Even Jeanette didn't realize it. She never thought about it, she said, thinking that's the way people see. Chiang called her shy because of the way she looked at him. Well maybe," I said, putting my hand on Jeanette's shoulder, "maybe you're shy sometimes, but the way you keep your head is to help yourself see better."

"Is there anything that can be done?" her father asked.

"Yes, everything. I will give you the names of two people who work specifically in this area with children. They will check for any other perceptual difficulties, then start her on an exercise program. Within weeks, you might see a difference. If she keeps at it, with your help, the problem will most likely disappear."

Both Daniel and Sue Ling seemed relieved. The trio exchanged smiles.

"Ah, I almost forgot," I said, lifting a small box onto the table. "This very ordinary grey paper box contains two absolutely delicious don-tats."

*   *   *

Three weeks later, Jeanette and I had a second session seated around our reserved table at the Joy Ling Tea Garden. She wore tiny wire-rimmed glasses and looked at me directly, though she shifted her eyes away quite often. Once the physiological reasons for indirect eye contact had been eased, she discovered she had other kinds of discomforts about facing people. What about it was uncomfortable? She saw herself being exposed. What did she mean? "Eyes tell other people about who you are inside." And why would that make

227

her uncomfortable? Somehow, if they knew her, they wouldn't like her. Why did she believe that? At that point, she presented a succession of beliefs: "I'm not smart, not really," "I'm the kind of person who makes people, especially my parents, unhappy," and "There must be something wrong with me." One by one, during the next four sessions, we explored each belief, most of which originated from judgments and self-recriminations in response to her early difficulties at school.

Since I didn't see her every week, our involvement spanned a period of three months. We made our fifth session our last. Jeanette's eyes had strengthened to such a degree that glasses were no longer required, though her exercises still had to be performed thirty minutes each day.

Having concluded during our previous meeting that there was, indeed, nothing wrong with her, she began this encounter offensively. "Today, Bears, I'd like to have a staring contest. Let's look into each other's eyes and see who can do it the longest."

"I warn you, I will not just let you win."

She nodded. Leaning forward on the table, we peered into each other's eyes.

"Not again," Daniel said happily, observing us at the table. Jeanette giggled. "I will hold up the food. I can see this might take a long time." With that statement, he disappeared.

"Do you want to talk about anything while we're doing this?" I asked.

"No," she replied succinctly. "Let's not talk."

For the next five minutes, I felt myself absorbed, consumed by her penetrating scrutiny. Each time my eyes went out of focus, I concentrated on sharpening the edges. Sometimes, we were very serious. Sometimes, we smiled. On at least two occasions, we laughed, enjoying this very special way of being with each other.

Breaking her edict, she said: "I learn about being happy this way too."

My turn to nod my agreement. "You're a student and a teacher at the very same time," I said.

We continued in silence. Finally, she suggested: "I can go on and on. If we stop together, then nobody wins."

"Fair deal."

She counted one, two, three and then we both looked away.

"You're doing fantastic."

"I'm not afraid any more," she noted. "And I haven't been sick in three whole months." Her confidence, combined with an evident weight gain, added strength to her delicate features.

Our session ended quietly in a rich wordless exchange. I embraced the little girl who no longer seemed so fragile.

Daniel Ling accompanied me through the restaurant. At the door, I turned to say goodbye. "Ah," he said, "before you go, I want you to see something." He pointed to the wall where his rewritten Buddhist saying hung. Now another piece, also written in beautifully stylized Chinese letters, had been framed and placed beside it.

"I call it my new addition," he boasted. "It is, unfortunately, not an old Chinese saying, although it is probable some wise Chinese philosopher might have said something similar thousands of years ago." He laughed, thoroughly enjoying his own humor. "No matter, it is still very special, although my grandfather might not agree. I will translate it. All those fancy symbols say, quite simply: 'To Love Is To Be Happy With.'"

THE BOOK OF ANGIE

Three people, silhouetted in the opened arch of the front door, touched glasses, toasting each other as part of a traditional celebration. The muffled music of a graduation party drifted lazily across the lawns, creating an immense umbrella of festivity around the entire house. Bursts of laughter cut through the soft rumble of voices coming from the stately stone building.

A young girl, thin, delicate and childlike, leaned on the arm of a rather husky, athletic young man. They giggled and kissed between sips of champagne as their third companion busily consumed a tumbler filled with scotch. The couple separated from the other boy as they skipped down the slate walk toward the parking lot. They mouthed an old Beatle tune, oblivious to their inability to reach any of the correct notes. Their friend followed them; his huge, lumbering hulk stumbled along the path, aptly reflecting the enormous quantity of liquor he had consumed.

A glass dropped to the pavement, splintering into hundreds of tiny pieces. The young girl placed her hands on her hips in an exaggerated gesture. She assumed a rather indignant pose, then giggled again. Her boyfriend offered his drink to replace the one lost to the ground. Laughing and singing, she slugged down the remaining pink liquid. After she tossed the glass high into the air, she held her ears, waiting for it to hit the macadam. Several seconds passed. No noise. No broken glass. She bowed theatrically. Both boys applauded wildly, their enthusiasm forced and transparent. But their female companion, too busy with her own antics, didn't notice. Throwing her arms around her date, she planted a wet, lingering kiss squarely on his lips. He responded in kind.

"C'mon, I want to be close to you, Angie," he said.

"But Ken, the party."

"Fuck the party," he said, feigning embarrassment over his words. "You're my girl, aren't you?"

She nodded her head shyly in support of his comment, protective of their three-month relationship.

They weaved through the crowd of parked cars. The moist evening air coated the lifeless metal with a wet blanket. The drone of distant music still enveloped them. No one spoke or even looked at each other. The couple slid into the back seat of a large, blue sedan. Their companion settled into the front, alone. Flipping on the radio, he stared out the windshield, rocking his head back and forth to a loud, frenzied rock tune.

The young man in the back seat began kissing his girl, his hands moving nervously across her clothed form. When she felt him pull on one of the buttons on her blouse, she pushed away and whispered: "Don't. I don't want to do this. Allen's right there in the front seat."

"Angie, he's just going to be our look-out," Ken assured her.

As if on cue, Allen turned around and tipped his head. He smiled peculiarly; his attention riveted on the activity in the back seat even after he resumed his original position.

Though more secure with the back of his head, she still hesitated. "Don't get uptight," Ken said, "I wouldn't want your reputation questioned any more than you do. Hey, you're my girl. You know I love you too much for that."

He slowly unbuttoned her blouse, slipping his hands underneath the silky garment and finding the warm flesh. She kept kissing him and pushing away at the same time.

"Ken, no more."

"Please. C'mon. Just a little more."

Her eyes scanned the interior of the car. The back of Allen's head reassured her. She relaxed her body and gave in to Ken's roving hands. He slid her down on her back, then pressed himself on top of her. His hands rubbed against her skin roughly. The harshness distracted her. Dizzy and slightly nauseous from the alcohol, she recoiled spastically when his teeth squeezed her lips to the point of pain.

"Please. No more. You're hurting me." Angie pushed against him to no avail. "Enough, Ken," she said, angered by his aggressiveness. Her vision blurred as she tried to clear the fog from her thoughts. She knew their drinking had been excessive. Closed in by the seats on either side of her, she became frightened.

Ken pulled her skirt up above her waist. She struggled to push it back down, but he overpowered her, locking her arms beneath the weight of his body. When she felt him remove her underpants, she began to kick her feet. Ripping her hands loose, she punched his face and chest. Everything became even more blurred. She opened her mouth to scream, then stopped, afraid to be caught in the car.

He pawed her exposed body with relentless hands. She grinded her teeth, still punching at him. Trying to avoid the blows, he pushed the skirt over her face, entangling her arms at the same time.

In disbelief, she pleaded with him: "Ken. Please don't do this. Are you crazy? Please don't!" Sensing a pause, she sighed, momentarily relieved. Then the familiar sound of a zipper being slid open filled her ears. She lifted her head to see him begin to remove his pants.

When she tried to gouge his face with her nails, Ken yelled to his friend. "Allen, get back here. Help me."

The door behind her opened. Two large hands grabbed her wrists and pulled them over her head. Screaming, she flapped her thighs back and forth, hoping to avoid what she knew would happen. Ken locked his knees against her legs and slammed into her. A sharp pain in her groin ended her virginity.

He kept moving up and down, hurting her with each thrust. She lost consciousness. Seconds later, she awoke wide-eyed, staring at the large, dark form jerking rhythmically on top of her. The inside of her body burned. Her limp legs ached from the assault.

A loud groan filled the car. Ken's body became stiff against her. She prayed that he was dying. Within seconds, he withdrew. Through the fog of her vision, she watched him pull up his pants quickly, close his zipper and buckle his belt. She wanted to jump at him, to hurt him in some unspeakable manner. But when she tried to move, her body did not respond. Disconnected. Numb. She tried desperately to convince herself that she would wake up from this watery dream, that it never happened. The sudden appearance of Allen looming over her immediately wiped away her momentary fantasy. He began to unbuckle his belt. A hand reached in around his throat and dragged his body outside of the car. Fists slapped against flesh. The door slammed abruptly closed.

Alone, she listened to the faint music and laughter. As she dragged herself from the floor, her right hand landed on her underpants. A hazy light filtered through the fogged windows of the car. Frosted images danced in the background. She struggled with the door handle, finally releasing the catch. The night air slapped her face. Sobered even more, she eased herself out of the car. Nervous fingers straightened her skirt and adjusted her blouse. She started to cry as she hobbled across the parking lot. Leaning against the fence, Angie tried desperately to control herself, afraid someone might hear her or see her. Covering her eyes with her hands, she managed to regain her composure slowly.

Heavy panting seeped through her private mourning. Her body braced as she whipped her head around; her eyes gaped at the dark form standing in front of her. It was Ken. She bolted from the fence and ran across the lawn. At first, he didn't pursue her; then, he darted after her receding figure. Halfway to the house, he caught her. Too scared to scream, Angie held her breath. His hands seemed gentle on her shoulders. She felt them trembling as she heard strange murmurs. When she looked up at him, she realized he was crying.

"God. Oh God, I'm sorry. I don't know what got into me. Can you ever..." His heavy, tight-fisted sobbing interrupted his words. "Can you ever forgive me. I...I didn't let Allen get near you. Please, please say something." He dropped to his knees and hugged her around the waist.

She pulled away slowly, dizzy from the pain inside her. She felt a strange liquid oozing down her leg. Her hand searched beneath her skirt. When she withdrew it, her fingers were covered with blood. The tears flowed down her face as she extended her arm, holding her hand in front of his face. When Ken looked up, his eyes bulged. He began to cough and choke on a dry vomit.

Rising to his feet, he turned and ran.

Angie just stood there, alone, her arm still extended as the stereo in the house blared across the lawn.

* * *

"Angie's a god damn stubborn idiot," her father snapped, "that's exactly what she is. Suddenly, the roles are reversed. I feel like I'm the progressive, the liberal, after the last couple of years listening to her bitch about how old fashioned and short-sighted her parents were. Not that we all don't love each other. Hey, no way, I don't want you to get me wrong. We've got a beautiful thing going, our family. And Angie is more important to me than anything else in the world."

Carl Striker turned away, his eyes drifting blankly across the terraced landscape which surrounded the plaza. Little children ran across the cobblestones, their hushed musical voices resounding through the narrow streets. Every Thursday, in this small, medieval mountain village in southern France, the baker's truck parked beside the fisherman's wagon. Women, dressed plainly, the tops of their blouses buttoned discreetly to their necks, bargained with the vendors in the late morning sunlight. A young boy bicycled past our table, a narrow three-foot loaf of bread strapped to his handlebars. Water dripped limply from a fountain in front of the old church. The facades of ancient shops, chipped and weathered by passing centuries, fractured the monotony of the interconnecting brown mortar walls. Our waiter delivered two more glasses of iced tea.

"Angie is . . . she's very dear to me," Carl continued. "I can't describe how much I adore that kid. Sometimes, I think maybe even too much. I guess that's what happens when you have only one kid. Fran and I used to talk about having more children. I don't know what happened. Too busy, too wrapped up. Shit, I didn't come here to bend your ear."

He put his hands over his head in a mock surrender gesture. "Yes, I did. I came to bend your ear and ask a favor. Wait! Wait! Don't open your mouth. I don't want to be confused by one of your questions. I know, don't say it . . . your questions can't confuse me, only I can do that to myself. Got it down pretty good. I can almost recite the whole scenario. I find it easy with you. I even find myself saying some of the things you say. Maybe it's contagious?" Carl laughed self-consciously. "Just remember I knew you when, Bears. You were just as crazy as me . . . no, much, much crazier. The Mad Hatter destined to burn out by thirty. Only you didn't. I've got to hand it to you; you really changed everything for yourself. I envy that." He stopped himself short, plastering his face with a Hollywood grin. "Good thing I see you from time to time; otherwise I'd be willing to swear someone else is inhabiting your body."

He rose from the table and leaned against the stone ledge behind his chair. The sun baked his balding crown. Fitted with flared pants, perfectly pressed, and matching double-breasted jacket, he modeled his clothes more than he wore them. His business trip to Nice and Cannes had been complicated by the recent arrival of his wife and daughter. He took a cigarette from a metal case, ignited the tip, then sucked the smoke in so heavily he seemed to gasp.

"Let me tell you about Angie," Carl continued. "She's become a very special young lady. A beautiful girl, a real head-turner. Impeccable dresser. Great student; straight A's until she joined that free school garbage . . . now who knows! That fancy-ass program doesn't have grades. Just pass and fail. How do you like that? Bright, articulate, special . . . now she's anonymous. Or maybe 'was' anonymous more aptly describes it. Oh, shit, let me just say it. She's pregnant. Angie's pregnant. Now that's no great catastrophe, no big deal. A shock, yes. An unpleasant surprise, yes. It's a little like someone sending you a box filled with shit for Christmas. But you deal with it. Okay, I'm ready to deal with it. Openly. Well, maybe, at first, not so openly. You know how it is; Christ, she's only fifteen. Sleeping around at that age. Sometimes I think the world's going too fast for me." Carl shook his head back and forth, then groaned. "But we lived through it. We always do. Anyway, that's not the problem. Would you believe Angie won't agree to have an abortion. Fran took it reasonably well. Here we are, ready to help, do what's necessary and she wants to think about it.

"Well, that was four weeks ago and still no decision," Carl declared. "Wow, you know what she had the nerve to say; it's her body and she'll decide. Well, if she had taken care of 'her' body, she wouldn't be in this mess...just offering herself to any young twerp who comes along. She wants to think it over. The little Queen of Sheba wants to think it over. I knew she always had this special thing about having a baby. You'd have to see her with kids to see what I mean. But, for God's sake, not this way! Talk, talk, talk! In the meantime, we're losing precious weeks. If she waits much longer, she won't be able to have an abortion safely. Me and my shotgun mouth. I had to be the one to suggest an abortion. Naturally, Angie would jump the opposite way. If I'd just let her suggest it, it would be done by now and there'd be no more problem."

"Is it your problem or her problem?"

"Listen, Bears. I know my Angie. She looks wrecked. The dark circles around her eyes tells me she isn't having much fun. If she wants to sleep with someone, I can't stop her; I can't put her in chains. Jesus, she's so young. She'll just have to learn. I think she's learned already. But if she doesn't quit this bullshit...," Carl interrupted himself. "I can't go over it any more."

"You mentioned a favor?" I said.

"Yep. You've always been one of her favorites. She'll talk to you. Maybe you can do your stuff with her?"

"What 'stuff' would you like me to do, Carl?"

"You know. The dialogues. Option. I know if she wasn't so busy defying us, she'd come to her senses."

"And do you define coming to her senses to mean her doing what you want her to do?"

"Oh, don't make it sound so provincial."

"That's only a question. What do you really want? Would you like me to help her clarify her own wants and thoughts for herself . . . or do you want me to lobby for your cause—in this case, an abortion?"

A smile creased his tan face. "Well, I can't complain that you're not direct. Sure, I'd like you to lobby for our side, but I knew you wouldn't even before I decided to talk to you. I know what my baby would do if she wasn't so busy fighting us. Help her unwind it. I know what she'll decide."

* * *

Small villages melted into the landscape dotted with vineyards and tiny farms. The road meandered lazily through the countryside as it descended from the mountains toward the coast. A beautiful, mellow journey. Suzi and I stared at the crystal-blue surface of Lake St. Cassien as the roadway curved down a steep slope toward the water. Bryn hung over the back of my seat, consuming the landscape with her alert eyes. Thea and Raun played with miniature cars in the back of our little Renault station wagon. We had rearranged our schedule, shifting several commitments and delaying work on my book so I could spend time with Angie. After leaving my family with friends just south of Cannes, I continued driving down the coastline, awed by the burnt brown soil and stone houses which jutted out into the Mediterranean.

Past La Napoule, the sign pointed to Theoule, a tiny fishing village which hugged the interior of a small bay. Fran stood beside her daughter, who used the hood of their rented Citroën as her seat. Everything about Fran exuded style and taste, from her dress to the way she moved her head and gestured with her hands. Capable of doing a quick study like her husband, she managed to alter her character to fit defined situations. Just six years ago, before Carl had successfully launched his own company, she worked with him from morning until night without questions or complaints. At that time, people accused her of being a workaholic with a highly pragmatic, no-nonsense attitude. Dressed in dark, simple clothes, she used to define herself as a "tough cookie" and she meant it. Now adorned in an elegant white suit, she affected the pose of second-generation royalty. Only the intrusion of the letter "r" in inappropriate places, such as in the words saw "r" and idea "r," betrayed her very modest beginnings in an interracial ghetto in lower Manhattan.

Angie, in contrast, appeared subdued in her jeans and blue polo shirt. Though well formed and fully matured physically at fifteen, at first glance her small, delicate figure suggested the body of a much younger person, perhaps only ten or twelve years old. Her darting black eyes, hovering above chiseled cheekbones, riveted themselves on my approaching car. She jumped off the hood, rushing to greet me. We hugged playfully. Fran touched my shoulders and kissed me from cheek to cheek. Three days out of New York and she had already gone native.

After exchanging ritual pleasantries, Fran said, "Okay, I'm off to Nice. Angie will show you the house if you decide to escape the sun later in the day. Enjoy. Enjoy. Thanks, Bears." She kissed Angie affectionately on the forehead. With a very French flourish, she started her car and left. Angie looked at me curiously.

"How about you and I taking a short sprint up the beach?" I suggested.

She nodded. We jogged together along the surf, our feet sinking below the surface of small, rounded stones. After wincing for more than five hundred yards, we stopped.

"I'm glad you're here." Angie spoke in a muffled voice.

"I am, too, Angie."

"Are you here for me or for Daddy?"

"What do you think?" I asked.

Angie turned her penetrating eyes on me. Cocking her head to the side, she shrugged her shoulders and said, "Probably for both of us."

"Do you mind?"

She shook her head.

"Although your father asked me to talk with you, while I'm here . . . I'm here for you. I want you to know that."

"I've never had a date with a married man before." Angie smiled awkwardly. "Do I start or do you?"

"What do you want to do?" I asked.

"I don't know what I want to do . . . about anything."

"How do you feel?"

Her face tensed, her voice strained. "Oh, on a good day, miserable. On a bad day, indescribable."

"Why?"

"I feel so alone. I guess it's been coming a long time. with my 'problem,' as Daddy calls it, all I get is one lecture after another. No one—" Her breathing became labored. Several minutes passed. Angie squatted on the sand, then extended her legs and proceeded to bury her feet. I sat beside her, helping her with the project. She giggled at the sight of my participation. Within seconds, her legs disappeared beneath mounds of sand and tiny polished stones.

"Do you want to talk?" I asked.

She nodded her head affirmatively, carefully smoothing an area directly in front of her. With her index finger, she wrote the word "yes" in the sand Slowly, like the gentle backwash of a receding wave, she erased the letters.

"What are you feeling?"

"Unhappy."

"What are you unhappy about?"

"Everything!" she said.

"For example?"

"For example, this trip to join Daddy. My mom called it our little mini-vacation. Meanwhile, Daddy's in Nice all day and she's on a shopping spree."

"And what about that upsets you?"

"They're pretending. They just wanted me here to try to make me have an . . ." Her voice trailed off. "Nobody asks me!"

"Asks you what?"

"What I want. What it means to me!"

"And what do you want?" I asked.

"Truly, I don't know. But I just can't stand being talked at."

"What upsets you about it?"

"They treat me like I'm an idiot."

"What do you mean?"

Angie's eyes glazed. "They never really ask, they just tell. They never wanted to understand, they just think of getting rid of the 'problem.' You know, I'm a person, too." Tears flooded her eyes, spilling down her cheeks.

"Why, if they deal with the situation in the way that they do . . . why does that make you unhappy?"

"Because . . . because they're so busy with so many things, they can't be bothered. It's just another problem to be solved. Efficiently . . . that's their style. But it's me . . . what about me?"

"What about you?"

"I have feelings, opinions. Sure, I know from the looks of what's going on, maybe I haven't been too smart. But if they really cared about me, they'd want to know more about how I feel and what it's like to be me."

"Do you believe that?"

"Believe what?" Angie questioned.

"Do you believe if they cared about you, then they would want to know how you feel?"

"Yes! Yes!"

"Okay. Why do you believe that?"

"Because when someone cares, when someone loves you, they want to know. If they don't really care, they don't ask."

"Are you saying that because they don't take your feelings and your thoughts into consideration, then they don't really care about you?"

Angie grinned. "When you say the question that way, I suddenly feel different about my answer. When I get angry, I'm not very considerate of them, yet I still love them; I still care."

"Then does someone not doing what you want them to do or believe they should do mean they don't care or want to care more?"

"No, it doesn't mean that at all. Maybe it means they're as miserable as me right now. Mom's been so weird, smiling twenty-four hours a day, trying to show it doesn't matter when it does. Daddy's so nervous. He can't believe his 'little girl' was . . ."

"Was what?"

She turned away. "That I slept with someone." Her eyes darted around, becoming fixed on my face. She searched my expression, then seemed to relax. Continuing, she said, "You should have heard him. 'Only fifteen!' he screamed at me. Then he shouted his favorite line—'What the hell's the world coming to?' His face got red. I thought he'd have a heart attack. Poor

Daddy." Angie sifted the sand through her fingers. "I guess they love me, in their way."

"And how do you feel about that?"

"Sometimes it's okay."

"And now?"

"It's almost okay."

"What part of it still upsets you?"

"I get scared."

"About what, Angie?"

"That I'm going to hate them."

"Why are you scared about hating them?"

"Because I don't want to."

"Angie, not wanting to hate them is very different from being scared you might hate them. Why does it scare you?"

"It's the same answer. Because I don't want to."

"What are you afraid would happen if you weren't scared about hating them?"

"Then I'd hate . . . them. I guess."

"Are you saying by being scared of hating them, you don't let yourself hate them?"

"Sounds kind of silly, doesn't it? But if I wasn't scared, maybe I might just hate them." She put her hand up to my face. "Wait. Let me say it again. If it's okay to hate them, then I would."

"Do you believe that?"

She shook her head emphatically, then wrote the word "no" in the sand. "I'm not scared right now and I don't hate them. Funny, but I feel better about them now than I have for the last three weeks . . . since all this began. You know, Bears, I don't even know what I mean when I say I'd hate them. I guess when I think they don't love me, I get scared I'll decide not to love them."

"Do you feel that way now?"

"No. Not any more. Even when I scream at them or curse them under my breath, I still love them. I guess it's the same for them. I never really thought about it this way before. But, Bears, it still doesn't change what they want me to do."

"What do they want you to do?"

"You know . . . to have an abortion."

"And how do you feel about that?"

"Can we walk?" she asked.

"Whatever you'd like," I replied. "That sounds fine to me."

Angie jumped to her feet and methodically brushed the sand off her pants. As we strolled on the beach, she began: "I didn't forget the question. At first, when I told them, I reacted just like they said. Daddy declared an abortion and I said no. I think at that time, if he had said to have a baby, I would have screamed for an abortion. Anyway, later when I told them it wasn't a 'no,' that I wanted time to think, they thought I was still being stubborn. But I wasn't."

She paused, her dark eyes flashed at mine, then she looked away. "Bears, can I hold your hand?" she asked, her voice barely above a whisper.

Smiling at her, I nodded. Her thin fingers trembled in my palm. We walked in silence for several minutes.

"You know what?" Angie asked.

"What?"

"I think I'm going to cry."

We continued walking along the beach for another ten minutes. Angie never let go. Finally, I said, "Why did you think you were going to cry?"

"Can I not answer that?"

"Sure. But why don't you want to answer it?"

"Let's go to the house," she suggested, ignoring the question.

The small two-bedroom villa rented by the Strikers hung over the sea. The arched entrance led to a ceramic tiled living room walled in glass. The front terrace beyond it, in square footage larger than the entire house, faced the beach. In the distance the city of Cannes loomed like a faded painting on the horizon.

"Would you like a drink?" Angie asked, quickly opening the liquor cabinet. Fran would have applauded her daughter's gesture, envisioning it to be a sign of quality breeding. Suddenly, the little-girl face seemed very mature and firm.

"No thanks. A little juice would be great," I said, deciding to wait for her on the terrace.

A cool breeze mixed with the heat of the sun, tempering its impact on our skin. I purposely moved my chair to face Angie's. We stared into each other's eyes for several seconds, then she turned away with obvious discomfort.

"What are you feeling?" I asked.

"Here we go again . . . huh?"

I smiled at her. "You decide, Angie. I ask questions, but you don't have to answer them. Not for me, not even for your parents."

"Then why answer at all?"

"For you. If you answer them, you answer them for yourself."

"That sounds so nice, Bears." Angie walked over to the other side of the terrace, squatted in the corner and started to cry. Her chest heaved spasmodically. Clenched fists rubbed along the top of her thighs. Her body shuddered, surrendering to the internal eruption. Finally, the crying subsided.

"What are you so unhappy about, Angie?"

"About a lot of things. About . . . about being pregnant."

"Why does that make you unhappy?"

"Because . . . oh, you know, I don't want to be pregnant."

"Sure. But that's different from being unhappy about being pregnant. . . . Why are you unhappy about it?"

Her face lost all its color. She squeezed her eyes shut

and said: "I don't want to be a murderer." Walking back across the terrace, she faced me directly and said, "That's what an abortion is ... isn't it?"

"What I think about abortions would come from my beliefs. My opinion might tell us a lot about me, but nothing about you or what you want to do. Angie, what do you mean when you say you don't want to be a murderer?"

"If I had an abortion, I'd be killing something alive in me. I know all the arguments. I once watched a debate about it on TV when it didn't matter. Before a certain period of time, the fetus is not considered alive. Well, that's easy to decide when it's not your body, your fetus. A priest who argued against abortion sounded crazier than those for it. It all didn't make much sense. Now, well, it's different."

"How is it different?"

"It's not a high school debate. It just seems like murder."

"Well, let's find out why you believe that. Why do you see abortion as murder?"

"You're stopping a life that could have been?"

"What do you mean 'could have been'?"

She inhaled deeply. "Well, if you didn't have the abortion, then, one day, a child would be born."

"Okay, that's what would happen, perhaps, if you didn't have the abortion," I said.

"And if I did ... ," Angie sighed. "What was the question again?"

"What do you think?"

"Why do I believe abortion is murdering?"

"Do you want to answer it?"

"Yes," she said. "I guess if you didn't want a child or couldn't handle children, it's better not to have one. I'm still not answering the question. Okay, if it's not alive, not thinking, not breathing, then it's no different than taking the pill like some of my friends do already.

I mean it's different, but it's still the same thing. I guess you could argue each egg could have also been a person. Oh, God, it all seems so complicated."

"Why is that?"

"Because I could just as easily argue that it could be murder, of sorts. It's like . . . pick a side and then justify it with reasons."

"Uh-huh," I said, awed by her ability to dissect the logic of her position. "That's quite an insight. Now, what does it mean to you?"

"Want more juice?" She asked. I nodded. She returned and sat opposite me. "It means anyone can argue either side and come out sounding right. I have as many reasons to see it as murder as not."

"What are you afraid would happen if you no longer believed it was murder?"

"Then I'd probably have it."

"Okay, are you saying by seeing it as murder, you insure that you won't do it?"

"Yes. I guess that's what I've been doing."

"Why?"

"Because I don't want to be pushed into it. I want to decide."

"If it were okay to have an abortion, does that mean you would have to decide to have one?"

"No. Not at all," Angie said.

"Do you believe abortion means murder?"

"No. It's funny, but I guess I never really believed it. I needed to weigh the scale on my side because my father and mother kept pushing and pushing. I never realized how much of the time I spent fighting them. I didn't want to be weak."

"What do you mean by 'weak'?"

"Giving in. Not doing what I wanted."

"And do you see yourself that way?"

"Then, yes. Not now. It's getting clearer for me, Bears. But I still don't know what I want to do."

"How do you feel about that?"

"Better about it than before. But I want to decide, because if I don't, I won't have a choice soon."

"What do you mean?"

"After three months, the doctors say it gets dangerous. Then I'll be forced to go through with having the baby."

"What do you mean by 'forced'?"

"If I wait too long, it'll be too late. I won't be able to have the abortion."

"And why do you call that being forced?"

"Oh...I see what you mean."

"I just asked you a question, Angie. What you see is what you mean."

She giggled her recognition. "If I wait and don't decide, then I actually decided to let it happen. So if I don't decide, it's still a decision."

"Doing 'nothing,' whatever that means, is a way of doing something. We're always choosing even when we think it's not apparent. What do you want, Angie?"

Her fingers tapped the handle of the chair. "It's not as easy as that. At least something beautiful could come from all this."

"What do you mean?"

"A baby, that's what I mean."

"Are you saying that's what you want?"

"I don't know. I want something good to come from..." Her hands trembled again.

"From what?" I asked.

Her face hardened. Her dark eyes glared as she plastered an artificial smile on her face. "Come, I want to show you the view from the point. C'mon, it's not too far from the house."

I followed her up a narrow path leading toward the sea. At the peak, Angie turned to me. "Bears, isn't it just magnificent? Just so beautiful."

"Kind of takes your breath away," I answered, dazzled by the birds-eye view of Theoule tucked into the hillside. To the left and the right, the jagged coastline spread out before us like an impressionistic painting on fire. Red and orange soil filled the angular forms facing the sea.

We sat down together in a small clearing just below the summit of the mountain. Angie fiddled with the brown soil. With her index finger, she wrote the following words on the ground: "Shall we continue?"

"Sounds very formal," I responded. "Okay, how 'shall' we continue?"

Suddenly her eyes became watery. A barely perceptible tremor rippled through her body. "Can I hold your hand again?"

I nodded, clasping her left hand gently in mine. Cupping her fingers together on the other hand, she clawed the letter "r" into the earth. Her breathing quickened. Then she scratched out the letter "a" beside it. She scrutinized my face for a reaction. When I smiled, tears flooded her eyes. Squeezing my hand with a surprising power, she wrote the letter "p" beside the others. I found myself trying to complete the word. An internal scrabble game. "Stop wandering," I counseled myself, wanting to be right there for her from moment to moment.

Pressing harder than before against the earth, her fingers carved out the letter "e," the last letter of the word "rape." A commentary chiseled in pain. She smeared the letters, then pounded them with her fist angrily. Rising to her feet, Angie stomped on the remaining indentations from the word she had written, completely obliterating any trace of her handiwork.

Her body stiffened. She let herself drop to the ground like a sack of old clothing. Her resistance was spent. Finally, Angie let go. A sharp, unearthly whine erupted from her throat. She shouted as loudly as she could before surrendering to the tears.

After several minutes, the intensity of her sobbing ebbed. Slowly, without lifting her bowed head, she extended her arm toward me. I gave her my hand, pressing softly on her fingers to communicate my presence.

We sat that way, together, the wind off the sea as the only sound between us.

"I'm ready," she said, breaking the silence with a raspy voice.

"What did you mean by the word 'rape'?" I asked.

"I know you know."

"Angie," I said, "it doesn't matter what I know or don't know. It's what you come to know that counts. What did you mean by the word 'rape'?"

"That's how I got pregnant. It was so horrible. And I can't remember it all. I keep trying to remember it... everything. I don't want to ever forget anything about that terrible night."

"Why was it terrible?"

Laughter mixed with sporadic crying. "Are you kidding? Try getting raped sometime."

"If, somehow, I was raped and I described the experience as terrible or horrible, that doesn't mean we'd both be talking about the same thing. We each have our own responses, our own impressions, our own memories. A word can mean one thing to me and something completely different to you."

"A stupid graduation party," she began. "Ken and I had too much to drink. God, he kept saying he just wanted to be closer to me... closer to me." Her voice broke. "We went outside to the parking lot. His friend Allen came along. I can't believe I let it happen."

"What do you mean?"

"I should have known. Every time I go over it, it's so damn obvious." The tone of her voice changed, becoming lower and slightly more muddled. Her eyes skipped back and forth in their sockets like the ball of an IBM electric typewriter. Her mouth dropped open, her face registering expressions momentarily as if she viewed a montage of images on some hidden movie screen. "When we were together in the back seat of his father's car. I was so uncomfortable. I couldn't stop thinking about Allen. He was right there in the car with us. Ken said Allen would watch out for us, making sure no one came. So I went along." She shouted her anger, pounding the ground with her fist as a punctuation for each word. "I went along! I went along!"

Inhaling deeply, she closed her eyes. "Even when he got on top of me on the seat, I thought we were just going to pet. When he pulled my skirt up, then I knew. I knew, but I couldn't get up. I kept praying it was a dream. It couldn't be happening. Not here. Not with Ken." Her hands trembled again.

"I don't remember exactly what I did, I . . . it's foggy. I kicked, pushed, scratched . . . anything. But nothing mattered. Oh, God, then Allen came and held my hands. I think I passed out. I wanted to die. Maybe I'll die, I kept thinking. The pain made it bearable. Gave me something to hold on to. The pain. It was my pain, mine." She held her hands together, exhaling a deep sigh. "Everything else was so out of control. He stopped Allen. At least the bastard stopped Allen from raping me too. At least? I should have called the police. I thought about it over and over again. Half drunk, Ken got down on his knees in front of me on the lawn and cried, cried like a baby. Big deal, he was sorry. He raped me like an animal, then he says he's sorry. I think I wanted to see him dead, more at that moment than when he raped me."

"Why?"

"He robbed me of my hate; being so pathetic. I wanted to hate him, but I couldn't any more."

"Why did you want to hate him?"

"So I wouldn't hate myself," she replied.

"Do you hate yourself?"

"Yes. More than anything else, I can't stand thinking how stupid, how dumb I was. It's like I asked for it."

"Do you believe you did?"

"I'm not sure," she moaned. "No, not really. God knows I didn't want to be raped. I didn't want it to happen that way, especially the first time." She started to cry.

"Angie, why are you crying?"

"To feel it again. To always remember."

"Why do you want to do that?"

"So it never happens again. Never. Never."

"Are you saying by feeling the pain, it wouldn't happen again?"

"Yes, then I'll make sure it doesn't ever happen again!"

"And what are you afraid would happen if you didn't remember the pain and feel the hurt?"

"Maybe I wouldn't be on guard. That's how it happened the first time."

"Are you believing that's how it could happen again?"

"I don't know," Angie proclaimed. "I don't know. Suppose I didn't feel the pain; then I might forget."

"Do you believe that?"

"No. I guess not. I'll never forget."

"So, do you have to be unhappy, in pain, whatever, in order to remember to take care of yourself?"

A half-smile creased the corner of her mouth. She bounced to her feet like a ballet dancer. Her eyes moved slowly along the distant horizon. "How come," she said, "it suddenly seems stupid to do that? I'm much smarter now; much, much smarter. It's a lousy way to learn, but I learned."

"How do you feel?"

"Okay about that, but still damn uncomfortable."

"What about?"

"For one thing, I'm uncomfortable I didn't do more."

"More about what?"

"About Ken and Allen," she said. "Oh, I don't care about Allen. But with Ken, I keep thinking I'm supposed to do more."

"What do you mean?"

"Report it. Have him locked in jail or something."

"And why do you believe you're supposed to do that?" I asked.

"Because he did something wrong, something awful, something crazy. Maybe, maybe he'll do it again. If I do something now, I could stop that."

"Then why don't you do it?"

"Because, I guess, oh, I guess I don't think he'll ever do it again. Before we left for France, I saw him. He looked like walking death; must've lost thirty pounds. He said he can't live with himself so he's seeing a shrink. He cried again, asking if I would forgive him." Tears flooded her eyes. "He offered to do anything. Pay for the abortion. Marry me. Even go to the police if I wanted him to." Angie paused, shaking her head. Her face became stern and unyielding. "If he really wants to do something, let him take it back. Let him start that day all over again and make it so it never happened. Then, then I'll tell him it was okay." Angie sighed, rubbing her face, relaxing the taut muscles in her jaw. "Funny, but I really think he might lose his mind over this. I'm in better shape than he is and I'm supposed to be the victim." She grinned weakly at the irony of her comment. "You know, when I just let my thoughts come, I see a lot better. There's nothing more for me to do about Ken. He's with a doctor, whatever good that'll do. Anyway, I think jail would really kill him. Oh, Bears, it's gone." She stretched her arms above her head. "I'm free of him. It doesn't matter to me, except—" she cut herself short.

"Except what?"

"Except I'm pregnant. Do you understand why I couldn't tell them? If my parents knew, they could force me to have an abortion. They could, couldn't they?"

"I don't know what their legal rights would be. You're a minor. Somehow, I don't think they can force you to have an operation if you don't want it. But Angie, I'm not sure of that."

"I'm still afraid to tell them."

"Why?"

"Before I had a chance to explain the pregnancy, Daddy bitched about me sleeping around. Somehow that seemed better than letting myself be raped by my own boyfriend in the back of his father's car."

"Why is that?"

"I'm embarrassed about being so stupid, so utterly stupid."

"What do you mean by stupid?"

"Not aware. Blind to what's obvious."

"What about being 'not aware' embarrasses you, Angie?"

"They'll say I can't take care of myself, that I'm a fool. And they'll never trust me." She put her head in her hands.

"What is it about that that disturbs you?"

"Everything would change."

"How?"

She talked through her tears. "You see, there's a funny thing about Mommy and Daddy. They're very efficient. If there's one thing they hate, it's stupidity. If I sleep around, we have a disagreement in morals. Somehow, as much as they'll argue and get crazy, they'll still see me as okay. But being stupid is not okay."

"If being stupid is not okay with them and they see you as stupid, why would you be unhappy?"

"Then I'd be not okay with them."

"And what about that disturbs you so much?"

"They wouldn't love me."

"Do you believe that?"

Angie hesitated. "Yes."

"Why do you believe that?"

"You have to hear the way they talk about my Uncle Charlie. He's not too bright, but he's such a wonderful man. We can't see him any more because Mommy and Daddy decided he's stupid."

"Do you believe the same thing would happen to you?"

"Not in the same way. They'd just ignore me, write me off as a lost cause."

"And if your worst fear came true, they wrote you off as you say, how would you feel about that?"

"Not good. Not good at all. I wouldn't want that. I know—you don't have to say it, Bears... not wanting something and feeling bad about it are two different things. I suddenly feel angry."

"What about?"

"It's like if I do what they think is good, then I'm alright with them; I meet with their approval. If not, I'm out."

"Why does that make you angry?"

"Why should they have that power? Who gives them the right? Just because they're my parents."

"Parents can judge their children if they want to. You can't stop that; you can't get inside their heads and pull the strings. Only they can do that for themselves. But what you can do is deal with your reactions, your responses, your beliefs about those judgments. If your parents saw you as stupid, wrote you off, why would you be angry?"

"Because I would believe them."

"Why would you believe them?"

"They're smarter than me," Angie said, ending her statement with an implicit question mark.

"Is that your answer or is that another question?"

"I think it's both," she said. "I've always thought of them as smarter than me. They came up with a hundred sensible reasons why I should have an abortion... my age, the unwed mother bit, school, the child's welfare, on and on. I don't think that fast."

"What do you believe that means?"

"I was going to say it's proof of their smartness. Now, I'm not sure. Ever since I was little, they always said they knew better, that I'm too young, I haven't lived enough. Silly, but I keep thinking about Grandpa."

"What about your grandpa?"

"He's twice as old as my mother and father, but he doesn't know half of what they know. It's a lousy argument."

"What argument?"

"That I can't know things because I haven't lived enough. So what? I can still know things." Angie suppressed a smile. "It's changing, Bears."

"What's changing?"

"I'm not afraid of them calling me stupid. That won't mean I am. And if they write me off... well, I'll be okay. I know that now. Somehow, right this minute, I don't really think they'd write me off. And if they did, maybe I could show them they're making a mistake."

"What do you want?"

"Back here again, huh?" she said, eyeing me like a mother who just caught her child in the cookie jar. "Would you think I'd be a jerk if I said I still want to go through with it?"

"Through with what, Angie?"

"Having a baby. Now that's it's okay to have an abortion, I'm clear on not wanting one. I know all the so-called problems. But I'm not fighting my parents any more... I know that! I'm not fighting myself." She touched her abdomen. "It's already growing in me; it's started. I want to let it happen. Having a baby is the most beautiful thing in the world. I know it's a great responsibility, but I'll make it work...I will! I've thought about it thousands of times even before all this. I can handle it."

"Are you sure?"

"Un-huh," she answered. "As long as I'm not crazy and angry like I was, I'll handle it."

"How do you feel now?"

"Like a new person. I felt so ugly, so mixed up before. I feel so beautiful now, so alive. Thanks, Bears."

Angie took my hand and led me back to the house. We stood together on the terrace, warmed by a waning sun. The clicking of the keys in the front door signaled Fran's return. Wisping into the room like an aging starlet, she touched my shoulder and did her cheek-to-cheek routine. Angie hugged her very tightly and said in a hushed voice, "I love you."

Visibly moved, Fran lifted her daughter's face. Her eyes watered as she kissed Angie on the forehead. Turning toward me, she said, "I don't know what you two did, but I feel like I got my old Angie back."

"Your new Angie, Mom," she said to her mother.

"Okay," Fran agreed, surprised by the sense of determination in her daughter's voice. Her child had suddenly grown up.

"Mommy, we have so much to talk about. We do."

"I have an idea," I suggested, consulting my watch. "I have about another hour until I have to pick up Suzi and my crew. I'll take a stroll on the beach and leave you two alone."

"No," Fran insisted. "We'll take a stroll on the beach and leave you with the comforts of home. Don't say anything. It's my house."

Angie ran into the kitchen and retrieved a tall glass of cold juice. Those huge black eyes reached out, showering me with their warmth. "Bears, do you want anything else?"

"I'm fine, really I am."

"We'll be back before you leave."

From the terrace, I watched them walk arm in arm along the beach. They shuffled their feet leisurely across the sand. Their slow cadence had an easy rhythm to it. Suddenly, Fran stopped dead in her tracks. I knew Angie had just said the word "rape." I would have liked to see the expression on her face, for somehow, despite her verbalizing such a dreaded word, I imagined she smiled after she said it.

The two figures lingered in the same spot for at least five minutes. They linked arms again and continued their promenade, moving more slowly; slightly more tentative in their steps.

The hour passed quickly. I heard laughter beneath the terrace as Angie and her mother rounded the side of the building and climbed the steps to the front door. When they entered, they both seemed aglow with similar energy. Fran caught a glimpse of her own face in the hall mirror. Grabbing a towel from the kitchen counter, she quickly wiped the mascara streaked down her cheeks.

"Now how do I tell this to Carl?" Fran said, smiling and shaking her head at the same time.

"You don't, Mom. I do."

"Okay, young lady, you do," she stated respectfully.

"You know how he is, Bears," Angie said. "Any ideas on how to begin with him?"

"Maybe this could be another nice opportunity to trust yourself again," I commented. "I don't know what you said to your mother, but, obviously, you found the words."

A little-girl giggle escaped through a big-girl smile. Her head rocked up and down. "It's really special to know that about yourself," Angie said.

"What have you too been eating?" Fran joked.

"As you say that, my stomach growls," I interjected. "We haven't had a thing all day, except some juice."

"Let me make you something."

"No, it's not necessary," I said. "I'm going to go now."

Angie took my hand and squeezed it tightly. We hugged.

"How about me? I'd like some of that," Fran said affectionately, her face registering a new openness. She threw her arms around me with her theatrical flair. Somehow, amid the sincerity, she still managed to retain an elegant, refined air . . . though a bit too studied to be natural.

As we walked to the car, Angie smiled and said, "I still feel beautiful. No one can take that away from me." Fran looked at her daughter in awe. We said our goodbyes once again and I left.

*　　*　　*

That evening, Suzi and I sat together on the second-floor balcony of the small country home which we had rented for our stay in France. In this short time, we had become addicted to watching the sun disappear over the distant mountains each evening. The miles of vineyards below us took on a silver-blue cast. Gliders from a nearby airfield soared and dipped through the air currents above the village. The houses, clustered together with common walls, clung to the hillside like some giant medieval castle. Tall and stately poplars swayed in the breeze.

After putting the children to sleep, we took a walk in the meadow beside the house. On returning, I settled down in front of the typewriter, my hands poised over the keys. Minutes drifted by; always that pause before beginning a new chapter, always that search through the landscape of ideas and words until I knew to begin. Suzi read in bed, studiously consuming a recent Broadway play. An hour later, she fell asleep.

Time passed quickly until an insistent knocking on

the outside door finally jarred me from my work. The clock indicated two-thirty in the morning. In the French countryside, the world closed down with the last flicker of daylight. Crossing through the kitchen, I saw a familiar Citroën parked beside the front entrance. Since we had met in Fayence and Nice only, I admired Carl's ability to track our house down on some dirt road in the middle of the night. In business circles, his associates had nicknamed him "the hunter."

Hesitating for several seconds, I thought about Angie and her dark eyes. I pulled the latch and the door swung open. Carl Striker just stood there, his right hand clenched in a fist. His hair hung sloppily in front of his face; his clothes looked soiled, an unlikely portrait for a fastidious man who dressed with impeccable taste.

He lifted his closed hand slowly and stared at it. His breathing sounded labored and accelerated, but his expression seemed peculiarly soft and vulnerable. Then, like some ancient warrior performing a solemn ritual, he tapped me on the shoulder three times with his fist.

I grabbed his forearm gently, wanting to acknowledge his smothered "thank you." "Any time, Carl," I said. "Any time."

He nodded his head and turned away without speaking. As his daughter once did, Carl Striker still held back much of his feelings... even those he might have suspected were beautiful and enriching to share. And yet, this night, he dared to relax his guard just enough to allow his closed hand to be his voice. A step. His step. The gift of Angie.

*   *   *

Ten months later I received the following letter from the small, fragile girl with large, black eyes.

261

Dear Bears,

I guess as you probably know, I gave birth five weeks ago. When I first saw Joshua, I knew there was a God; I knew why it all happened. He's so beautiful, but I guess that's what every mother says. Just six pounds, which is pretty good considering I'm not the world's largest person.

You had to see Daddy with the cigars, the whole bit. Even though he's been great all these months, I thought he'd be embarrassed when it happened. But he wasn't. Maybe Josh is the son he never had. Mom's been terrific, too. They both really surprised me.

At first, the kids at school did a whole number; it wasn't too much fun for me. Now they're curious, even excited.

I'm so glad. I'll always remember our day in Theoule. I think I can recite every word we both said, especially those questions. They're the best. Bears, every time I look at Joshua, I think beauty can come from anything, if we want it to.

Love, Angie

P.S. I don't know what you and Daddy talked about when he visited you that night, but he came back so much more open.

THE BOOK OF DOMINIQUE

A group of boys shouted and heckled each other as they played stickball in the middle of the street. A long drive hit by the batter sent three of them scrambling over the hoods and roofs of parked cars in search of the ball. The front-runner tripped over a plastic garbage bag, one of twenty such containers piled in a small mountain in front of an anonymous six-story building. Huddled together, these small stone apartment houses no longer reflected the fashion of the first part of this century. Cracks, deep gouges and the casual insult of graffiti scarred their brick faces.

The first time I walked down One Hundred and Ninth Street on Manhattan's West Side, my system locked into a primitive state of alert. Shadowed faces and glaring eyes followed my movements with the coolness of radar. Blaring radios mixed with the occasional pop of a bottle hitting the sidewalk. Over the past several months, certain physical aspects of the street had become familiar, though its character remained somber and unpredictable.

After parking the Jeep beyond what the street players used for left field, I strolled past an assembly of people gathered at their front stoop. Their children sat opposite them on the fender of a truck. A handsome little boy flashed his teeth at me as he urinated between two parked cars. I waved to Chico Sanchez, the superintendent of my friend's building, who walked briskly by with his wife and four children. Eddie Shaw, an off-Broadway actor, shouted his hello from across the street. A yellow Eldorado, with wide white-wall tires, screeched to a halt. A tall man escorted two young women from the car into the corner building. A second man, sitting at the wheel of the Cadillac, moved his head mechanically like the periscope of a submarine, surveying the street with a detached, professional air.

I pushed the buzzer several times until I heard the familiar gravel of Nick's voice. He released the catch on the inside door. We met often during the past several months, pooling our energies for a book of sayings I had written and he had illustrated. I hopped off the elevator at the sixth floor. The lyrical sound of a flute caught my attention. I knew that Dominique, a young girl who lived down the hall, had to be practicing on the roof. She often watched Nick work his magic with an airbrush, reconstructing and illustrating faces and bodies to suit the needs of his clients. On several occasions, the three of us engaged in lengthy conversations. Once, Dominique invited me to have breakfast with her and her grandmother.

Her music stopped abruptly in the midst of a melody. The voices of children filtered down the staircase as I walked toward Nick's apartment. At first their muted sounds seemed easy and playful, but as I listened more carefully, though the words were indistinct, a quality of their speech sounded very sharp, even aggressive. Then I heard Dominique scream "stop!" several times. Almost without thinking, I lunged for the stairs behind me. Within seconds, I rounded the first landing. I catapulted myself up the next flight, using the side banisters as leverage. When I reached the door to the roof, I kicked it open and instinctively shouted. I could feel a trembling sensation in my hands.

On the other side of the expanse, a group of three boys and a girl circled Dominique, tormenting her with a shiny object she tried desperately to grab from the tallest boy's hand.

"Hey!" I shouted again as I ran toward them. They froze in their tracks, gaped at me, then fled across an adjoining roof.

The tallest boy, apparently the leader, stopped in mid-flight and faced me. Holding Dominique's flute in his hand, he approached us slowly. At a distance of thirty yards, he placed the instrument on the ground very carefully, put his palms up to indicate he had not harmed it, then turned and walked nonchalantly away.

Dominique picked up her flute. As I approached, she moved away, purposely hiding her face. She held the instrument tightly to her chest.

"Are you okay?" I asked.

She nodded.

"Is your flute okay?"

Without even checking it, she shook her head affirmatively.

"Do you know who they are?"

"Yes," she said, obviously unwilling to pursue the subject.

"Can I help you in some way?" I asked.

"I could have taken care of it," she insisted. "I didn't need anybody's help."

"Oh, I know that," I agreed. "But sometimes, it's nice to have another person with you, sort of, well, to lend a hand."

She eyed me suspiciously, then looked away. Without further comment, Dominique let her fingers dance across the thin silver instrument as she flexed her lips and jaw, sending a channel of air expertly into the small, metal mouthpiece. Her dark, wet eyes stared at the pigeons on a ledge. Although dressed in a baggy blue sweatshirt and dungarees, she had a very feminine appearance. Her curly hair, cut into a pixie, appeared curiously exotic against her sandy-colored skin. Her wide forehead furrowed each time she expended extra energy to hit a high note. When she completed the exercise, I clapped enthusiastically.

Turning her head slowly, she smiled at me. The roofline of taller buildings and the steeple of a church formed a powerful landscape behind her.

"Bravo," I said.

"I'd give it a 'ho-ho' instead of a bravo," she replied.

"Does that happen often?" I asked.

"Does what happen often?"

"Problems with the other kids in the neighborhood."

"Oh no, not really," she answered. "They're just some jerks from school. Claude is the big troublemaker. If you're black, you're his friend. If you're white, you're his enemy. And if you're any color in-between, you're somebody to make fun of."

"How do you feel about that?"

"I don't feel anything about it," she said, rubbing the side of her flute. "That's just the way it is. Anyway, it's a long story."

"I'm willing to listen."

"Bears, I don't want to insult you or anything, but I don't want to talk about it."

"Okay," I said.

She began to walk away, then stopped. Without facing me, she whispered. "I'm sorry, I didn't mean to sound that way." Dominique spun around, sporting a warm smile. "Do you want to hear a new piece I've learned?"

"Sure, I'll join the pigeons and we'll all listen."

Casting her twelve-year-old face into that of a serious concert artist, Dominique played a Bach piece with great ease.

I clapped after she finished. "Wonderful. You're really a fine musician . . . a fine artist."

"I feel funny when you tell me that. Especially now. My teacher said if I keep at it, one day I'll play Carnegie Hall. Could you just imagine that?"

"Bright Eyes, you can be anything you want to be."

She blushed, then quickly changed the subject. "Bears, are you and Nick working today?"

"Yes. If you want to come down and see the new drawings, you're welcome. I've also completed another section of the book, so you will have something to read as well. We can call it a trade."

"What do you mean?" she asked.

"You've given me something special . . . a beautiful solo. Now, I can give you something special from me, especially since chasing away unfriendly people doesn't count."

"I have another twenty minutes to practice," she said. "I'm sure it'll be okay, but I want to tell my grandmother first. Okay?"

"Whatever you want. And how about practicing in your grandmother's apartment instead of up here?"

"I know I don't look like much, but I can take care of myself, really I can."

"Then I'll see you later." As I left the roof, her soft, lyrical music followed me into the building.

His unkempt hair fell lazily over his ears and into his face. Nick put the finishing touches on the New

York City skyline as it might look in the midst of a severe earthquake.

"Aren't you doing the wrong city?" I asked.

"That's exactly why it works. The unexpected. Zap— there goes the Empire State Building. Down comes the World Trade Center. Crumble, crumble to the dear old Rockefeller complex. Coffee is . . . ah, excuse me, tea is simmering on the stove. You're late, you know."

"I know," I said as I walked through the dining room, which looked like the warehouse of an art supply store. "Saw Dominique on the roof. Some kids were giving her a hard time."

"That's the least of her problems which, incidentally, leads us naturally into our next subject."

"Hey, Nick, who turned you on this morning?"

"You noticed. Fantastic. I'm touched, redeemed," he shouted. "You're witnessing the aesthetic joy of an artist who just loves his work. You know, when I put this brush in my hand, I can do no wrong. Divine guidance!"

I handed him a cup of tea, then continued to admire the vast panorama. "Hey, I don't want to blow you away, but is this supposed to be the way the skyline looks today?"

"Of course. I took this off the latest shot done by the city's tourist board." He glared at me wide-eyed. "Oh Christ, man, lay it on me. What's missing?"

"When I come over the 59th Street Bridge, a favorite new building which just fascinates me is the one with the slanted top, the one that was going to use solar energy."

"Say no more," Nick moaned. He slapped his leg and cursed the huge painting. "This thing's supposed to be delivered tomorrow and it's missing the damn Citicorp building. Okay, smart guy, while you're here, do you notice anything else missing?"

"St. Peter's Cathedral."

"What? Where the hell's that?"

"Oh," I said. "Sorry, that's in Rome."

He pointed the airbrush gun at me.

"You bird. This time I'll spare you, but next time, you're in big trouble."

"Nick, you started to say something about Dominique?"

"Yeah. Her grandmother caught me in the hall yesterday. You must' a really impressed the old lady over eggs that morning. When I told her what you do, she asked if you'd talk with Dominique. I said I'd have you call her, but she doesn't have a phone, which means she also doesn't have any bread."

"So what else is new?"

"Boy, you come downtown and you get right into the swing of things."

"The word is flexible. This block isn't exactly what I'd choose for a backyard, but it's here, so you deal with it. You know, during the past couple of weeks, I've noticed Dominique getting more and more uncomfortable . . . kind of snappy."

"I can vouch for that," Nick concurred. "I almost threw her out of here a couple of days ago. She did this whole criticism trip on one of my watercolors. I'm not saying she has to like my stuff, but she had this chip on, like she wanted anything to hit and I was the closest person around. There's another thing. She used to stay up here with her grandmother when her parents worked during the day. Now, she also hangs out in the evenings. Something lousy is going down between her old man and old lady."

"She's really a special kid, Nick. I guess all kids are really special if you give them a chance."

"Wait, before you get on your soap box, let's go over the drawings."

For the next fifteen minutes, we reviewed his new sketches for the book. Just as I opened the envelope with the pages to be added to the manuscript, the buzzer rang. We heard three clear notes from a flute.

"Be there in a sec, Bright Eyes," I called. After studiously unlatching three locks, I opened the door.

Dominique smiled at me, then paraded into the living room, carrying her flute like a stick over her shoulder. She stopped abruptly in front of the painting.

"Wow. That's unbelievable. It looks so real. How do you make it look so real?"

"Me and Rembrandt have the same touch."

"Who's Rembrandt?"

"Oh," Nick said, "a very famous artist who lived many years ago. When you look at the people in his paintings, they're very alive."

She studied the painting, twisting her head comically as she tried to see into the windows of falling structures. Then she turned to me. "Bears, can I read more of your book?"

"Sure," I said, handing the envelope to her.

"Hey, I didn't even see that yet," Nick protested.

"We still have to go over the drawings from last week anyway."

As we leafed through some of his rough sketches, Dominique curled into a corner of the couch, consuming page after page. About ten minutes later, when I turned to check her progress, I realized she was crying. I tapped Nick on the shoulder, then sat beside her.

"Is the book that bad?"

She smiled weakly.

"You want to talk about it?" I asked.

She glanced up at Nick uncomfortably.

"Listen," he said. "I can split. Haven't been to the market in four whole weeks . . . it would be a nice experience to visit with some potatoes and carrots."

"No, Nick. I have to leave now," Dominique said, turning to me apologetically. "Thanks, Bears, I appreciate your wanting to talk to me, really, but there's nothing you could do."

"It's not what I can do, but maybe what you can do . . . at least for yourself. Sometimes when we look at something, understand it better, we feel and see differently . . . even, sometimes, think new ways to deal with old situations."

"I really have to go."

"It's okay, Dominique. I don't want to push you to do something you don't want to do. I'll see you next Wednesday."

She smiled awkwardly, then left quickly.

The following week, Dominique's grandmother waited for me in the lobby of the building. "Bears, over here," she shouted in a husky voice as I came through the front door. A bright smile stretched the thick rubber features of her face. She kept motioning with her hand.

"Hi," I said, startled to see her. "You look wonderful, so I don't have to ask you how you are." I took her hand and patted it. "I guess the question is—how's Dominique?"

The old woman wet her lips, then replied.

"To her parents, who are too busy fighting to look, she's fine. To the school, she's a good student, and in this neighborhood, that's a prize. To her music teacher, he only sees her name in lights. To the old grandma, I see the pain in this child. My daughter and her husband, Dominique's parents, are getting divorced. She had told you, huh?"

"No, we've never talked about it."

"Ah, another bad sign."

"If it helps us know more about her, maybe," I suggested, "it's neither good nor bad, but just a sign . . . like a road sign, tells you what street you're on."

"Okay. I'll give you your road sign," she muttered. "She won't talk to me, you know, I'm an old lady. Kids! They think old people have their heads filled with sand. Well, there's no sand in my head. If she came to me, I could help her. I want you to know that, Bears."

I nodded.

"But she doesn't come to me, the little dummy. When I was a kid, older meant wiser. Now everything's changed. Nick says you talk to people, help them understand things about themselves. Maybe you could talk to Dominique. I don't have any money, but I don't want something for nothing. I thought maybe we could bargain. What do you think?"

"That sounds reasonable. What do you suggest?"

"What about plants? You like plants?" she asked.

"Sure."

"I've been growing two rubber trees for over four years. They're beauties—won't find anything like them in all of Manhattan. How about two rubber trees and I'll throw in dinner for you and Nick?"

"Two rubber trees sounds like too much. How about just dinner for me and Nick?"

"That's all?" she blurted.

"That's all," I assured her.

"Now I don't know any more. If you're supposed to be so good, how come you make such a lousy bargain for yourself?"

"If it satisfies me, then it's not a lousy deal. After all, I want a very fancy meal."

She smiled at me through layers of cracked skin. "Okay, young man, then we have a deal."

I shook her hand enthusiastically. "We have a deal."

"Nothing fishy, huh?"

"Nothing fishy," I said.

"Come then, I have things to do," she said, guiding me gently toward the elevator.

"Tell your granddaughter to either meet me at Nick's in an hour or come by now and watch us work if she likes. Do you mind if I take her with me for a half-hour? I want to try to see something before five. It'll be fun for her."

"Will that be part of our deal?"

"Yes, if you'd like. But actually, I'd enjoy taking her. It's a museum just a couple of blocks from here."

"Then it's settled, it's part of our deal," she insisted. "Listen, I'm a reasonable lady—you sure you don't want a rubber tree?"

"Yes, very sure. The price of one session is a meal."

As the elevator ascended toward the sixth floor, she kept shaking her head. "Fair is fair. If you agreed, I guess it's fair."

"It would seem that way to me," I smiled and winked at her. "I can't stay for a meal tonight. I'll let Dominique know when Nick and I can come. Do you need much advance notice?"

"Listen, sonny, at my age you're always ready. You be sure to come."

"Don't worry, I'll collect," I assured her.

She waddled down the hallway, then turned around and indicated for me to wait. As she drew closer, she said, "I want to shake your hand again. Such a strong hand."

"Ah, a second honor to touch the green thumb of rubber plants," I said.

"Some honor," she mused. "Okay, I'm leaving now." Immediately after taking her first step, she paused again. "Thank you. And that thank you is over and above our bargain, you know. Just thought you deserved it."

An hour later, after my meeting with Nick, I decided to fetch Dominique myself since she had not come to the apartment. Her presence on the stairs leading to the roof interrupted my short trip down the hallway.

"There you are. I was coming to get you."

"I know. My grandmother told me. I don't know if I'll be very good at it."

"At what?"

"Talking."

"It doesn't matter, Bright Eyes. C'mon. First we're

273

going to take a quick trip to a museum close by."

As we crossed Broadway, she took my hand.

"Bears, I don't know what to say. Can I ask you a question?"

"Shoot."

"Do you only talk to crazy people?"

I laughed. "No. In fact, I've never talked to a crazy person. That's just somebody's label. When people are confused about what they're thinking, they often get unhappy and act in strange ways. They're not crazy, just unhappy. And most people have been there at one time or another during their lives. All I do is ask questions, which often helps a person figure out what they're thinking about and why. When you look at something and see it for what it is, you have a chance to change it or, at least, change how you feel about it."

"Sounds simple."

"The questions are. Sometimes the path to the answer curves around like a mountain road, but we can get there if we want to. For a lot of people, Dominique, it's a very beautiful journey, too."

We made a right turn on One Hundred and Seventh and strolled toward Riverside Drive. A small, dignified brownstone housed the Roerich Museum. A handwritten note attached to the antique door at the front of the building said the museum would reopen again in fifteen minutes.

"Rather than sit here, how about a walk in the park?" Dominique nodded, cocking her head in a fashion which reminded me of my daughter, Bryn. We glided down several flights of stairs before reaching the criss-crossing paths which meandered through the trees and planted fields.

"If Grandma asked you to talk to me, I guess it's pretty obvious," she said.

"What is?"

"That I'm bitchy. I don't mean to be that way. It's like I can't help it. I just feel so angry."

"What are you angry about?"

"Didn't my grandmother tell you?"

"No, Dominique, not really. We didn't discuss details," I said as we walked slowly along the path closest to the river. "She mentioned there were problems at home."

"Well, it's not just problems. My mother and father are getting divorced." The muscles in her face quivered.

"How do you feel about that?"

"Angry. They didn't ask me; they're just going to do it. Well, damn, I'm part of the family, aren't I? How about me?" She stared at her feet as she walked. "I'm just so scared, Bears."

"About what?"

"I don't know. Everything's different. What's going to happen to all of us?"

"What do you think?" I asked.

"My father will be all alone. He already took another apartment. He said I'd see him every weekend, maybe even every other day. But I don't want that. I want to see him every night, just like it used to be." She began to cry.

"What are you unhappy about?"

"I won't see him every night."

"And what about that makes you so uncomfortable?"

"Well, plenty of my friends have divorced parents. At first, their fathers came all the time. Then, after awhile, they only came maybe once a week, and then, sometimes, they skipped a week." She paused, running the nail on her index finger back and forth along the edge of her bottom teeth. "I'm afraid that's going to happen."

"Why do you believe that?"

"Just look at Collene, Rico, Malcolm, Maria. I could go on and on."

"Why do you believe if it happened to them, it'll happen to you?"

"You mean it happened to all of them, but it's not

going to happen to me!" she said, pondering the possibility with amazement.

"No, I'm just asking you a question." I paused, wanting her to hear my words. "Why do you believe because it happened to them, it will happen to you?"

"Well, I guess it's not really the reason. It doesn't *have* to happen to me when I really think about it. Maybe I . . . I just know my father."

"What do you know about him?"

"He's kind of lazy, you know what I mean. Like when it's raining, he won't go out because it's too much trouble. I guess if it's raining and that's the day he's supposed to see me, he won't go out either."

Dominique sat on a bench facing the river. A large tanker passed by. Her eyes jumped nervously along the horizon.

"And if your father doesn't come over?"

"That would be awful," she said in a firm, unforgiving voice.

"Why, Dominique?"

"Because it'll show me something."

"What do you mean?"

"It'll show me he doesn't really care enough." Her voice cracked as she spoke.

"Why do you believe if he doesn't come over, it means he doesn't care enough?"

"Wouldn't it be obvious?" she asked.

"If it seemed that way to you, you'd have your reasons," I interjected. "Why do you believe it would mean that?"

"'Cause if he really cared about me, he'd come over."

"Do you believe that?"

"Yes."

"Why?" I asked.

"That's what I would do."

"Okay, but if your dad doesn't do what you would

do or what you would expect him to do, why does that mean he doesn't care?"

"I don't know, Bears. You see, I told you I'm not very good at this." She shook her head from side to side, physically trying to reaffirm her statement.

"Dominique, why don't you guess at an answer?"

"That's silly," she replied.

"Maybe not. Why don't you try?"

"Okay." She put her hands over her face. "Only now I've forgotten the question. What was it?"

"Why don't you see if you can remember?"

"Something about if he didn't do what I did or what I want, why does that mean he doesn't care ... that's it."

"You want to answer it?"

"Well, when you love someone, you don't want to be away from them, you just don't."

"What are you saying?" I asked.

"He wouldn't move away if he loved me."

"Are you saying that by his leaving, it means he doesn't love you?"

"Yes." She looked away. "Can I take something back?"

I nodded.

"I don't think it means that. I know he still loves me. I really do ... maybe right now more than before. But I think maybe it's a little true."

"What are you afraid would happen if you didn't think that?"

"Then it would be fine with me if he lived somewhere else. And it can't be, Bears, it just can't be." Her breathing became labored.

"And if it was, why would you be uncomfortable about that?"

"Then maybe he'd think I didn't care."

"Are you saying by being unhappy he'll know how much you care?"

"Yeah, I guess so. How else will he know?"

"How do you think?"

"I could tell him, but I do that already. There's something else."

"What's that?"

"I heard them talking one night. My mother said they should stay together until I'm older. He didn't agree. He said I'd be alright, but I'm not."

"How come?"

"I don't know, I'm just not."

"What are you afraid would happen if you were alright?"

"Then he'd never consider coming back, never!"

"So are you being not alright to convince him to come back?"

Dominique walked away. Her face reddened as she rubbed her eyes furiously. "I guess that's what I'm doing. Okay, so why can't I do that if I want to?"

"You can, but do you want to?" I asked. "Does it get you what you want?"

"At first, I thought it did. But last time he saw me, he got so angry at me for being bitchy, he left early. It felt like I couldn't help myself."

"Do you believe that?"

"Then, I guess I did."

"And now?"

"No. It's pretty obvious why I did it." Suddenly, she smiled broadly.

"Why are you smiling?"

"I feel better. I guess being sad won't get them back together again. Sometimes, Bears, it's all I can think about."

"You can't force them to do what they don't want to do, but you can look at it and maybe change how you feel about it and how you act toward them and yourself But that's only if you want to, Dominique."

"I want to," she said.

I looked at my watch. "Hey, in another five minutes, we're going to miss the museum completely. How are you at running?"

"I'll keep up."

Holding hands, we sprinted across the lawn and up three flights of stone stairs. The green light on Riverside Drive allowed us to continue our race uninterrupted. We jogged down One Hundred and Seventh Street, then charged up the stairs of the stately brownstone, only to find the door locked. A discreet bronze sign indicated the museum had closed for the day.

"It wasn't for us to go today," I said, panting. "Next week. Next week—okay?" "Yes," Dominique said, breathless. Observing each other's red faces, we burst out laughing.

The following week, Dominique appeared at Nick's door a full hour early. Though she listened to our conversation and peeked over our shoulders at the sketches, she seemed distant despite the warm smile dancing on her face. Somehow, I sensed her desire to get on with it, wanting very much to continue our dialogue from the previous week. Perhaps her aloofness merely signaled her impatience.

Once on the street, I said, "I didn't feel you with us in Nick's apartment. Were you thinking of other things?"

She furrowed her forehead in the exact same way she did when trying to reach those high notes on her flute. "I guess I wanted to tell you about what happened this week."

"Ah, I thought so. Listen, why don't we hold the talk until after the museum so we don't have to stop in the middle. Nick wants me to look at a couple of paintings, then I'm yours. Okay?"

"Okay."

The sun glittered on the surface of small puddles which still remained in the streets after the morning rain. We turned into One Hundred and Seventh.

"This time, we get in," I said. "That, my dear young lady, is today's prediction."

As we climbed the steps, I sensed a quiet in the interior of the building. Very gently, I tried the handle. The door was locked. Dominique began to giggle.

"Not so fast. I've yet to try my famous knock." I rapped my knuckles against the thick wood panel. Within seconds, a pleasant-looking man dressed in a suit opened the door.

"Welcome to the Roerich Museum," he said, greeting us as if we had been expected and honored guests.

"Thank you," I said.

Although I had been there on a previous occasion, I didn't stop him from reciting his monologue on Nickolas Roerich. Dominique listened wide-eyed to the stories about this Russian painter who traveled the world, though most of his energies involved his depictions of the Tibetan mountains and people. She held my hand tightly as we were then treated to a picture-by-picture tour, complete with descriptions and related background material.

On the second floor, an older Russian gentleman showed us more of Roerich's paintings, including some luminous, semi-abstract murals of ominous white and blue mountains set against a flattened sky. An elderly woman accompanied us through the third floor, talking non-stop about the unique inner light in the paintings resulting from the use of tempera on canvas.

As we left the museum, the man in the lobby handed us several circulars.

"Oh, Bears, that was fantastic. How could that place be right here on a Hundred and Seventh? Thanks, that was a super place. They treated me like a real person."

"I knew you'd love it. There's something about that museum and flute music which go together. If you like one, you'd like the other. Want to find our bench and talk?"

"Can we go up on the roof?"

"If that's what you'd like, let's go."

We crossed Broadway, then headed uptown. "You mentioned you wanted to tell me about this week."

"I told my father about our talk. He listened a lot, but didn't say too much. He laughed like crazy about Grandma—thought she was a riot. We . . . uh . . . we had a wonderful time together. But not the best because I just can't feel comfortable with him or my mother any more . . . not like I used to."

"Why not?" I asked.

"I feel like they're both trying to get me on their side. My father calls my mother a pain. And she, well, she's always saying how rotten he's been, how he never keeps a job more than a year, how he screams at her for no reason. The whole bit. I know she doesn't want me to like him more than her, but I get creepy listening to her."

"Why?"

"She talks so much about it, I kind of agree after awhile. Then at night, when I'm alone, I get annoyed at myself for agreeing with her. I don't want to hate him like she does. He's my father."

"Do you hate him?"

"No, of course not."

"Then why do you believe you might?"

"Because I almost do when she goes on and on. After all, he left us . . . any jerk can see that." She lagged behind as we entered her street. "They used to fight every night. Sometimes I'd listen by the door. One time he hit her. I think she hit him back. Then he said something about her using me to chain him with. And then . . ." Suddenly, she became very still.

"Then what happened, Dominique?"

"My mother said it was no picnic working all day and then coming home to cook and clean for some . . ." She closed her eyes. The tears flowed down her cheeks. "For some pain-in-the-ass kid." A choking sound erupted from her throat. Dominique cried quietly, hunching her shoulders into her neck like a turtle withdrawing into its body for protection. She continued to walk, pushing herself, struggling to control the sobbing while refusing the support of my arm. Several neighbors watched us pass, their eyes cool and impenetrable.

When we entered her apartment building, she hid her face so as to appear inconspicuous to the other tenants in the lobby. In the elevator, she turned toward the wall. The door opened on every level, further disrupting her privacy. Finally, we reached the sixth floor. Once on the roof, we sat on top of an interior ledge.

"Why does what your mother said upset you so much?"

"Neither of them really wants me. I'm just something that messes up their lives."

"What do you mean?"

"If I wasn't here, my mother wouldn't have all those problems and my father wouldn't feel . . . chained." She spit the words through clenched teeth.

"Let's suppose it's exactly the way you see it. If they feel that way—angry, troubled, chained—what about that makes you so unhappy?"

"I love them. I want them to love me too."

"Are you saying they don't?"

"Yeah. Maybe. Why would they say all those things if they loved me?"

"Why do you think?" I asked.

"I don't know."

"You want to guess at it?"

She smiled weakly. "Again, huh?"

"If you want."

"Maybe they're just mad, you know, like I was with my father. I acted like an awful bitch to him, but I love him, really I do. I know when you get angry, you say a lot of things you don't mean. Maybe they didn't mean it, but I still feel like maybe I'm the reason."

"The reason for what?"

"The divorce," she said. "If they didn't have me, everything would be much easier."

"What do you mean?"

"Well, then my mother wouldn't have to rush home to cook dinner, to watch out for me all the time, and my father would be freer."

"If you didn't exist, perhaps, and only perhaps," I suggested, "your parents might do different things. But how do you see yourself as the reason for their problems, or the reason for their unhappiness?"

"If they're unhappy taking care of me, then isn't it my fault?"

"How does that make it your fault?" I asked.

"I don't know. I don't know. It just does." Jumping to her feet, she ran through the exit door and disappeared down the steps. Moments later she reappeared, shouting at the top of her lungs. "I don't want to be blamed! It's not fair! I didn't do anything! I didn't!" She bent over like a monk before an altar. "When I was little," she began in a raspy whisper, "they were happy. If I was such a damn pain, why weren't they miserable *then*?" She sank to the ground in front of me.

"Why do you believe it's your fault?" I asked again.

"I don't know any more. Honest. I guess when I heard them fighting over me, that's what I thought. But they fight over everything."

"So what could you know from that?"

"That they're miserable? But maybe I make them more miserable."

"How would you do that?"

"Being a kid they have to take care of," she declared.

"Do they have to be miserable about taking care of a kid?"

She pondered the question for a long time before answering. "No. Grandma loves it when I'm with her; I know she does. So do my mother and father when they're not acting crazy."

"Then sometimes when your parents are with you,

they're happy, and at other times, they're unhappy. How do you see yourself as doing it to them?"

"I guess I really don't. It's like when I'm with my father, sometimes I'm nice, sometimes I'm not. It depends on me. So I guess it depends on them." After sighing noisily, she furrowed her forehead. "It's funny, when my mother blames my father for making her miserable, I know it's not true. I can actually watch her get furious all by herself and then blame it on him. Sometimes I think she's mad at herself. You know, I never thought about that before." A smile rippled across her face.

"How do you feel now?"

"Much better. But what should I do when they complain to me about each other?"

"What do you want to do?"

"To make them stop. I guess I could ask them to stop, but suppose they won't listen?"

"Then how would you feel?"

"Not good."

"Why not?"

"Maybe I'll start to believe them, but no, I know I won't. Especially Mommy. She's so scared I'll want to live with him. We never talk about it, but I know what she's thinking." Dominique nodded. "You ought'a hear them. My father told me my mother used to steal money from his pants pockets at night. And my mother complains how he never brought much money home because he spent it on booze. I love them both—it's just hard."

"What's hard about it?"

"Half the time, I don't know who to agree with. I shake my head like an idiot, but I try not to listen. I'd love to tell them to shut up." She pressed the palms of her hands against her eyes. "I wish I could just be me, but that's so scary."

"What's scary about being you?" I asked.

Dominique pulled her hands away from her face. "Well, it would be just saying what I felt. Suppose I tell my mother I know she's jealous of me with Daddy—God, she'd freak."

"Why do you believe that?"

"You don't know my mother."

"Let's say she freaks. Then what?"

"She'll scream at me and, oh, maybe, she won't want me any more." Her face became somber. "You think she might not want me any more?"

"I can't answer that for you, Bright Eyes. Only your mother can answer that question. How would you feel if she said she didn't want you?"

Her face became very red again. "Oh God, that would be awful. I don't know what I'd do. Maybe I could live with my father. Or Grandma," she sighed. "Grandma would let me live with her. But that's not the point. It would be awful if your own mother didn't want you."

"Why, Dominique?"

"Because if she didn't want you, then who would?"

"What do you think it means about you if your mom doesn't want to be with you?"

"That I'm no good." Her voice faltered. "That something's wrong with me if my own parents don't even want me."

"Do you believe that?"

"I guess so."

"Why do you believe that if everything you feared came to pass—that neither your mother nor your father wanted you—why would that mean something was wrong with you?"

"Grandma would want me," she mumbled.

"Okay—what could you know from that?"

"She's the only happy person in my whole family. Maybe it doesn't mean something is wrong with me. And I know Francisca would let me live with her family, too. She's my best friend. Bears, my parents are really crazy right now—maybe they just can't think straight because they're so unhappy."

"You use the word 'maybe.' Do you still think there's a possibility it would mean something is wrong with you?"

"I guess so. Kind of."

"Why do you believe that?"

"I don't know," she said. "I don't have a reason, not really."

"What are you afraid would happen if you no longer believed it?"

She turned away, hiding her face self-consciously. "Then I'd be me."

"And what would that mean?"

"I'd say what I thought. Then they'd probably hate me and not want me and . . . oh, it's so crazy, I was going to say it would mean I'm rotten, but that's not true— I know that much by now. And you know what else?"

"What?"

"I don't think they'd hate me anyway. When I was honest with my father last week, it was okay. No—it was better than okay."

During the remainder of our talk, Dominique explored her discomforts with her friends' opinions concerning her family situation. She felt embarrassed about the impending divorce, about the judgments of others . . . most specifically, they would think her parents, especially her father, didn't care about her. Dominique saw herself as vulnerable in the face of those opinions until she confronted them and began to trust her own clarity.

As we prepared to leave the roof, Dominique glanced at me shyly and said: "I learned a new piece of music. Before you go, Bears, would you like to hear it?"

"Absolutely."

She raced down the stairs and returned with her instrument. She then played an hypnotic nocturne originally written by Chopin for the piano. When she finished, she smiled brightly, her eyes glimmering in the late afternoon light.

"Wow, you really let yourself go with that flute. That's beautiful."

She blushed.

"See you next week—yes or no?" I asked.

"Why did you ask me like that?"

"Oh, I guess to give you an opportunity to decide each time whether you want to talk more."

"I do. It's . . . like you said, it's sort of fun. Bears, my grandmother wanted me to ask you when you're going to collect those fancy meals she agreed to make. According to her, she owes you three already."

"I think it's only two."

"No, she says you're spending more time than she figured; so she's looking out for your interest since you don't."

We both laughed.

"Okay, set a date for next week, definitely. Next Wednesday. I'll tell Nick."

Dominique touched my hand lightly. "Thanks, Bears—for listening to me play. It's hard to get an audience around here for a flute solo."

"You can count on me. And I don't mean as a favor to you. Your music is a gift to anyone who takes the time to listen."

Her cheeks flushed. "And the talks really help."

"I'm glad."

We exchanged smiles as we left the roof together.

* * *

Dominique curled her legs underneath her as she squatted on the ledge created by the two-foot recess framing the window. From the second floor, she could easily observe the activity on the street. A light drizzle frosted the glass and softened the edges of the cars and garbage cans lining the curb. The little girl with bright eyes snapped her head around in order to consult the large wall clock. Her father was already late, having promised an early start this Saturday morning. Dominique held a small brown bag in her right hand. It contained the two peanut butter sandwiches she had prepared for their outing at the zoo.

"Sitting there isn't going to make him come any faster," her mother chimed. "I'll never understand you. He up and walks out on us and you just wait for him every Saturday like a puppy dog. Well, you're not a baby any more—if that's what you want do do...do it," she said, feigning a casual pose which defied the obvious stress in her voice. "Tell him the rent is due on Wednesday. And tell him I don't care how many apartments he has to support—Wednesday is the day."

"Okay," Dominique replied. Although she heard her mother's request, she refused to relinquish her watch, even for a second.

Gretchen Celine eyed her daughter suspiously. She pranced across the room, then stood by the window ledge with her arms crossed. "Does that 'okay' mean you'll tell him?"

"Yes, I will."

"Listen, honey, I don't mean to jump at you, but this whole thing is very new...for all of us. Who knew I married such a souse? The bastard! Will you look at that," she barked as she looked at the clock, "twenty minutes late already. I don't think it'd matter if his life depended on it. Why don't you just forget it and come along with me today?"

"Oh, Mom, I can't—you kn w that. We have the whole day planned. He'll be here."

"Yeah, after taking his sweet-ass time." She kissed her daughter lightly on the cheek. "I'll see you tonight. Don't forget to lock the door when you leave."

Dominique nodded her head, still maintaining her intense scrutiny of the street. Although the slamming door jarred her, she felt relieved, finally alone and free to pick and choose her fantasies without her mother's intrusion. Images of her father's distinctive walk dominated her thoughts. He tended to rock backwards and forwards with each complete step; a slightly uncoordinated gait choreographed to a continually changing rhythm. That awkward characteristic allowed her to identify him at great distances and focus easily on his lumbering figure even amid large crowds.

Each person on the street came under her surveillance. Suddenly, a tall man whipped around the corner, jogging down the sidewalk at a fast pace. Adrenalin flooded her system. Dominique created an instant scenario about the unexpressed devotion of her father, using his running figure as evidence. She would dismiss the half-hour wait.

Standing on the ledge, she waved furiously, awaiting that moment when he would look up at her in the window—part of an unspoken ritual that developed between them after he had moved out of the house. As the figure neared the building, she held her breath. Though the man seemed a touch too tall and a bit too agile, Dominique clutched her original impression and moved her arms back and forth over her head. Even after the man passed the building, never once looking up, she continued to wave. Finally, her hand went limp and she slumped back down on the ledge.

Her smile disappeared when she turned to consult the clock again. An hour passed. Dominique hopped off the sill and dialed her father's phone number. No answer. She assured herself that he had to be on his way, detained only briefly by a business call or some other pressing responsibility. Nevertheless, he would be here . . . she could feel it in her bones. Back on the ledge, she cuddled against the recessed wall, oblivious to the chipped paint which crumbled under the pressure of her body.

A woman with a baby carriage passed by. Two groups of men loitered by the entrance of a neighboring building. A young man, dressed neatly in a three-piece suit, glanced up as he strolled along the street. He waved at the little girl framed in the second-story window. A smile creased his face when she returned the gesture, though her movements lacked enthusiasm.

Another hour passed. Again Dominique dialed her father's telephone number to no avail. Her fingers expertly spun the knobs on the radio. This time, when she continued her vigil, her body pulsated to a hard rock tune. But her response seemed forced, mechanical. The shrill blare of the noon news punctuated the passage of three hours since the time of her father's promised arrival. Had he forgotten? Impossible! Was he angry because she spoke openly and honestly with him the week before? The questions flooded her and the absence of answers made her tense.

Rain pelted the pavement, darkening the brick buildings on the opposite side of the street. Water eroded several piles of paper bags filled with garbage; their debris of empty milk cartons, bottletops and soiled napkins floated on the surface of spontaneous rivers rushing beside the curb. Her mood turned somber. *He'll come*, she insisted. *There's still time, he'll come.* But another hour elapsed and another. Her attention wandered. Suddenly, the music seemed sad and distorted. Dominique flipped the radio off and paced the living room. Grabbing her flute, she jumped back on the sill and began practicing. Her head bobbed to the rhythm of a Mozart piece she had just mastered. Dominique fantasized a private recital for her father—at Carnegie Hall or, perhaps, Lincoln Center. The daydream renewed her energy. He would come, she assured herself.

By three in the afternoon, six hours after their appointed rendezvous, she returned the flute to its case, then leaped up on the ledge again. The rain had stopped, giving way to a late afternoon sun which danced along the surface of the slick pavement. She scrutinized every man who turned the corner until she fell asleep.

A noise at the front door woke her at five o'clock. She jerked her head around, facing the entranceway. The sounds of hands fumbling with keys filled the quiet room. *That's just like him,* she thought, *not only late, but clumsy.* She quickly adjusted her blouse and pressed her hair down. Within seconds, the door opened.

When Mrs. Celine met her daughter's wide-eyed stare, she surmised what had occurred. "Oh wow—you poor kid. I just don't believe it!" she hissed while literally stomping into the apartment. "I just don't *believe* it! That son of a bitch never showed. I'm so sorry, baby. Jesus, you had to wait here all day by yourself. If I had known, I would have come home sooner—honest, I would have."

"It's okay, Mom. Gave me a chance to practice." Her voice cracked.

"I just can't believe he'd do this to you. Now do you see what I mean? You can't count on him for anything. Wait till I see him . . . just wait!"

"Maybe something important happened so he couldn't come."

"You're always so ready to make excuses for him. That's just wonderful for him, but you see that's exactly what I did these last fifteen years and look where it landed me."

Dominique turned away. She pressed her cheek against the cold glass.

Gretchen Celine sat opposite her daughter on the sill, suddenly self-conscious about the harshness of her comments. Leaning forward, she embraced Dominique, rubbing her back in an effort to erase the pain. For the first time since her husband's abrupt exit, she felt herself giving in to the sadness which now overwhelmed her. Her body convulsed as she cried.

Her mother's sobbing surprised her. At first she felt confused, impotent—not knowing what to say or do. Then Dominique's hands moved instinctively as she began to caress the woman who had seemed so stern and distant during the past few weeks. While she stroked her mother in gentle, rhythmic motions, tears filled her eyes. "It's okay, mom. We'll be alright, I promise."

*   *   *

When I entered Nick's apartment the following week, Dominique had not only arrived, but worked busily at preparing the surfaces of several stretched canvases. White gesso caked her hands.

"Can you dig my new assistant?" Nick asked while scratching his head frantically with the paint brush handle. "She finally got off the bleachers and went to work."

"Is she slave labor or skilled help?" I questioned.

The bright-eyed little girl in the corner of the room smiled mischievously.

"A trade," he replied. "Would you believe that? You got her and her grandmother all fired up about the barter system."

"Bears, he's going to give me that small painting, the one over there against the couch." She pointed to an impressionistic illustration of children dancing in a circle.

"Lucky me," Nick said. "If my generous clients didn't give the pieces back to me after they used them, I'd be short on things to trade."

"Isn't that wonderful, Bears?" Dominique blurted as

she eyed the framed painting proudly.

"You picked a beauty," I said.

Nick and I began to review the next series of sketches he had prepared, pinning our choices to the corkboard behind his drawing table.

Dominique worked non-stop, her face spotted by the white undercoating she applied to each canvas. Her fingers held the brush with a light, caring touch; each stroke precise and professional.

"I'm finished," she yelled.

"Great," Nick answered. "Wash that stuff off before it dries."

Just after she disappeared into the bathroom, we concluded our own discussion about the drawings and the book. Nick excused himself to make a late delivery to a client.

Dominique marched back into the living room, her face and hands still dripping. I threw her a towel from the linen closet.

"I'm ready any time you are," I said.

"Do you want to talk here?" she asked.

"Any place is fine. If we use Nick's apartment, I can make some lemon grass tea." She nodded. "Good. Just let me put up some water and find the strainer." After concluding my business in the kitchen, I returned to find that Dominique had cleared a space for each of us on either side of the coffee table.

"I did it," she said coyly.

"Did what?"

"It's kind of a long story. You see, last Saturday, my dad didn't show up and my mom, well, she got real upset. She kind of cried in front of me for the first time since Daddy left and I think I helped her—I think I really did. Does it sound silly to say that?"

"What do you think?"

Dominique smiled. "No, I guess not—it's just that it never happened that way before. Anyway, I...

uh ... felt, you know, stronger. And the next day I did it. I told her everything ... that I thought she was jealous and afraid and that's why she always talked mean about Daddy. I knew she'd freak and she did ... kept screaming at me, even when I told her I loved her she yelled at me to shut up."

"How come you're telling me all this with a big grin on your face?"

"You didn't give me a chance to get to the end of the story." Dominique bowed her head, then wrinkled her forehead. "My mom woke me up before school the next morning and told me that what I said was true. She said sometimes people don't want to hear what's true. When I told her I was afraid she might not want me to live with her any more, she hugged me ... real tight." Her expression suddenly changed.

"What are you feeling?"

"I was thinking about my father. I didn't do so good with him. He didn't believe what I told him was my idea. He kept saying Mommy had gotten to me and turned me against him. And that wasn't all—like I said, he didn't pick me up this weekend. Bears, I try not to be unhappy about it, but I guess I am ... a little."

"It's okay to be unhappy. If you feel it, you feel it. It's not bad—there are no bad and good feelings. It's just an opportunity to understand what you're thinking."

"I know that. I felt so good after I talked to him, even when he didn't listen and said things that weren't true. But on Saturday, I sat by the window all day until it got dark." Her voice thinned. "I felt so sad."

"What were you sad about?"

She put her palms over her eyes. "I really know it doesn't mean I'm a bad person if he doesn't want to see me. That makes it different. But you know, I still want to see him."

"Sure. But wanting to see him and feeling sad when

you don't are two distinctly different things. Why do you feel sad?"

"I want to see Daddy," she said in a voice that sounded infantile.

"I know. But what's so upsetting about not seeing him?"

"Maybe he'll never come back?"

"Do you believe that?"

"I don't know, but it could happen. He could just decide it's too much hassle to see me. That'd be really shitty."

"What do you mean?"

"I talked to him so we'd have a better time. But he didn't listen. Now I don't have any time with him at all. What if I never see him again?"

"What about it?" I asked.

"I want to see him every weekend, like before. It's because of what I said."

"What do you mean?"

"If I hadn't said anything, everything would be the same."

"That might be so, but is that what you would have wanted?"

"No, damn it. No and yes."

The whistle from the tea kettle interrupted us. "Dominique, give me a second, I'll be right back." I made our tea very quickly and sat opposite her on the side of the coffee table.

"I've been thinking," she said. "I'm glad I told him what I felt. I don't want to be just the little kid. I'm a person too. I just got scared he'd never come back."

"Why do you believe he'll never come back?"

"That's stupid, isn't it," she said.

"Not really—if that's what you thought, you can ask yourself why?"

"He left my mother, didn't he? He could do the same with me." She sighed, then shook her head. "I don't really believe that . . . well, only sometimes."

"Let's take the sometimes. Suppose what you feared happened and he didn't come back, what about that would be most disturbing?"

Her eyes jumped nervously back and forth across the table. "I would miss him."

"What do you mean?"

"I'd think about him a lot," she asserted.

"And how do you feel when you think about him?"

"Okay. It would be different if I thought he would never come back."

"What would make it different?"

"There would be no hope."

"Do you believe there's no hope?"

"I guess it could always change. He could change his mind. He could, you know." She looked at me surprised. "I think I knew that all along. It's like a make-believe reason."

"Dominique, what are you afraid would happen if you weren't upset about his not seeing you last weekend?"

"Then I wouldn't do anything about it."

"Are you saying by being unhappy about it, you'll make sure you'll do something?"

"Yeah, I guess that's what I'm saying."

"Why do you believe you have to be unhappy in order to do something?" I asked.

"I don't really believe that."

"Could you feel okay about something and still want to change it?"

She smiled softly. "Sure. How come I didn't think about that before? I do a lot of things that way. I've always thought if it was okay, you just left it that way."

"Do you believe that now?"

"It's silly. And you know what? I didn't change it by being unhappy anyway," she said.

"What do you want?" I asked.

"To see my father again. That's it," she declared emphatically. "I'm going to call him. Maybe he'll listen to me now."

"And if he doesn't?"

Dominique giggled. "I'll call him again and again and again until he does. Boy, it's nice not to be afraid."

During the next hour, she explored her feelings and thoughts about school and her peer group. While we talked we drew a picture using Nick's magic markers. It depicted her grandmother on a throne in the middle of New York harbor—an updated Statue of Liberty. Dominique drew a huge rubber tree, instead of a torch, in her right hand. On the bottom of this mini-masterpiece, I wrote an inscription.

"To Grandma . . . 'Nothing Fishy' by Dominique and the Bear."

THE BOOK OF SAM

The sun baked her face, sizzling the perspiration on her forehead and reddening the tip of her nose. Her fingers embraced the steering wheel of her convertible. She maneuvered the car to the curb directly in front of the main entrance of a huge, three-story building which stretched the length of the entire block. This brick-and-stone high school, built in the late nineteen-thirties, loomed like a fortress, cold and uninviting. Drawings decorated the bottom panels of one classroom, a dramatic counterpoint to the acres of empty glass panes. Lisa Millen released the clutch of her ancient Fiat, purposely stalling it in gear beneath a sign which indicated no parking. Somehow, today, especially today, it did not matter. Nothing mattered.

Black sunglasses hid her eyes; blond, windblown hair danced in front of her face. She stared at the familiar wood doors, their heavy brass hinges sealing

them tightly together in the stone frame...a mauso-
leum for grades eight through twelve. Though frozen
like stone in her seat, Lisa occasionally dragged heavily on the cigarette dangling from her mouth, oblivious
to the ashes collecting on her lap. Even the passing
students, who shouted suggestive remarks, could not
invade her space. Insulated. Numb. Detached from her
body, even her thoughts. She had dreamed about this
morning for many months, rehearsing the words to
herself, mouthing them in the mirror. Ironically, she
had not been elected, but volunteered. "Why did I offer?" she muttered to herself. Nausea licked the back
of her throat. Her father had expressed his willingness
to go, as did Chuck, a neighbor and friend. Yet, despite
her dread, the chore fell to her, supported her awareness that she had always known she would be the one
to tell Sammy.

The car door opened easily, too easily. Lisa walked
along the sidewalk hesitantly, then mounted the staircase with resistant legs. Her breathing seemed unusually heavy. She held her hand on the door handle for
several minutes. Faded conversations flooded her ears,
old faces drifted before her...memories aged and
slightly muddled since her graduation four years ago.
Once inside, she turned right and walked down the
familiar corridor, her eyes scrambling across bulletin
boards she had once helped decorate. Another century,
another lifetime, she mused.

No one in the office recognized her. The reception-
ist's curt greeting jarred her. As soon as she explained
her presence to a secretary, she was ushered into the
principal's office immediately. Within moments, a
monitor left in search of Sam. Lisa declined an offer to
use the office as a place to meet her brother. "Tell him
I'll be waiting for him outside the front entrance."

She sat on the stone stairs, her tall figure draped
over several steps. Popping another cigarette into her

mouth, she ignited it expertly while gazing into the park across the street. A group of boys, in blue-and-orange uniforms, played hockey under the supervision of two coaches. An airborne volley ball bounced off the head of a short, heavy girl and flew over the net menacingly. Several people played racket ball against huge walls designed expressly for that purpose. Everything seemed in its natural order; so steady, so unshakable. These people had replaced the ones she once knew, part of an endless cycle which confused her. Though she had spent four years of her life in this school, at this moment, it was as if she had never existed. Was death the same? she wondered... your chair, your bed, your clothes ultimately filled by other people, little by little eradicating your presence, leaving your life and loves locked in the memory of a few who, one day, might also forget.

The door opened behind her, but she did not turn around. Instead, Lisa held her breath, keeping her eyes focused on the activity across the street. Sam stared at his sister's back, holding his large hand over his mouth. Almost six feet tall, his lanky, surprisingly athletic form suggested a person much older than fourteen. His face seemed almost prematurely lined. He touched her shoulder, but withdrew his hand quickly when she did not respond.

"Lisa?" he said.

She rose slowly and faced him. The tears rolled down her cheeks to her own amazement. Despite the rehearsals, she had lost control.

"What?" Sam asked urgently, denying his own awareness.

When Lisa tried to talk, no words came. She put her arm around her brother and walked with him down the steps.

"Tell me," he insisted.

Drawing in a deep breath, she blurted out a garbled

sentence with only one very clear word ... "died."

"Who died? For God's sake. Grandma?"

Lisa shook her head as she bit her bottom lip. Very clearly, in a low and penetrating voice, she said, "Mommy. Not Grandma. Mommy died."

Sam stared wide-eyed at his sister. Adrenalin flooded his system, accelerating his heartbeat, lathering his skin with cold sweat. He pushed away from her, throwing his arm out over his head and twisting his body awkwardly as if responding to some internal eruption. Suddenly, his legs lunged forward, carrying him in a full sprint across the lawn into the street.

"Sammy, Sammy!" Lisa shouted, running after him.

When he reached the park, he ran onto the track, at first slipping on the leather soles of his shoes. Rebalancing himself, he plunged like a horse moving out of the starter's gate. His legs stretched in long, controlled strides. After the first quarter mile, he gained more speed, obviously moving faster and faster. His eyes appeared vacant; his movement studied.

Sitting on the empty bleachers, Lisa watched her brother, wanting to help, to comfort him, to be there and share the pain. But, like her, he had his own private way to absorb it, to integrate what they had all silently anticipated but had not accepted.

One of Sam's friends separated from the hockey team, apparently at the request of the coach, and jogged toward the track in search of an explanation for Sam's unauthorized appearance during what would normally be his third period English class. When Brian spotted Lisa, he slowed his pace, then finally stopped. He turned around, knowing not to intrude.

Sam pushed himself to continue even after completing the second mile. For him, track had been not only a sport, but also a way to find a certain energy level within, a surge akin to meditation. His arms reached forward; his fingertips gripping the air in an effort to propel his body at greater speeds. Not once did he look at his sister. Not once did he break his concentration. After three miles at a frenzied pace, he lost his momentum, having run himself out. Nevertheless, he continued, pursuing the face of his mother; hearing their last conversation repeated; knowing all the words had ended; aware he had said goodbye but wanting another chance . . . just one more minute, ten more seconds to tell her he loved her and would remember, would always remember.

Winded and drained, he dropped to the ground beside the track and rolled over onto his back. Beads of sweat bubbled on the surface of his face. His chest heaved, his body pulsating to the rhythm of his breathing. Lisa joined him, putting his head in her lap. Her fingers slid over his wet forehead and through his hair. She had never felt so loving toward him, so affectionate, so caring, so motherly.

He glared up at the clouds. "Funny," he said, his voice thin and cracking, "this was her favorite kind of day . . . those big cotton-candy clouds hanging so low. How come she died on her favorite day?"

Lisa hugged him. "Sammy, let go. If you want to cry . . . cry!"

"Do we have to go back now?"

"When you're ready, we'll go home."

"Is she still there?"

"No, Sammy, I think she's gone."

He rose to his feet, then helped his sister up. They walked hand in hand across the field. Sam hummed a melody from the *Peer Gynt* Suite, music his mother adored. He envisioned her lying in her bed, her eyes closed, a half-smile on her face as music filled her bedroom. Turning to his sister, he said, "Lisa, can I hug you?"

She nodded and held him tightly, feeling his body convulse as he cried.

*　　*　　*

He draped his long legs across the coffee table, letting his hands dangle from the sides of the chair. The growth of his nose had outpaced the rest of his face, giving him an awkward, gangly appearance, though not diminishing the strength of his deep-set eyes and angular jaw. His curly hair had been cropped close to his head with little regard for style.

Silence reigned for the last fifteen minutes. Sam's face tensed. He tapped out a drum rhythm on the table, while glancing around the room nervously, hopping from object to object without any sustained interest. Finally, he said: "There's nothing wrong with stopping track. It's a dumb sport anyway."

"How do you feel about that?" I asked.

"Great! Fine, just fine," he insisted.

"Then why the question?"

"You know why. Okay, it's not a dumb sport. I like track. I'm the best long distance runner in the county. But . . . but I can't, not now. Not while Ma's sick."

"What do you mean?"

"I have to get home and help after school. We take turns. My sister even comes from Manhattan a couple of times each week. Do we have to talk about this?"

"Is there something about our talk which disturbs you?"

"Yes. How can I feel better if all I think about is her being sick?" He turned his head, visibly upset.

"What are you disturbed about?"

"The damn game. It's called the smile game. Before my mother got sick, we smiled at lots of things. Now we're supposed to smile at everything. But you know what...nobody really feels the smiles. They're silly and I can't stand them!"

"What is it about them that you can't stand?"

"It's a lie, everybody's lying—me, Dad, Sis. Everybody's so full of shit with my mother. Dad says it's just a matter of time until Ma gets better." Sam rubbed his hands together. "Two nights ago, when I showed her my biology project, she smiled...and I could see the blood between her teeth." He winced uncomfortably. "That's why I can't go back to track."

"Because of the blood between her teeth?" I asked.

"Well...like all those kinds of things."

"I'm not sure what you mean...how does that relate to track?"

"Hey, man, my mother's very, very sick," Sam said. "I care about her, know what I mean? How can I go out and spend time at track?"

"What is it about spending time at track that you see as not okay to do since your mother's sick?"

"It's like laughing and horsing around while someone in the next room is not well...it's like making fun."

"Do you believe that?"

"Yes," Sam said firmly.

"Why do you believe that?"

"'Cause it's true."

"Okay...could you explain how it happens, how track would be making fun?"

He rose from the chair and walked out onto the deck. Sam shook his head like a young colt. Within seconds, he spun around and marched back into the room. "Look, track for me is having fun, having a good time. How could I have fun while she's so darn sick?"

"What do you believe that would mean?" I asked.

"That I didn't care."

"Why do you believe it would mean you didn't care?"

"When someone you care about doesn't feel good," he asserted, "you don't feel good either."

"Sammy, that might be your experience, but why does it happen?"

"It's natural."

"What do you mean?"

"That's the way it happens." He flopped down on the couch, his long limbs dangling in every direction.

"I understand that's what you have usually experienced," I said. "But what is it about your mother's feeling bad that makes you feel bad?"

"Because I don't want her to feel bad and be sick."

"Not wanting her to feel bad is very different than your feeling bad when she does. Why do you feel bad, Sammy?"

"I don't know any more. I'm getting confused. You ask the weirdest questions."

I smiled at him, then suggested: "Let me try another one on you. Sammy, what are you afraid would happen if you didn't feel bad when your mother died?"

"It'd mean I didn't care about her," he said shaking his head as if denying his words.

"Do you believe that?"

"Yes, no. Maybe more no. Last week, we went to the countywide debating match. Our school placed second. I really had a great time, a fantastic time 'cause I knew my stuff cold. I was so into it, I forgot about everything. I wasn't feeling bad then, but I know I still, somehow, cared about Ma."

"So does having fun mean you don't care," I queried.

"I guess not. They're two different things. I can see that now. Guess I thought I was supposed to be miserable all the time."

"And now?"

"I don't have to do that. But . . . but wait a minute. Everyone else won't understand . . . they won't agree, they'll be like I was before today. If they see me laughing or horsing around, they'll think I don't care."

"Who's they?"

"My dad, sis, my friends at school. That'll be really awful!"

"Why?" I asked.

"Because it wouldn't be true."

"And if what they thought was untrue, why would that disturb you?"

"It wouldn't matter that it was untrue. I just wouldn't want them to think that."

"Why not?"

"I know it's going to sound stupid," he said, 'but I'd feel embarrassed."

"Why, Sammy?"

"They'd, maybe, think bad things about me, not want to be with me, ignore me like a freak."

"Do you believe that?"

He looked away sheepishly. "No," he grinned, "not really. Boy I say a lot of things I don't believe."

"Sometimes, Sammy, when we say and hear what we think, we can see it more clearly. Maybe that's why so many people talk to themselves, to get it out there and look at it."

"I'm the kind that doesn't talk to himself," he observed. "You know what I said before about them thinking I didn't care ... well, I don't know if that's true. Maybe some would, you know, put me down ... that's a great sport in my class. At least Brian and Allen would understand. But what about Dad?"

"What about him?"

"He loves Ma so much, he's so miserable about what's going on ... I mean, underneath all those smiles. He wouldn't understand about track. He'd tell me I was thinking only about myself and not Ma."

"And how would you feel about that?"

"It wouldn't be true. I could still help out, just like I do. The coach said I could work out with the team two afternoons each week, then practice on my own. Lisa comes Tuesday and Thursday, so they don't really need me. Besides, on those days, all I do is sit around the living room depressed."

"How come, Sammy?"

"I don't know. There's nothing to do. Sometimes, I think I'm just there to show them I care, to show Ma it matters," he blurted out. His mouth dropped open in response to his own words.

"What is it?" I asked.

"You know, that's what I'm doing. It's like all the other games in my house. I never realized I was doing that. It felt so automatic." He laughed self-consciously, then nodded. "You want to hear something crazy I just remembered? One time I got into the football game on TV and started rooting for the Jets. As soon as I heard someone coming downstairs, I looked away from the set. I can almost remember making sure I looked sad so they'd know and not think the wrong things. Wow!" He cleared his throat and continued. "I don't know if they would understand about track. Maybe, if I explained it to them ... but, but I'm afraid."

"Afraid of what?"

"What happens if they don't understand?"

"Maybe that would be a nice question for you to answer," I said.

He laughed. "I guess I could go back to hanging around in the living room with a sad face." He smiled, shaking his head up and down. "You know, that's the first time I laughed in a long time. I guess I didn't think it was okay to laugh while Ma's so sick."

"And now?"

"It's okay. I mean here I am doing it. So what!" He paused, inhaled a deep breath and said, "Yeah, maybe I could go back to track ... maybe if I talked to them. Ma could be sick a long time and what's the difference since she's going to get ... to get better." He looked down in his lap. "That's another thing, Bears, suppose, just suppose, she doesn't get better."

"What about it?"

"Well, you see, the kind of cancer she has is with her bones. I don't understand all of it, but now her bones break easy. She had a bad cold two weeks ago and, from coughing, she broke two ribs. Now she's bandaged all around her chest. There's other things, too. She's awful sick, I know it—but nobody really talks to me about it. Maybe my father's wrong, maybe the doctors are wrong, maybe they're all lying. That really scares me."

"What about it frightens you?"

Sam squeezed his eyes shut, holding back. "I don't want her to . . . to not be here."

"I understand. But what about that possibility frightens you?"

His breathing came forced. "It's my mother. Nobody else cares about me like her. She's, well, sort of my best friend, you know what I mean. I need, I . . ." The words became garbled as he started to cry. Several minutes passed before he could continue. "No matter what I do, I'm always, kind of, you know, okay with her. It's not the same with Dad or Sis. Ma and I have something special." Sam bowed his head, then put his hand over his eyes.

"What is it, right now, that you're most unhappy about?"

"Think it might be over and she wouldn't be here and I'd be all alone."

"What do you mean, Sammy?"

"Nobody would feel about me the way she does. Dad's into his work, Lisa's doing her bit at college. Nobody really has time for me except my mother. That's pretty special. I know it sounds silly. I'm almost fifteen and I have a lot of friends and stuff," he sighed. "I guess I never thought about any of this until she got sick last year. When I was in the sixth grade, Ellen Ringer's mother died. She used to be such a great kid, but ever since then she's different...weird, alone. I know she's miserable. Maybe that's what happens."

"Do you believe that?"

A half-smile creased his face. "Not really. There I go again with my 'not really.' Even when everyone said Ellen was a great person, I thought she was weird. Only, I guess, she got weirder." His eyes filled with tears. "I just can't imagine Ma not being here."

"What about her not being here disturbs you?"

"It's not fair."

"In what way?"

"Most people live till they're old, even really old like my grandparents." He paused, then closed his eyes. "I don't think I'd be okay without her."

"What do you mean?" I asked.

"Well," Sam said, "if I can't talk to anybody like I do to her, then I'd be more mixed up."

"Do you believe that?"

"Sort of."

"Why?" I asked.

"I don't know. I guess I'd get along, but it doesn't feel like it."

"What are you afraid would happen if you felt you'd be okay without her?"

"Then she wouldn't matter," he declared.

"Are you saying by seeing yourself unhappy about her, she then becomes more important...she matters more?"

"Yeah, I guess," he said. "If I wasn't unhappy about her not being here, then she couldn't have mattered."

"Do you believe that, Sammy?"

He smirked.

"Why are you smiling?"

"'Cause it's like what we talked about before with the track team. Not having fun, feeling bad to know you cared and to show it."

"Could you not worry about being unhappy and still care?"

"Yes," he admitted. "I don't know if that's so easy, but yeah. You know, sometimes I think I made the whole thing up...that stuff about a special relationship with Ma. I want to do what's right!"

"What do you mean?"

"I want to care. Sometimes, it's a pain to help her all the time and I feel awful when I think it's a pain."

"Why?"

"'Cause if I was a good son," he said, "I wouldn't think those kinds of things."

"Do you believe that?"

"Well, Lisa never complains, nor does my father. At least they never tell me. When I think about staying with the guys and playing some ball after school, I feel horrible."

"Why?" I asked.

"'Cause I shouldn't think about those things, at least not now."

"Why not?"

He crossed his legs and vibrated his left foot nervously. "Everybody in the house is counting on me, for my part anyway."

"What are you afraid would happen if you didn't feel bad about those kinds of thoughts...like staying after school?" I queried.

"That maybe I'd think about them more often and maybe I'd stay," he declared.

"Do you believe that?"

"I did when I said it, but as soon as you asked that question, I knew it wasn't true. The answer is no...I wouldn't stay, I'd go home."

"Okay. Then do you still see those thoughts as bad?"

"I guess they're okay. I kept thinking they'd mean I'd suddenly decide not to help. You know what, I like this talking out loud stuff." He rubbed his eyes and sighed. "Bears, do you think it's okay to sometimes feel helping with Ma is a pain?"

"If I told you what I thought, Sammy, I'd just be telling you about my beliefs and my reasons. It wouldn't really help you focus on what you believe. So maybe, it'd be more productive if you answered the question. Is it okay to see helping out as a pain?"

"This morning it wasn't—now, well, it's okay. I could still care and sometimes think that."

"Sammy, what does the word pain mean?"

He smiled. "When I don't want to do it, I call it a pain. Silly, huh? I guess if you said it wasn't okay to do that, then I wouldn't know what to think."

"Why, Sammy?"

"Because maybe," he said purposely avoiding my eyes, "maybe, I'm only being selfish."

"Do you believe that?"

"In a way," he said.

"Why do you believe it?" I questioned.

"Everybody else just thinks about Mom all the time. With me, it's different."

"Let's talk about your observation. Unless you can crawl inside someone else's head, you can't really know what they're thinking all the time. Maybe your father and sister think about your mom all the time, maybe not. But you can never be sure of either conclusion," I said, allowing a lapse of several seconds before I continued. "For the moment, let's assume your assessment is correct . . . they only think about your mother and you are different, you think about other things as well. What's selfish about that?"

"I'm only thinking about me, things that are important to me. With my mother, it's different."

"What do you mean?"

"When I'm with my mother," he asserted, "I'm there for her, not me."

"How's that?"

"Well, I help her get things, make her tea. Sometimes, when she's tired, I feed her like she used to feed me when I was sick."

"Okay, you help her when you are there, you do things to make it easier for her. But why are you there?"

"To do that, to make things easier for her. That's what I want to do."

"Why do you want to do that?" I asked.

"There's no answer," he insisted. "I just want to do it, Bears."

"Maybe if you can guess at an answer, something will come. Hear the question. Why do you want to help make things easier for your mother?"

"For her and, if I guessed, I'd say it makes me feel good inside."

"Now that you've said that, does it sound true for you?"

"Yes," he smiled.

"So then a reason for doing it is the good feelings you get inside. If you didn't get that good feeling, do you think you'd want to do it?"

"Probably not," he answered. "I'd still do it, but I don't think I'd want to."

"So are you saying you want to?"

"Uh-huh."

"Then if you want to and you get this good feeling, are you there for you?"

He nodded. "I never realized that before. Somehow it all got mixed up. I always thought when you are there for yourself, that's selfish, that's bad, but I guess you're always there for yourself in some way. That's incredible! I really understand a lot more now. But what about staying after school?"

"What about it? Is it okay to want to stay with your friends after school?"

"Yeah!" he replied. "Definitely. But you know what,

I still want to go home and help out more. Funny, I was afraid, deep down, I really didn't want to help, like I had to and that was the only reason." As he rose to leave, he nodded his head. "I love my mother. I guess I don't use that word too often out there. It's nice to know I love her and still can think about going back to the track team. I'm going to try."

"To try for what?"

"To help out at home," he reaffirmed, "and, at the same time, train with the team on my free afternoons. I know I'm smiling, Bears. I feel good about what we talked about, but there's things I didn't say." He shuddered.

"If you want, next time, we can explore some of the things we didn't get to today. There will always be something to know, Sammy, if you look. See you next week."

*   *   *

The incessant drone of the television filtered through the house like stale smoke, infectious and anonymous. Shafts of sunlight bathed the early American furniture in the living room and danced off antique picture frames housing tapestries of another era. The dining room set, a modest reproduction of a museum piece, appeared so neat that the chairs seemed as if they might have been unoccupied for many years. A wooden cane leaned against the wall in the entrance foyer, a room noticeably clean and spartan.

In contrast, the kitchen, cluttered with empty plates, soiled napkins and silverware, seemed the victim of a recent cyclone. Three bags of garbage stood in front of the cabinet under the sink.

Sam threw his books on the kitchen table, narrowly missing two bowls which represented breakfast for both him and his father. After he poured a glass of milk, he searched the breadbox for rolls or doughnuts, a scavenger willing to accept whatever he could find. Only stale bread greeted his probing fingers. He muttered when he opened the refrigerator. Suddenly, he groaned, pausing in the midst of his hunt. He quickly slammed the door, walked back into the entrance hall, and scooted up the stairs three at a time.

Propped up with pillows against the headboard, Darlene Millen slept uncomfortably in a sitting position. Her drawn and bony face seemed oddly strained. Wisps of brown hair fell stiffly like straw against her hollow cheeks. Her lips were parched and cracked; her eyelids puffy and black. The crow's feet around her eyes suggested a perpetual grimace, aging her face in excess of her forty-two years.

In one hand, she held the remote control unit for the barking television set, which continued to perform in spite of the lack of audience. In the other hand she gripped an empty coffee cup, her thin fingers wrapped tightly around the handle. On the floor beside her, a stainless steel bedpan, filled to the brim, grew like a mechanical mushroom out of the floral design of the thick oriental rug. Piles of books, magazines and newspapers decorated the top of the bureau. A portable hospital tray, complete with casters, hung over the bed. A half-eaten meal lay wasted on its shiny Formica surface. A thick odor embraced the room like an invisible wreath.

Mrs. Millen winced as she coughed, her hands automatically holding her chest. She never opened her eyes, just let herself slip back into the comfort of sleep. Sam watched from the doorway. He barely remembered his mother before the sickness ravaged her body. The smooth skin and bright eyes were gone. Her new face, as he called it, dominated his vision of her. For him, the last two years had all but eradicated the twelve preceding. The trips to the beach, Sunday breakfasts in the kitchen, and barbecues on the back lawn had become mere footnotes of a distant memory; a faded photograph he could not restore.

As he stood at the foot of the bed, he surveyed the tense face contorted in sleep, a bleak testament to pain and endurance.

"Ma," he whispered. No response. "Ma, it's me, Sammy. I'm here."

Lifting her eyelids like weights, Darlene managed a slight smile. "Oh, Sammy, how come you're here?"

"It's Wednesday, Ma, my day," he said.

"Why did I think it was Thursday? Guess when you live in one room, one day isn't much different than the next. Come, sit down, tell me about school."

The ritual bored him, yet he proceeded to describe his day, discussing his math lesson with inflated enthusiasm, then detailing a chemistry experiment in depth. His mother, occasionally letting her eyes close for short periods of time, seemed more relaxed than before. Her son's voice comforted her, bringing activity and life into her shrinking world.

"If I had to learn what you kids learn, I could never make it today," she observed.

"Ah, it's not that hard, Ma," he observed. "Do you want something?"

"No. I'm not hungry—must be those new pills Dr. Walker gave me. Been nauseous all morning." She struggled with her next request.

"Um, ah . . ."

Sam, correctly anticipating her words, interrupted her. "I'm going to empty the pan. Be back in a second." He lifted the metal container, balancing it carefully in his arms. Breathing only through his mouth, he avoided looking directly into the murky liquid. After he poured the contents into the toilet, he used the bathtub spout to run water into the pain. The room began to spin. Sam sat on the rim of the tub, bent down over his knees and placed his head between his legs until the dizziness passed. Once the water ran clear in the pan, he returned to the bedroom.

His mother became absorbed in a soap opera, although her eyes wavered at half-staff. "Sammy, sit with me for awhile."

"In a minute, Ma. Let me take this stuff downstairs," he said, indicating the half-empty yogurt container and bowl of tuna salad. After dumping the leftover food into a bulging garbage bag in the kitchen, he sat down at the table. He held his head in his hands, trying to overcome the nausea. Every afternoon started the same way ... with the bedpan, then the stomach pains. He ignored the glass of milk on the counter, rocking back and forth on the chair like an infant soothing himself with the rhythm of his own body. Twenty minutes passed before he could bring himself to return.

"Come, sit," his mother motioned. Sammy eased onto the other side of the bed, then focused on the television. More than an hour passed without either of them speaking.

Sam broke the silence. "Do you want something to drink?"

"No. I'm okay. If there's anything you want to do, don't mind me, I'll be alright."

"Well," he said, "maybe I could do some homework, but the TV wigs me out."

She flicked the remote control switch with her thumb, extinguishing both sound and picture.

Parking himself on the floor, Sam started his math assignment. He chewed on a pencil as he worked. Darlene Millen leafed through a mystery novel until she located a folded page. She cleared her throat several times as if she intended to speak, but then lowered her head to begin reading. They both became absorbed in their separate involvements. Another hour passed.

Darlene muffled a cough, throwing a quick smile to her son. She tried unsuccessfully to suppress a second cough, then a third. Wide-eyed, she held her ribs as her body convulsed, overcome by the hacking spasms. Sam ran into the bathroom, then sprinted back into the room, spilling half the water out of the glass. She sipped some, but her coughing continued. Frightened, Sam pressed his hands against her ribs. They both pushed desperately against her chest cavity. His mother managed another weak smile, coughed several more times, then collapsed against the pillows. Perspiration dripped from her forehead. The muscles on the right side of her face twitched. Sam used a towel to dry her skin. He tried to steady his hand as he offered her more water.

"I'll be okay," she assured him, pushing away. "It's probably a reaction to the new medicine. Now don't look so concerned, Sammy, I'm fine."

He smiled, swallowing his own vomit several times. "I'm not so concerned," he said. "You're going to be fine. Maybe next month, you'll be out of bed. Dad said so." His mother turned away, focusing her attention out the window. "Anyway," he continued, "I'm not the greatest nurse."

"You do fine," she said authoritatively.

He stared into her face, tongue-tied, wanting to scream, choking on the knot growing in his stomach. "Well," Sam suggested in a purposely sedated voice, "want to watch more of the boob-tube?" When she nodded, he picked up the remote unit and tuned in a game show. Too upset to return to his homework, he watched the program with her, barely absorbing the electronic pantomime.

Another hour passed until Chad Millen arrived home, carrying Chinese food in a brown paper bag. Tall and slender, he moved with an easy agility, but his eyes seemed aged and sad.

"Well, well, two of my three favorite people in one room," he declared as he kissed his wife and tapped his son on the shoulder. "How did it go today, honey?"

"Fine," Darlene smiled. "Just fine. You know, Sammy's doing wonderful things in chemistry. Right, Sammy?" He nodded his affirmation.

"You guys mind if I go downstairs now?" Sam asked his parents.

"Hey, I just got home," Chad said. "How about a little time together? All of us."

Sam sat down on the edge of the bed. "What do you want to talk about, Dad?"

"Everything. Anything. You see the Jets' game to-day? Some spectacular quarterbacking." Suddenly he stopped himself. "Hey, Darl, I'm sorry, that's got to be boring for you."

"No, no, please go on," she said, settling back for the inevitable—an intense commentary on football, followed by some quips about his office and the inequity of taxes.

Sam watched his father's lips, but never heard a word.

* * *

The evening dew wet the lawn beneath my sneakers as I walked toward the track. The school building and athletic fields, alive with students during the day, were deserted. A brisk wind pushed the clouds rapidly along the horizon. Darkness enveloped the fence and the black gravel path which formed into an oval behind it.

Sam had phoned two days before, requesting this as the site for his next session. He convinced me quite easily, since I usually jogged several times each week. He called it a celebration. After what he characterized as an easy discussion with his parents, he had visited his coach and rejoined the team.

Stepping in front of the bleachers, I searched the blackness, finally detecting the hazy figure of a runner moving gracefully into the far turn. His legs glided out easily from beneath his athletic form, touching the ground so lightly, so silently that I questioned my vision.

Then a familiar voice bellowed across the field. "Hey, Bears."

"Hey, Sam," I shouted back. If we were both on schedule, as planned, he would be finishing his seventh mile. We would do the last three together.

"Number seven going down. Go ahead," he counseled, "start, I'll catch up."

After taking three deep cleansing breaths, I leaned forward slightly to generate that initial thrust, pushing off with my toes until the motion of my legs began to carry me. The wind filled my lungs with an invigorating coolness. It whipped through my hair and made my eyes tear. As I rounded the first turn, Sam came alongside. No strained face. No panting chest. He seemed perfectly relaxed, like a casual stroller; his long limber strides awesome in their ease.

"You're serious about this, right?" I questioned. "If you can ask the question, I can answer it," he assured me. "The wind works against you on this side, but it'll carry you on the way back. Fall into it with your body—it'll help."

"Will do," I acknowledged.

"You know, both my parents really understood about the team," he began, speaking in a loud voice. "What a surprise! In fact, they called it a mature move ... get that, a mature move," he repeated, delighted with the words. "Everybody on the team has been so nice. I really missed it." He smiled and nodded at the same time. "Been thinking a lot about caring this week. Good stuff. Except, well, there's something that bothers me."

"What?" I asked.

"The pains in my stomach ... right here," he said, pointing to an area just below his diaphragm.

"What about them?"

"They're getting worse. Especially on certain days."

"Which days are those, Sammy?"

"I know you know. The days I help out with my mother. They really take over. Last time I really got scared."

"What about them frightened you?"

"I know it'll sound crazy, being I'm still young and all, but I don't want to get sick or get an ulcer. A kid in my class has one. He's a wreck. Boy, that's all we need now."

"Do you think your stomach pains means you're getting sick?"

"Yes. I don't care what the doctor said. A couple of weeks ago I told Papa Max, my grandfather. I didn't want to worry Dad. Papa Max promised he wouldn't tell anyone if I went to the doctor with him. I had to drink this white chalk for the X-rays—it was awful. Big deal, the man said I was as healthy as a horse, nothing wrong except I had to learn to relax. He gave me some medicine, but it makes me sleepy. I'm not stupid, they were tranquilizers—I could tell because some of the kids sell the same stuff in the lunchroom. Maybe the pills made the pain better, but they sure don't stop them from happening."

"Okay," I said as we rounded the first quarter mile. "Describe the pains, when do you first notice them, how long do they last?"

"Like I said, they happen mostly when I'm with Ma. Sometimes I just lift the bedpan and I can feel them. They get so bad I think I'm going to choke. Once it starts, it can last all night. I want to be with her, I do," he asserted adamantly. "I want to help, but it's really hard."

"What's hard about it?"

"Have you ever carted what's in a bedpan?" I nodded my head. He seemed surprised. "Then you know!"

"Sammy, my reaction to carting a bedpan is mine,

yours is yours. Although we might have done the exact same activity, our feelings about it could be very different. What's hard for you in carrying the pan?"

"The shit, for Christ's sake, the shit. I get nauseous every time I look at it and let me tell you, I never, never look directly into it. I get sick just from the little I catch out of the corner of my eye."

"What's sickening about it?"

"What it looks like. The odor."

"Why is that sickening?" I asked as we completed our second full revolution of the track, marking the first half mile.

"It's just sickening," he answered. "Maybe I'm just allergic to it or something. Every time I pick it up, I feel that way."

"What's your first thought when you pick it up?"

"That it's hers. My own mother's." He shook his head several times. "I think if it was someone else's, then, maybe, it'd be different. But it's not somebody else's."

"Sammy, why because it's your mother's do you find it so sickening?"

"I know what it means, damn. I really do," he said, shouting his response.

"What do you think it means?" I asked.

"She's . . . she's . . ." He aborted the sentence, squinting his eyes angrily.

"She's what, Sammy?"

"I can't say it. I can't think it. At first, I thought I couldn't because nobody in the house ever talked about it. But it's different. I can't say it."

"Why not?"

"Maybe it'll happen if I do," he said.

"Are you saying that if you say something, that will cause it to happen?"

"Sounds crazy, doesn't it? Somehow, if you say it, it becomes real, and I don't want it to be real. Yet I can't stop thinking about it. I can't."

"Why do you believe saying it will make it come true?"

"I don't know, Bears. I don't know why I believe it. Maybe it's like thinking a bad thought."

"What do you mean?"

"Look what happens every time I pick up the bedpan. I feel nauseous, dizzy, like I'm going to puke."

"Are you saying the thought makes you that way?" I asked.

"Not exactly," he replied. "When I think it, that's the way I feel."

"Why is that?"

"'Cause I don't want it to happen. Sometimes I can talk about her not being here, but not the other way?"

"Using the word," he said. "How come words are so powerful?"

"They're not. They only have the power we give them. One man screams something vulgar and another person gets upset. Another man screams the same thing and nobody cares. It depends, Sammy. It depends on what we believe about the words."

"Well," he said, "in my house, certain words are very important. They're the ones nobody uses. It's like that word . . . cancer. Ma had it all the time, yet my father only said cancer once and by accident. He never used the other word. Never!"

"Do you want to share what that other word is?"

"Not yet. I'm not ready yet. Could we stop talking now?"

"Why?"

"Let's just finish. I'll meet you on the bleachers." He lunged forward, increasing his speed significantly for the last mile. I followed his lead, pushing myself until I came alongside of him. Sam held his mouth strangely ajar; his eyes bulged. His strained appearance had little to do with his running.

When I became winded, I concentrated on one distant point . . . the marker at the far end of the track. Sam broke through the imaginary barrier first, completing his tenth mile. I finished my third, easing into a trot, then finally a walk. We paced each other around for another quarter-mile. Sam kept a substantial distance between us.

I sat half-Lotus style on the top bench of the bleachers. Sam dangled his body over three levels. A silver light bathed his face.

"I'm . . . I, it," he stuttered, squeezing out the words with extreme difficulty. "When I . . . lift the, the pan, I know! I know! I know!" He began to shout. His fingers dug into his face. "I know. Nobody will tell me, but I know! She's . . . she's . . . she's going to . . . die." He stood up, snapping his body off the wood plank, and gaped at me—surprised, confused, relieved. For a long time, he held his breath, his body remaining rigid, frozen at attention like a young soldier. The wind rippled through his hair moving his curls like grain in the fields. Suddenly, he groaned and dropped down on the bench.

"Sammy, how do you feel?"

"Weak. Like I have a fever." He stared down at the track and said, "Die. Die. Die. Oh, God, I was so scared to say it. Thought it a thousand times, but couldn't say it. And now, look. Die. Die." He smiled queerly. "It's not so bad. Why did I think it would be so bad? When I was eight, I had a parakeet. Its name was Chipper. Boy, I loved that dumb bird, always getting out of the cage and flying all over the house. One day when I came home from school, it wasn't there. They said it flew away, out the door. Well, I looked for it for days and days. I kept calling him in the backyard. Maybe Chipper was cold or hungry. I cried myself to sleep every night for weeks. Then, Lisa, I guess she couldn't stand listening to me any more, came into my room and told me. She said my parents lied, that Chipper had died and there was no use in looking for him any more. No use at all. I hated my parents for that, for all the times I looked for nothing. Then I thought, if they couldn't tell me, dying must be terrible. Everything clanged. Chipper wasn't coming back. Dying meant not coming back, no hope to make it change."

"How does the word apply in your mom's case?"

"It's like making it real by saying it could happen. I guess I don't want it to be real." Tears flooded his eyes. "But it is, Bears, I know it is. In my history book, pictures of all the great men have dates under them. When they were born; when they died. It's so matter of fact in class. You never think about it being you or someone you know. I wonder if she knows?"

"Who?"

"My mother. Sometimes, I see her looking at her face in the mirror. I wonder what she's thinking. But she's doing it, too. Nobody talks about it. I wish...I wish we would. It's much more scary when we don't." He began to cry.

"What is it, Sammy?"

"Why can't dying be happy? Why does it have to be so sad?"

"Why does it make you unhappy?" I questioned.

"Because I'll miss her, I really will. I thought about what I said...about our special relationship. That was a lie, it really was. She's always nice to me, but we don't talk. There's so many things I can't tell her...or him."

"Why not?"

"It's that same stuff again. In my house, you don't talk about everything, just some things."

"What are you afraid would happen if you talked about the things you wanted to talk about?"

"They'd get mad."

"Since you don't talk about those things, how do you know that?"

He grinned weakly. "Well, maybe they wouldn't—but maybe they would."

"And if they did get mad, then what?" I asked.

"Then nothing," he concluded, shrugging his shoulders. "That's the big joke. They'd get mad, maybe yell, and that would be the worst of it." He shook his head back and forth. "Isn't it a riot? The way it felt, you'd think the atomic bomb would go off when I opened my mouth."

"And now?"

"It's all beginning to look different. I've always been afraid of words, but you don't have to be, you can use them . . . like now, like right now. I'm sick of the football crap, the TV, the 'what-did-you-do-in-school' questions. Nobody asks me how I feel. Never. And I guess I learned really well, because I don't tell them either."

"What do you want, Sammy?"

"To talk more, like this."

"How are you feeling?"

"Better. Everything doesn't seem so dark."

* * *

Chad Millen cleared the table, rinsed the dishes before placing them into the dishwasher, then wiped the counter with fast, efficient movements. No hesitations. No wasted energy. He took special pride in his ability to meet any challenge, any difficulty. As a stockbroker, he endured a roller-coaster economy, managing to earn a substantial income despite the dramatic fluctuations in the market. If he could accomplish that feat, he believed he could do anything. Although he never viewed himself as a winner, he took refuge in the fact he always found a way to survive.

Initially, his wife's illness threatened to disturb the balance, placing a foreign, unwelcome pressure on him. Yet, despite the erosion of his confidence and the increased demands on his time, he met every obligation . . . bread-winner, father, surrogate mother, part-time cook and house cleaner. Again, he proved he could survive. When the doctor suggested a full-time nurse, he wouldn't hear of it, volunteering himself and his children to care for his wife. There was never a question of money . . . only, perhaps, a question of style. He considered his alternative highly successful not only in rendering the needed services to his wife, but also in bringing the family closer together. Not once did Chad ever doubt his own conclusion, nor did he ever substantiate them by soliciting the feelings of his children.

The ceiling in the kitchen acted like a baffle for the television set which blared from the master bedroom above. The crackling of gunfire, explosions and screams filled the room. Chad found the noise soothing, a predictable lullabye, a mindless anti-depressant. "Thank God for that set," he thought to himself, paying silent tribute to the electronic companion which he believed had diverted Darlene from thinking about her situation. The buzzer on the coffee machine drew his attention. He pushed a blue button, then poured himself a cup of the black liquid. Settling down by the table, he immersed himself in the *Wall Street Journal*. Though he had read the paper once on the train, he took comfort in a second reading, occasionally testing his memory and surprising himself with his ability to retain information.

Sam walked into the kitchen silently, his sneakers cushioning his footsteps. His father looked up, startled. "Hey, how about a little noise or something? You could scare someone half to death that way."

The word lunged out of the sentence—the very word which had dominated Sam's thoughts since his last session. Death. Dying. The taboo subject, one among many. Ironically his father had used it, though in an impersonal context. "I'll be sure to wear my boots next time," Sam said.

"No sarcastic remarks now. Sit down, I'll be finished

in a minute." Chad scanned the last several pages quickly. The self-satisfied smile on his face seemed stiff and oddly familiar to his son, like an old mask, overused and unconvincing. Rubbing his hands together briskly, he said, "So, how'd it go at school today?"

"You really want to know?"

"Yes, I really want to know!" his father insisted, slightly offended by his son's question.

"Well, in Social Science II, we watched film strips on inventors and their early inventions like the cotton gin, the telephone, the steam engine. In math, we learned two more theorems in solid geometry. In English, my teacher bored us to death with a lecture on *A Portrait of the Artist As a Young Man* by James Joyce. Boy, he writes a lot better than my teacher talks. In gym... let me see, oh yes, in gym we did the same old calisthenics, the same old running and jumping exercises. What else? Wait, wait, I know there's something else." Itemizing his courses with his fingers and his words, he said: "Social science, math, English, gym... ah, yes, yes, I have it. How could I forget? Dear Dr. Jacobs, my chem instructor, started a fire in the lab. That was the most exciting part of the day." He noticed his father stealing glances at the paper while he talked. "Dad?"

"Uh-huh?"

"What book did we discuss in my English class?"

"Whatever you said."

"I know what I said, I just wanted to see if you were listening."

"Sammy, I was listening and I refuse to be tested," Chad said, his face flushed. "I don't know what's getting into you lately. I thought those sessions would calm you down."

"I don't need to be calmed down. I'm not the one who's angry!"

Chad eyed his son suspiciously. "I'm not changing

my mind; we all decided, especially your take-charge grandfather, that it would be good for you to talk to Mr. Kaufman. But what do you get out of those conversations anyway?"

"Plenty," he replied. "They really help."

"Good, that's good," Chad said. He forced a smile, unwilling to probe further, than allowed the paper to attract his attention once again.

"Dad, can we talk?"

Detecting a change in his son's voice, Chad, camouflaging his annoyance, folded his hands on the table and said, "Sure. We always talk. You don't need to make an announcement."

"Maybe I do," Sam said. "Maybe I do because I don't mean the kind of talk we just began. I'm talking about saying things straight to each other."

"I still don't understand what you're talking about," his father retorted. "I always talk straight to you. That's the way everyone is in this house. What are you getting at?"

"What about Ma?"

"What about her?" Chad barked.

"Please," Sam said. "I don't want you to be angry."

Chad exhaled a deep breath, then said, "I'm not angry. Just a little short these days. I don't mean to jump on you. What about your mother?"

"How is she?" Sam asked, his voice almost a whisper.

"Well, Dr. Welker changed the medicine again. The results are promising. Nothing for you to worry about. She'll probably be up and around in a month. By that time, you won't remember she was ever sick."

"But, Dad, that's what you said two months ago."

"What is this ... an inquisition? Forget what I said two months ago. Listen to what I say now. She'll be fine."

"How can you be sure? Did the doctor say she would be fine in a month?"

Folding the paper carefully, Chad fumed. "I don't think I like you talking this way to me, do you hear?" Sam nodded his head. "Furthermore, we're all under a great strain. Let's not quarrel."

"Do you want some juice?" Sam asked, retreating from the table.

"No. I'm still not finished with this cup of coffee."

Edging back toward his father, Sam spoke quietly. "I really don't want to fight. I'd like to talk. Can't we talk?"

"Well, I think we talked enough for tonight." Chad looked down at the folded paper and started to read the two exposed columns.

"Is Ma going to die?"

"Where the hell did you get that idea? She's doing fine. You hear! That's it, that's it, she's doing fine." He shook his head, avoiding his son's eyes. "I don't want any more of that kind of talk. No more."

"But I think about it, Dad, all the time. If I think about it, why can't I talk about it?"

"That's not the question. The question is whether you're going to listen to me or not. If I say the discussion is over, it's over. Finished! Now I don't have to keep going on with you. It's late, go to bed."

Sam left the kitchen, only to return several minutes later. "Dad?"

"You're really pushing it tonight, Sammy. I thought I told you to go to bed."

"I care about Ma very much, very much. So I'd like to say something."

"I guess you'll go on forever unless I let you get it off your chest," Chad sighed. "Okay, you care about your mother. Now what?"

Drawing in a deep breath, Sam's eyelids quivered as he faced his father directly and said: "I think she's going to die . . . soon."

Jumping out of his chair, Chad slapped Sam across

the face; the impact threw him against the cabinets. He grabbed his son by the shirt and raised his hand again.

"Go ahead," Sam said coldly. "It won't change what I think, it won't change it." Chad hesitated. His body trembled as he glared at his son. Then he surrendered himself to his anger and brought his hand down against his son for the second time, slamming him to the floor. The boy started crying. His father turned away swiftly and stormed out of the house.

Holding on to the side of the counter, he pulled himself off the floor, dazed, beyond tears. Like a zombie, he began to clear the table, going through the motions, the ritual, mechanically rinsing the coffee cup and juice glass, then placing them neatly into the dishwasher. He couldn't remember the last time his father hit him. His face felt hot and swollen. Sam stopped himself from crying again.

"Dad," he called, inching his way toward the entrance hall. "Dad, are you there?"

The front door was wide open. Nervously, Sam backed into the kitchen. Had his father gone crazy? Without delaying any longer, he ran outside, never looking back, never noticing his mother balanced uncomfortably on her cane as she leaned against the wall at the top of the stairs.

The street was deserted. He searched the darkness, looking for his father in the shadows. "Pop! Pop!" No response. Suddenly, he noticed the figure of a man sitting on a bench in front of the park. He ran down the street, feeling very alone. The sound of his sneakers slapping the pavement bounced off the houses and reverberated in his ears. As he approached the bench, he stopped running, becoming more cautious with each step. Sam recognized the man's shirt. Then he heard it; the unfamiliar and devastating sound of his father sobbing. He had never seen him cry. He thought of running away, but stopped himself. Fighting back his own tears, he drew nearer to the bench, peering at the hunched figure and the hands cupping his head. Sam was no longer afraid.

Sitting beside his father, he put his hand on the man's shoulder. He didn't speak, just sat there quietly, waiting. After several minutes, the sobbing ended. Chad had spent his emotions.

He rose from the bench unsteadily, turned away from his son, then spoke in a voice barely audible. "I'm sorry, Sammy. If I could cut off my hand, I would. I know I can't take it back. In a way, it had nothing to do with you."

"It's okay, Dad. I got a hard head."

Chad nodded. "Thought I had it under control. I guess I don't. You see, Sammy, I believed if we all just thought good thoughts, remained positive, everything would turn out. But I guess that's like living a lie. I know it sounds childish, but I didn't know what else to do. Christ, you're only fourteen and you knew." He smiled warmly at his son. "I kept kidding myself I was doing it for you and Lisa, but when you said that in the kitchen, I realized I was doing it for myself. I didn't want to hear what you said. I didn't want to think it. I . . . I really don't know what I'd do . . . without her. You know what I mean?" Tears poured down his face.

Sam wiped his eyes continually as he peered at his father. "Maybe if we talked, like now. Maybe it'll help. That's what I've been doing in the sessions and it really makes a difference."

He stared at his son proudly. "I don't know if I could go through that, the talking. Thinking about her not being here. Maybe we could try." Chad took a deep breath and threw out his chest like a sergeant drilling his troops. "Okay, Sammy, try, try me. Go ahead, right now. Talk. Ask a question."

"You know what I'm going to ask you, don't you?"

"Just ask, Sammy, just ask."

"Is Ma going to die soon?"

The muscles in his face quivered as he riveted his eyes to his son's. In a very soft, controlled voice, he said. "Nobody can know that for sure. We've changed the medicine many times now...many times." He sighed loudly, forcing himself to continue. "Her blood count is getting worse and worse...and worse. I think it's possible, very possible that it could happen soon."

Sam wrapped his arms around his father. "Thanks for telling me, Dad."

"Thank you, Sammy. You're really quite a kid. Maybe it's time we all stopped running away from it."

As they walked back to the house, arm in arm, Sam nudged his father. "What about Ma?"

"What about her?"

"Does she know?"

"No, not really. I don't know what she guesses. I keep telling her it's getting better when it's not. She has to keep her spirits up. That's so, so important."

"But maybe she thinks about it too...like me and you. Maybe she'd want to talk about it."

Chad clamped his hand down hard on his son's shoulder. "I know what you're going to say next. Now, forget it. You hear? Don't you dare talk to your mother about her sickness. Don't you dare use that word in front of her! She needs all the strength she can get." He pulled his son close to him, embracing him tightly. "Sammy, listen to me. I'll talk to you about it, any part of it, any time. I won't keep anything from you any more. I promise. Only, your mother stays out of this. Please, Sammy, trust me."

*   *   *

The moon, peeking through the heavy overcast, spotlighted the field. The metal rim around the track glowed in the darkness. Trees stood unruffled in the silence of the night. Sammy rounded the far curve. He moved like a deer; relaxed, graceful, as if his body belonged to the motion, playing out its own inner rhythm. His legs sliced through the air like long, thin needles, choreographed for maximum speed. Everything, from the position of his hands to the slight upward tilt of his head, carried him forward.

"Six, Bears. Six. You're early," he shouted.

"I'll let you go around one more time," I said. Sam raised his hand and saluted like an Olympic athlete.

After performing some quick calisthenics, I waited, poised by the side of the track until I heard rubber against gravel. Pushing off, I eased myself into a slow jog, then quickly gained momentum. Just as Sam glided along side of me, it began to drizzle.

"Hey, it's nice," he declared, turning palms up to catch the thin spray.

"Did you ever run on a beach when it rains?" I asked. Sam shook his head. "Well," I said, "it's quite a beautiful experience." We ran the remainder of the quarter-mile in silence. As we began our second revolution, I turned to him and said, "What would you like to work on?"

"My dad and me, I guess."

"What about it?"

"Sometimes I can't believe it's me. I told him how I felt, straight out, no bullshit. He rapped me a couple of times, real hard. I kept thinking he lost his mind. Anyway, we talked. It was the first time we ever talked like that. He said it . . . she could die soon, that it was really possible. How come I feel better now that I know?"

"What do you think?"

"Maybe I'm just getting used to it," he said. "Not knowing is worse than knowing. Before I kept making circles in my head. Now they're gone. I can think about other things. I really like our talks. You know what's funny . . . you're going to laugh when I tell you, but since it's now okay to think about it and talk about it, I don't any more . . . at least not all the time like I used to."

"Sammy, it's like the story of a child left in a room. Just say to the kid, listen, do anything you want, play with anything, but don't do one thing, don't open the closet. Well, from then on, all the kid thinks about is the closet. Sometimes he'll just open it immediately. Sometimes, if he's scared enough, he won't touch the door, but he'll sure play with the idea all the time, worry about it, nurse it, reject it and then reconsider it again. In your house, death is a little like the closet. Everybody knows it's there, but nobody's allowed to open the door because maybe you'll find something terrible. And then if you believe that, you never get to deal with the closet, you're too busy dealing with your fears about the closet."

"And when you finally get to it, it's not the same," he said. "So maybe I'll work more of it out, like I'm doing right now. But with my father, it's different. I'm still kind of glad I talked to him, but I feel bad about what I did."

"What do you feel bad about?" I asked.

"That I hurt him by what I said."

"What do you mean, Sammy?"

"I told him that I thought she was going to die and he just went crazy. He go so angry and upset. But if I hadn't said that, nothing would have happened."

"Maybe that's true. You said something and then your father responded. But how did you hurt him?"

"I just told you," Sam insisted, "by saying what I did."

"How do your words hurt him?"

"Well, the words don't hurt him. It's what he thinks about the words; you know, I had the same problem before."

"Let's explore it again . . . what you experienced.

When someone talked about death and people dying, did you get upset?"

"Sometimes. Not in my history class, but when I thought about my mother."

"Okay, then sometimes you heard about death and didn't get upset; at other times, you did. Is that so?"

"Yes."

"When you did get upset, did the person who said the word get you upset, was he or she responsible for your feeling sad or unhappy?"

"No, because what they said didn't always matter," Sam replied. "I guess it depended on where I was and what I was thinking about."

"So who gets you upset . . . who does it to you?"

He smiled hesitantly. "Well, if it's not them, and it's not, then it must be me. I do it to me. Wow, that's really neat, Bears. I see what you mean."

"It would be nice for you to see that's what 'you' mean. Your 'wow' is not over my question, but your answer, your own realization." He meditated on my comment, then nodded enthusiastically. "Okay," I continued, "back to your father. Do you believe you hurt him?"

"No," he answered. "I guess not. But there's a catch—suppose I know he gets himself upset when I talk about certain things and then I talk about them . . . isn't that kind of doing it to him?"

"What do you think?"

"My answer is no and yes. He'd still do it to himself, but I pressed the button."

"Sammy, you have brown curly hair. If someone told you they hated brown curly hair and they got unhappy everytime you walked into the room with your brown curly hair, did you press their button?"

"That would be ridiculous," he mused. "Then anyone could make up a reason to get upset and blame it on you. I think they would have the problem. It'd be the same for me. It's like my friend Jane—she gets upset when anyone mentions she's tall, then screams at them for getting her upset. You gotta see her. She drives herself crazy." Sam paused, allowing a half-grin to surface. "I can see this all now."

"Back to your dad. Did you hurt him?"

"No, but I want to go through it . . . okay?"

"Sure."

"I talked about my mother dying. To my father that's like brown curly hair and he freaks. He does that because he has . . . his reasons, but he doesn't have to get unhappy. So I don't do it to him. That's really clear. I wish I knew this before; it would have been easier to talk to him. Maybe I could have made him understand instead of feeling so guilty . . . like I did something terrible."

His continuous talking and running at the same time winded him. Sam concentrated on regulating his breathing, then spoke again. "You know what, I'm glad I did it, for me and for him—I think it was good he talked. You know? And things have been different since then. He's been friendlier the last two days . . . I mean, he smiles at me more. He also told me they're going to try a new kind of chemo . . . um . . . chemotherapy next week. He kept his word."

"How do you feel, Sammy?"

"Like I have a father. Really good. But not so good about my mother. We still do the smiles all the time, like everything was the same. I feel so uncomfortable with her, like I'm a phony. And, maybe, she knows."

Just as he completed the last sentence, it began to rain heavily. We laughed at each other. Soaked during the first seconds of the downpour, I said; "You want to finish out the last mile?"

"Then what?"

"My Jeep's in the parking lot. We can go back to the house on the hill and continue talking."

"I'm for finishing," he affirmed. "Finishing the mile and finishing the session."

We increased our pace around the track, moving faster into the turns than before. The coolness of the water refreshed me. My body perked with a new strength. The last quarter-mile was easier than the others. Sam completed first, then I followed quickly behind. We walked briskly to the truck.

After showering at the house, I threw our clothes into a dryer. Sam looked comical outfitted in one of my old sweatsuits. We sprinted up the hill, leaped onto the deck and ran into the one-room studio. Rain pelted the roof and windows.

Once we were seated, Sam said, "Where was I?"

"Do you remember?" I asked.

"Yeah, I think so. About my mother, my feeling uncomfortable when I'm with her."

"What is it about being with your mother that makes you uncomfortable?"

"The lie."

"What lie, Sammy?"

"Smiling all the time, saying everything's getting better when it's getting worse, making believe I'm interested in all the things we talk about when I'm not. Feeling one way and acting another way."

"What about doing those things disturbs you?" I asked.

"I want to tell her about how I feel. Maybe she would want to tell me how she feels."

"That might be what you want to do, but that's different than getting unhappy about not doing it. Why does it make you unhappy when you realize you're not sharing your real feelings?"

"Because if it happens, then we never talked, never had that special thing."

"What do you mean?' I asked.

"She could...die, and we would never have been together, not really."

"If that came to pass—what you fear—why would you be unhappy?"

"I just would."

"But why, Sammy?"

He stood up and paced the room. "Because at least one time, I'd like to be me. That's the special thing."

"What are you afraid would happen if you weren't unhappy about not having a special thing?"

"Then I wouldn't have it," he asserted, dropping back onto the couch.

"Ah, are you saying by being unhappy, it'll happen easier or be more possible?"

"Yes," he said. "If I weren't unhappy about it, then it wouldn't matter. I'd just let it slide."

"Why do you believe that?" I asked.

"I don't know. I'm getting confused again, Bears. Wouldn't I just forget about it if I wasn't unhappy?"

"Sammy, that might be a nice question for you to answer," I suggested.

He stared at the floor and rubbed his hands together. "Okay," he said, "I wouldn't have to forget about it. I could still want it, I guess."

"Do you have some doubts?"

He shrugged his shoulder.

"Sammy, do you think you have to be unhappy in order to remember you want that special thing, as you call it?"

"No. I don't have to be unhappy to remember. That feels right! It's different from what I thought before, but it feels right." He shook his head, courting a slight smile. "First I think one thing, then when I look at it, I really don't believe it at all. It's all so weird," he concluded, "but I like it."

"What do you want, Sammy?"

"To talk to her," he asserted a second time, his voice dramatically stronger. "What do you think I should do?"

"There's no should, except the ones we decide to put

there," I said. "It's that same point we've talked about before. If I give you my opinion, it would tell you what I would do, which, in a real way, has little to do with you. It's your decision. And nobody knows more about you than you do. Not me, not anybody."

"Yeah, but I'm only a kid," he said sarcastically.

"What does that mean?"

"You know, kids don't really know the answers; they haven't lived long enough."

"Do you believe that?"

"Isn't that the line? I hear it in my house, in school, everywhere. 'You're too young, kid, what do you know?'"

"But do you believe it?"

"Sometimes," he answered.

"And now?"

"A little bit."

"Why do you believe it?"

"Maybe I don't know, maybe all I'll do is make the wrong decision."

"What do you mean by the wrong decision?"

"It's not only me. It's my mother and my father. Suppose she doesn't want to talk about it like me. That would be awful."

"Why, Sammy?"

"Because then I would have . . . " He threw his head back, stared at the ceiling and held his breath.

"Why did you stop?" I questioned.

"I was going to say I would have hurt her. But as I thought of the words, I knew they weren't true. I just don't want to see her get any more unhappy."

"Do you believe that's what will happen if you talk to her?"

"Bears, I really don't," he said. "If I was sick, really sick, I'd want someone to talk to me . . . just like she did once. I used to have asthma, a real bad case. I remember being in the hospital, all by myself. It seemed forever.

God, I was so scared. Then my mother came and sat with me all day one day and just explained what was wrong; how my lungs were filled with stuff and how the doctors were giving me special medicine to stop the infection so I could breathe better. I think I loved her on that day more than any other day. I wasn't scared after we talked. Maybe I could do that for her, but, somewhere, I'm still afraid."

"Of what?"

"I don't know any more. Could I just be afraid without a reason?"

"What do you think?" I asked.

"That's what it feels like."

"Well, if you don't have a reason to be afraid, why would you be?"

"I guess I wouldn't, Bears. It's going, this fear thing, but I still feel something, just a tiny bit," he acknowledged.

"Sammy, what are you afraid would happen if you weren't afraid?"

He laughed. "You know the answer as well as I do. Then, I'd do it."

"Are you saying you're afraid in order to stop yourself from doing it?"

"Yes. That's kind of dumb—scaring myself. I do it all the time, don't I? Well, I don't feel scared now. I feel freer ... to decide. And you know what, I want that special thing even more now. Ma would understand, I know she would. But, damn, I wish I never talked to my father."

"Why, Sammy?"

"Because he asked me not to talk to her and he's been great. He wouldn't understand. He'd think I didn't care about anything he said. But do, Bears, I do."

"You know you do and I know you do, but suppose, as you said, he doesn't know it—how would you feel?"

"Pretty shitty," he snapped.

"Why?"

"It's like he trusted me, told me everything and then I did this. I guess I think he'd never trust me again."

"And what about that would make you unhappy?"

"I'd be alone, all over again."

"What's disturbing about being alone?"

"No one to talk to," he said. "Round and round in circles."

"Why would that make you unhappy?"

"It'd be okay for awhile, until I saw he would never talk to me."

"And then what would happen?"

"There would be no way out . . . I'd just be there."

"Do you believe that?"

"I knew you were going to ask me that. I guess, if I wanted, I could find a way. After all, I did it last week. But it seems so hard."

"Why?"

He sighed, dipped his head and spoke in a strained voice. "You really want to know? It's hard because I'm not used to saying what I really feel to people."

"Why does that make it hard?"

"Because I never know what they're going to do. That's really it. I guess I've always dreaded them walking away or hitting me, like my father did." He furrowed his eyebrows. "But that wasn't so bad. It's really worth it." Sam smiled at me. "You know, we seem to talk about everything but my mother."

"Do you think so?"

"I don't know why I said that. I thought I'd be crying a lot, but I'm not. I don't want my mother to die. But if that's going to happen, maybe at least this can be a special time." He wiped his eyes. "You know, I've got this thing about a special time."

"Why the tears, Sammy?"

"I'm not unhappy. It's a new feeling for me. It's like saying, hey, Sammy, what you want is okay. So do it, ask yourself and see what you say. That's what, I guess, I've been doing here. Asking me—not my father, not a teacher, not you...just me."

"And how do you feel about that?"

"Like I just found a new person. Me. The kid who really cares about his mother and father."

*   *   *

Taking the steps three at a time, Sam sprinted up the stairs, his books barely contained in the backpack strapped to his shoulders. The chattering television bombarded him when he reached the second-floor landing. He walked directly into his mother's bedroom without his ritualistic hestitation.

Darlene Millen's head hung forward, dangling in front of her chest at such a sharp angle that it appeared disconnected from her body. A thick, green bathrobe bunched up in front of her chest. Another half-eaten meal decorated the hospital tray.

Sam's smile, a carefully rehearsed and orchestrated greeting, dissipated as he lingered near the bureau. Was something different? With each passing second, his stomach tightened like a vise; the blood crashing through his arteries as his heart rate accelerated rapidly. His mother's hands were stiff and still. No movements. He focused on her chest, fixating on every fold in the robe; waiting, praying for the material to move, quiver...anything. It couldn't be, a voice screamed within him. What about that special time? He started to approach her, fighting the numbness which spread from his fingers into his hands. Then he stopped, as if confronted by a physical barrier. Slowly, in nervous little steps, he backed out of the room into the hall. His vision blurred. Placing one foot in front of the other carefully, he moved down the staircase. Suddenly, he stopped. A sharp, distinct cough filled his ears. Spinning around, he charged back up the stairs, jumped the last four steps and leaped into the bedroom.

Startled by his frenzy, Darlene looked at him wide-eyed. He stared at her, smiling so broadly he thought his face would crack. They both laughed, but for very different reasons.

"I'm flattered," she said. "I never saw you in such a hurry to see me."

He nodded his head up and down, speechless.

"Well, are you going to move from that spot and kiss me?" she asked. Sam obeyed immediately. "That's better." She turned her face away from him to cough. The hacking spasms in her throat dominated her, forcing her to hunch over and hold her ribs until it passed. When she looked up again, her eyes were glazed and bloodshot.

"Do you want some water or juice, something for your throat?" Sam asked.

In a raspy, hoarse voice, she indicated the juice. He filled the glass and gave it to her. He could hear her teeth rattling against the glazed rim.

"How's school?" she asked.

"Would you mind if I didn't answer that question?" he said.

"It's okay, Sammy, I don't want to pry."

"You're not prying. I love when you ask me questions . . . just not that one. That one's such bull. I mean, who cares?"

"I do," Darlene said to her son. "I want to know what you're doing. There's not much else I can really experience from this bed. But, if you don't want to talk, it's okay. Want to play cards?"

"Ma, that's just it. Today, I'd like to talk."

"I don't understand. I thought you just said you—"

"I mean," he interrupted, "I didn't want to talk about that kind of stuff. I wanted to talk about you." He frowned and looked away.

"You don't have to get upset about me, I'm fine," she countered. "I feel better each day."

Uncomfortable, feeling he had trespassed, Sam nodded. "Let me empty this," he said, picking up the bedpan. For perhaps the hundredth time, he dumped its contents in the toilet, then rinsed it in the tub. He completed the chore quickly, but remained in the bathroom, leaning against the window, mumbling about the words he found so difficult to use. He grabbed the pan and returned to the bedroom, unaware that for the first time, he was neither dizzy nor nauseous.

The whine of the TV tuner, jumping from station to station, filled the room in direct response to the gadget in his mother's hand.

"Hey, you want to play cards?" Sam asked.

Clicking off the set, she nodded. Darlene rubbed the back of her neck with her hands, displaying considerable discomfort.

"Let me do that," Sam insisted. "The guys sometimes do it to each other before a track meet—it kinds of loosens us up." He kneaded the muscles around her shoulder blades, then massaged her neck with a professional flair.

"That's great. Your hands are like a man's. They're strong, like your father's."

"Ma?"

"Yes, Sammy."

"How does it feel being so sick?" he said, trying to keep his voice steady. He could feel the muscles in her neck tense.

"Oh, you get used to it."

"But how does it feel?"

"Not as good as your hands on my neck. You can stop now," she counseled, "it feels much better."

"No, I'll do some more," he said, not wanting to face her. He felt freer to ask the questions when their eyes did not meet.

"Well?"

"Well, what?" Darlene asked.

"How does it feel?"

"The pain is the easiest part. Not being able to get around like I used to, well, that's more difficult for me to handle. There's so many things I'd like to do for you and Daddy and Lisa. You get to feel a little bit useless."

"We're doing just fine, Ma, I swear."

"Oh, I know you're taking of yourself. But you should have a mother who can be with you—oh, you know, play tennis with, go to a restaurant, make your favorite dessert . . . meet your teacher at school." Darlene started to cry.

"Ma, it's okay, really it is. None of that matters. It used to, but it doesn't matter any more." He held his hands tightly on her shoulders.

"I'm sorry," she whispered. "You shouldn't see me like this."

"But I want to help," he said, now willing to sit on the bed in front of her and look directly into her eyes. It was she who now avoided him. "Remember when I was in the hospital a long time ago." She nodded. "Well," he continued, "the best day of my life happened then. I was so darn scared and alone until you came and sat down on the bed. I didn't know what was happening. And you know what you did?" Darlene smiled through her tears, envisioning a scene which had taken place seven years before. "You asked me what I was frightened about and then you just explained everything about what was going on. It made such a difference that you just really talked to me honest. I'll never forget that. Never. So," he said, sighing rather noisily, "what I thought is, maybe, well . . . maybe now I could sit here and talk to you. You know. About how I feel and you feel and what we both think. That kind of stuff."

"I think I'd like that," she asserted. "Before, when

you asked me what it feels like, there's one thing I didn't tell you. It can get very lonely being sick because everyone's afraid of talking about it. Even the person who's sick. Except . . . " Her voice cracked as she struggled to continue. "Except if they're lucky enough to have a son like you."

"You're not mad, then?"

"No, Sammy." She stroked his arm affectionately.

"Do you ever thing about . . . about . . . " He paused, unable to say the word.

Darlene smiled at her son. "Do I ever think about dying? Is that what you wanted to ask me?" He bowed his head, undecided, unsure, until she lifted his chin. "Do you want to continue this?"

"Ma, I've been wanting to really talk like this to you for a whole year."

"Okay," she said. "Then let's do it. There's so many things I'd like to tell you too."

For the next three hours, Darlene Millen and her son shared their thoughts, their fears and their love. When her husband arrived home that evening, he noticed a glow on his wife's face. Very gently, she described to him a most beautiful afternoon she had had with Sammy. They, too, then exchanged thoughts which had so long been suppressed beneath false smiles. Sam joined their discussion after dinner and the three of them talked into the early morning hours.

Two weeks and two days later, on her favorite kind of day when thick white clouds hang low like cotton-candy, Darlene Millen died. For her, for her husband and for Sammy, there had been a special time.

POSTSCRIPT

If you are happy and doing what you want,
you are helping the world and yourself.
But if you are unhappy and not doing what
you are wanting, then you are not helping
the world or yourself. I'm wanting you
to read this because it is true.

By me, Thea (seven years old)

ACKNOWLEDGMENTS

To Suzi; mentor, alter-ego, whose hand moves silently through the pages of this book.

To Bryn, Thea and Raun—my special teachers.

To the faces behind Dawn, Robertito, Sam, David, Angie, Jonathan, Dominique and Jeanette.

To Jane, the "Houdini" of Fifty-first Street; this book carries the scent of her red roses.

To Pat, whose energy made this sharing possible.

To Laura and Nancy, whose loving presence enriched this giving.

And to Rita, a very special Option lady.

ABOUT THE AUTHORS

Barry Neil Kaufman and Suzi Lyte Kaufman, both born and raised in New York City, teach a uniquely loving lifestyle and vision called the Option Process, which has both educational and therapeutic applications. They are mentors and teachers to individuals and groups (The Option Institute and Fellowship, R.D. #1, Box 174A, Sheffield, Mass. 01257) and lecture in universities, hospitals, and have appeared often in mass media throughout the country.

As a result of their innovative and successful "Option" program for their once-autistic child and other developmentally delayed or brain-impaired children, the Kaufmans also counsel and instruct families wanting to create home-based teaching environments for their own special children. They also teach professionals in this area.

Mr. Kaufman has written seven books, co-authored two screenplays with his wife (winning the coveted Christopher Award twice and also the Humanitas Award), and has had articles featured in major publications. His first book, "Son-Rise," which details his family's inspiring journey with their once-autistic child, was dramatized as an NBC-TV special network presentation. "To Love Is To Be Happy With" shares the specific applications of their nonjudgmental living and learning process as it applies to different life situations. In "Giant Steps," Barry Neil Kaufman gives us very caring, intimate, and uplifting portraits of young people he has worked with and touched during times of extreme crisis. "A Miracle To Believe In" recounts the emotional and oftentimes miraculous story of the Kaufmans' teaching another family and group of volunteers to love themselves and, in turn, to love a little Mexican boy back to life in defiance of all medical professionals who turn their backs after labeling the little boy's case hopeless. "A Land Beyond Tears" presents a liberating approach to death and dying. His latest book, "A Sense of Warning," shares the stranger-than-fiction, life-changing psychic experiences that led the Kaufmans to their current work and teaching.

Currently, in addition to working with others, Bears (as he is called) and Suzi Kaufman are at work on two new books, one fiction and one nonfiction, both of which have their seeds in the Option experience.